THE NAVY IN THE POST–COLD WAR WORLD

COLIN S. GRAY

THE NAVY IN THE POST–COLD WAR WORLD

The Uses and Value of Strategic Sea Power

The Pennsylvania State University Press
University Park, Pennsylvania

Library of Congress Cataloging-in-Publication Data

Gray, Colin S.
    The Navy in the post–Cold War world : the uses and value of strategic sea power /
by Colin S. Gray.
      p.   cm.
    Includes bibliographical references and index.
    ISBN 0-271-01107-6—ISBN 0-271-01108-4 (pbk.)
    1. Sea-power.   2. Naval strategy.   3. Unified operations (Military
science)   4. United States.   Navy.   5. Sea-power—United States.
I. Title.
V25.G733   1994
359′.03—dc20   93-6462
                                                  CIP

Published by The Pennsylvania State University Press,
University Park, PA 16802-1003

It is the policy of The Pennsylvania State University Press to use acid-free paper for the
first printing of all clothbound books. Publications on uncoated stock satisfy the minimum requirements of American National Standard for Information Sciences—
Permanence of Paper for Printed Library Materials, ANSI Z39.48–1984.

For Valerie, with love, as always

Contents

Prologue

What is the strategic value of the Navy in the 1990s and beyond? Is the strategic history of naval power in ancient, medieval, and even modern times, really relevant to policymaking and defense planning today and tomorrow? How do the forces of the land, the sea, the air, space, and the electromagnetic spectrum interrelate to comprise a unitary military capability geared to generate overall strategic effectiveness in times of peace, crisis, and war? These questions dominate this analysis.

In this book I develop in greater depth some of the themes woven into my previous work, *The Leverage of Sea Power: The Strategic Advantage of Navies in War* (New York: Free Press, 1992). In that book I treated the theory of sea power briskly, outlined repertoires of strategies for sea power and land power, and proceeded to let a historical framework advance the argument. In the interests of brevity and clarity, *Leverage of Sea Power* did not dwell at length on particular aspects of land power–sea power relations, nor did it seek to analyze the future of sea power, save with reference to lessons of the past.

The analysis here falls naturally into three parts. Part I introduces the debate over the value of sea power (Chapter 1), develops the idea of sea power as a "great enabler" and contrasts the purposes and value of command at sea and on land (Chapter 2), and brings historical and strategic theoretical concerns together by examining the contemporary relevance for the United States of the British experience with sea power from the late sixteenth century until 1945 (Chapter 3). Part II, the heart of the book, analyzes from different complementary perspectives the long struggle for strategic advantage of land powers and sea powers and land power and sea power. Part III looks in detail at a key emerging relationship treated only in passing in *Leverage of Sea Power*, the connections between maritime power and space strategy (Chapter 7) and examines the U.S. geostrategic condition in the post–Cold

War world and speculates about the future strategic demand for the effectiveness that can be generated by U.S. naval power (Chapter 8).

The themes and topics addressed here are all directly or indirectly relevant to the challenges to refashion national security and naval policy and strategy for the post-Soviet era. It is paradoxical that just as optimistic commentators announce that "history, as such" is ending,[1] contemporary events in—where else?—the Balkans bear witness yet again to the triumph of history. In Chapter 8, "The Strategic Demand for Naval Power," I argue, with due gratitude to Carl von Clausewitz,[2] that there is both a logic and a grammar to naval power that smooths the transition from a Cold War to a post–Cold War U.S. Navy. The difficulty today is to oversee some evolution of the Fleet to a more regionally focused and shallow-water-capable force, still able to respond to policy demand when the next great balance-of-power struggle gets under way—as surely it will. Furthermore, it is well to remember that even in local or regional crises, U.S. opponents are more and more likely to be armed with late-model information-age weaponry and support systems.

It is a useful axiom that although the last war should help inform strategy, operational art, tactics, and doctrine, that war should not dominate in those categories to the exclusion of other sources of inspiration. The reason is clear; each war is unique. I wrote and revised these chapters against the backdrop of Desert Storm, but I am skeptical of sweeping reinterpretations of military affairs that rest on but one brief passage of arms. Much has been made of, and even more has been claimed for, the future of air power as a result of its operational leading-edge role in the Gulf in 1991.[3] It is far too soon to say how (or whether!) the current interservice debate over the relative strategic utility of air power will be concluded. It is true that the *promise* of air power from World War I through Vietnam seems to have been fulfilled, finally, against Iraq in 1991. The issue, however, is not so much exactly what did how much damage to Iraq's ability to fight, but whether Iraq as a target set was unhelpfully unique (as a basis for the reconstruction of strategic theory and military doctrine), and just how combined were the elements that wrought its downfall. The weight of history and common sense is with me on this issue, though current U.S. authority is not. (In this book I employ "combined arms" in its commonplace sense of cooperating arms,

1. See Francis Fukuyama, *The End of History and the Last Man* (New York: Free Press, 1992).

2. Carl von Clausewitz, *On War*, ed. and trans. Michael Howard and Peter Paret (Princeton, N.J.: Princeton University Press, 1976; first pub. 1832), 605.

3. Richard P. Hallion, *Storm over Iraq. Air Power in the Gulf War* (Washington, D.C · Smithsonian Institution Press, 1992), is useful.

differently focused. In other words, my "combined" equates to what the U.S. military establishment prefers to call "joint.")

Apart from considerations of undesirable complexity in analysis, the case remains strong for treating sea power and land power and sea powers and land powers as the key players in this story. There are times when it is not inappropriate to think of the United States as an *air power*, a *space power*, and a ("strategic") *nuclear power*, much as it is viewed as a sea and a land power. Nonetheless, those occasions remain episodic and noticeably specialized. It is entirely possible that with capabilities such as those provided by the B-2 bomber the United States will be able, more and more often, to function strategically in a distinctive sense as an air power, independent of local land facilities or forward-deployed maritime platforms. When that era dawns, I will be pleased to adjust my thinking, categories, and conclusions.

None of the above denies the changing, but probably case-specific, terms of operational cooperation among land, sea, air, and space elements. Although in this book I tend to treat air power as an adjunct to, even a component of, land and sea power, there are indeed likely to be more and more instances when U.S. land and sea forces function as adjuncts to air power. Given the key role I assign here to the concept of sea power as a great *enabling* agent, I have no serious intellectual difficulties with such a development.

Questions of definition invite scholarly pedantry, but they can be important also. Two such questions beg for clear treatment here. The idea of a sea power as contrasted with a land power is central to my argument, as is the distinction between a maritime and a continental alliance (or coalition). But one might well ask, is it useful or accurate to make those distinctions?[4] Is it not more helpful to think of states on a continuum of sea power–land power, recognizing that most countries have some of both kinds of power, are at some liberty to emphasize either over the other, and may fluctuate more or less uneasily between them?

There is much to be said in favor of eschewing a sharp distinction between sea power and land power. Nonetheless, in many cases geography and historical experience have encouraged the maturing of a strategic culture unquestionably maritime or continental in preference and style. That polities with navies also have armies and, these days, air forces should not be permitted to obscure a traditional military orientation toward the sea or the land.[5]

---

4. I am grateful to Professor Jan S. Breemer of the Naval Postgraduate School, Monterey, California, for pressing on me the need to clarify my meaning on this point.
5. Which is not to claim that polities always choose wisely when they have scope for choice

The question of definition of a maritime alliance, so-called, yields readily enough to common sense. Most maritime alliances have in fact been mixed maritime-continental alliances, as sea powers and land powers formed teams against rival alliances. To label an enterprise a maritime alliance is not to ignore its continental dimensions. Such labeling, however, claims that the most important member, or members, of the alliance are maritime in principal strategic orientation and that sea, rather than land, communications are the more vital binding element. For example, for all their mighty land power the anti-German grand alliances of World Wars I and II "worked" because of their maritime superiority. The contrast with the German contexts could hardly be plainer.

The attention paid in these chapters to basic ideas, long-standing relationships, and historical illustrations much older than yesterday's newspaper headlines is at least a partial answer to the black hole that menaces U.S. national security policy and defense strategy today. Naval commentators, scarcely less frequently than other pundits, are tempted to modernize their arguments to suit fashion rather than evolving convictions. I do not presume here that another great balance-of-power struggle *must* emerge over the next several decades, but I do assume that the possibility of such a struggle is sufficiently probable to be relevant to defense planning today. When a major military vehicle can have a design hull (or airframe) life of thirty years and may well take in excess of ten years to develop and construct, the need for prudence is more important than ever.

---

among geostrategic emphases See Michael D. Hobkirk, *Land, Sea or Air? Military Priorities: Historical Choices* (London: Macmillan, 1992).

Part I
INTRODUCTION

1

Strategic Sea Power

By its very nature as an enabling agent sea power is a strategic force that can make a very positive difference in support of high policy. The landward focus of human affairs requires that the strategic value of navies ultimately be felt ashore. These facts transcend different periods, polities, and technologies and speak to the historical continuities that are to be found in the strategic effect of sea power. Navalist theorizing, particularly that of Alfred Thayer Mahan, has been overly criticized by strategic commentators who neglect to see much of the truth in Mahan's voluminous writings. Despite a glittering record of strategic accomplishment in the twentieth century, sea power has not attracted the balanced appreciation that it deserves.

CONTINUITIES

In this book I explore the strategic value of sea power in the post–Cold War world. Because the human race occupies and can live only on the land, sea power derives its strategic meaning strictly from its influence over events on land. Whatever their wartime duties, navies are the policy instruments of territorially organized states. It follows logically, indeed inexorably, in the words of Vice Admiral William Ledyard Rodgers, that "in its nature maritime war is secondary to that on land."[1] Strategic studies finds no difficulty in asserting the necessary primacy of the land over the sea, as a relationship mandated by human ecology. However, the obvious truth that all wars, ultimately, must have a landward focus, says next to nothing about how and to what effect sea power functions strategically.

In these pages I lean heavily on historical evidence shaped and guided by strategic ideas. American naval theorist Admiral Alfred T. Mahan was given to the issuing of pontifical declamations, which, no matter how definitively or inspirationally they read, should not be confused with divine inspiration. Nonetheless, he is more right than wrong when he advises that "from time to time the superstructure of tactics has to be altered or wholly torn down; but the old foundations of strategy so far remain, as though laid down upon a rock."[2] It is a working assumption of this analysis that there are important continuities from sea power as wielded by the empire of Athens in the fifth century B.C. to sea power as wielded by a United States seeking to define, craft, and defend a world order for the post–Cold War period. History serves as the essential basis on which educated understanding of the utility and limitations of sea power in the future can be formed.

The theorists and practitioners of every age are impressed, indeed overimpressed, with the novelty of the problems that beset their particular generation. Mahan, for one, was acutely sensitive to the charge that an analysis of sea power based wholly on the period of "fighting sail"—a span of three and a half centuries—might have little to say for an age of steam propulsion.[3] Moreover, although the late Soviet empire was admittedly relatively inaccessible from the sea, a geostrategic fact that works two ways in wartime, the

1. William Ledyard Rodgers, *Greek and Roman Naval Warfare: A Study of Strategy, Tactics, and Ship Design from Salamis (480 B.C.) to Actium (31 B.C.)* (Annapolis, Md.· Naval Institute Press, 1983; first pub 1937), 5.

2. Alfred Thayer Mahan, *The Influence of Sea Power upon History, 1660–1783* (London: Methuen, 1965; first pub. 1890), 88.

3. Alfred Thayer Mahan, *Naval Strategy Compared and Contrasted with the Principles and Practice of Military Operations on Land* (Boston: Little, Brown, 1919; first pub. 1911), 222. Mahan persistently affirmed "the permanence of the great general principles of strategy," though that affirmation tended to be broad rather than specific He recognized that "steam has introduced a relative certainty and precision into the movements of fleets" (115), but noted also that steam "has imposed upon [fleets] such fetters, by the need of renewing their fuel, that naval enterprises can no longer have the daring, far-reaching sweep that once they had" (381).

problem of maritime reach against continental power, and vice versa, is far from unique to recent decades. In the 1850s the British and French strategists who organized and executed the grand raid that became the misnamed Crimean War confronted challenges familiar in kind to those which faced U.S. defense planners during the Cold War period.[4]

A book such as this all but invites the criticisms that the strategic world was made over anew by the atomic fact in 1945 or by the end of the Cold War. Whether or not history jumped tracks in 1945 or 1989–91, the implication is the same: events prior to the discontinuity are of no more than antiquarian interest. In this book I demonstrate, or at least illustrate, continuities across the centuries, and am less than convinced by the argument that the fall of the Soviet empire means a lasting revolution in the terms and relevance of geostrategy.

MAKING A STRATEGIC DIFFERENCE

It has long been fashionable to find extensive fault with Mahan. With some justice he is charged with deficient scholarship, attempting to derive timeless wisdom from challengeable studies of a particular historical era, a romantic attachment to the age of sail, persistently understating the importance of land power and of the influence of land power on sea power, rather simple-mindedly searching for formulaic certainties après the Baron Antoine Henri de Jomini instead of recognizing the rich tapestry of confusion and uncertainty conveyed by a careful reading of the emphatically nonmaritime Carl von Clausewitz, and generally functioning as a propagandist putting history to contemporary political purposes.[5] There is much to criticize in Mahan's writings. He does exaggerate the influence of sea power over land power,

4. The outstanding study is Andrew D. Lambert, *The Crimean War: British Grand Strategy Against Russia, 1853–56* (Manchester, U.K.: Manchester University Press, 1990).

5. Geoffrey Perret, *A Country Made by War: From the Revolution to Vietnam—the Story of America's Rise to Power* (New York: Vintage, 1990; first pub. 1989), 276; Antoine Henri de Jomini, *The Art of War* (1862; reprint, Westport, Conn.. Greenwood Press, 1971); and Carl von Clausewitz, *On War*, ed. and trans. Michael Howard and Peter Paret (Princeton, N J.: Princeton University Press, 1976; first pub. 1832). Also see Paul M. Kennedy, *The Rise and Fall of British Naval Mastery* (New York: Charles Scribner's Sons, 1976), 1–9, and Philip A. Crowl, "Alfred Thayer Mahan: The Naval Historian," in *Makers of Modern Strategy: From Machiavelli to the Nuclear Age*, ed. Peter Paret (Princeton, N.J.· Princeton University Press, 1986), 444–77. By way of some contrast, see the excellent and balanced collection of essays, John B. Hattendorf, ed., *The Influence of History on Mahan* (Newport, R.I.: Naval War College Press, 1991).

and his narrow terms of historical reference do exclude cases of the growth of some great empires wholly bereft of anything remotely resembling his broad notion of sea power. Nonetheless, as British historian Paul Kennedy affirms, "Mahan is, and will always remain, the point of reference and departure for any work upon 'sea power.' "[6] Above all else, Mahan's treatment of "the elements of sea power," providing it is not treated as holy writ, remains incomparable and of enduring relevance.[7] For all the criticism his writings have attracted, few authors have attempted systematically to correct his partial mistreatment of the sea power–land power nexus in a work that combines history and theory.[8] C. E. Callwell's pioneering studies, *The Effect of Maritime Command on Land Campaigns Since Waterloo* and *Military Operations and Maritime Preponderance*,[9] though valuable, bear the hallmark limitation of antedating the experience of global war in this century.

The outstanding work of recent decades is Kennedy's *Rise and Fall of British Naval Mastery*. In it Kennedy traces brilliantly the intimate connection between general British economic strength and the capacity to maintain a navy of the first class, for long periods a class in which Britain was alone. Furthermore, Kennedy discerns rightly that Mahan thought of economic strength unduly narrowly in terms of trade. Kennedy emphasizes, if anything overemphasizes, the continental dimension to British grand strategy. In his preface, he summarizes his thesis as follows: "It was not by maritime methods alone, but by a judicious blending of both sea power and land power, that Britain rose to become the leading world power."[10]

After the manner of Edward N. Luttwak's invention of a territorially oriented grand strategy for the non–territorially minded Roman Empire,[11] it

6. Kennedy, *Rise and Fall of British Naval Mastery*, 9.
7. Mahan, *Influence of Sea Power upon History*, chap. 1.
8. But see the pioneering work by Clark G. Reynolds, *Command of the Sea: The History and Strategy of Maritime Empires*, 2 vols. (Malabar, Fla.: Robert E. Krieger, 1983, first pub. 1974). Also see Colin S. Gray, *The Leverage of Sea Power: The Strategic Advantage of Navies in War* (New York: Free Press, 1992).
9. C. E. Callwell, *The Effect of Maritime Command on Land Campaigns Since Waterloo* (Edinburgh: William Blackwood & Sons, 1897) and *Military Operations and Maritime Preponderance: Their Relations and Interdependence* (Edinburgh: William Blackwood & Sons, 1905). The former work suffers somewhat from having been written in the shadow cast by Mahan's "discovery" of sea power. The latter is a more mature and balanced exercise.
10. Kennedy, *Rise and Fall of British Naval Mastery*, xvi.
11. Edward N. Luttwak, *The Grand Strategy of the Roman Empire: From the First Century A.D. to the Third* (Baltimore: Johns Hopkins University Press, 1976). See the critique in Benjamin Isaac, *The Limits of Empire: The Roman Army in the East* (Oxford: Clarendon Press, 1990), chap. 9 and "Epilogue."

is distinctly possible that Kennedy discovered more than there was to be discovered. He identified a "judicious blending" of sea power and land power which should have been true, had British statesmen thought and behaved as Kennedy and Michael Howard have claimed,[12] but probably was not. At least one thoughtful scholar of the Royal Navy in the eighteenth century, Daniel A. Baugh,[13] has found little historical merit in the Kennedy thesis; and another, David French, measured the continental or maritime tilt in British policy (via expenditure and deployments) and found British strategy to have been "essentially adaptive."[14]

It is little short of remarkable, given the maritime-dependent character of Anglo-American grand strategy in World War II and the effectively unchallenged preponderance of U.S. naval power for at least two decades thereafter, that no modern major works of theory or policy advice have been written on the influence of sea power on war. It is remarkable because both of the world wars of this century attested in obvious, as well as subtle, ways to the literally vital contributions that sea power makes to victory in war. Furthermore, what came to be known as a *Pax Americana* in the 1950s and 1960s, though underwritten by the sword of so-called *strategic* nuclear air, and later missile, power, really was a U.S. guardianship of a Western structure of international order largely sustained and made sustainable by the global reach of sea power and the freedom of strategic access that that sea power conferred. Of logistic necessity, the organizing security instrument of the West was a maritime alliance; a contemporary Delian League, though with an alliance leader far less arrogant and rapacious than was imperial Athens. Operations Desert Shield and Desert Storm in 1990–91 demonstrated that the need for a maritime basis to U.S. power projection is mandated by an enduring strategic geography and has not evaporated with the demise of the Cold War.

Public debate in the 1980s over the strategic merit in the U.S. Navy's

12. Kennedy, *Rise and Fall of British Naval Mastery*, and Michael Howard, "The British Way in Warfare. A Reappraisal," in *The Causes of Wars and Other Essays* (London. Unwin Paperbacks, 1984; first pub. 1983), 189–207.

13. Daniel A. Baugh, "British Strategy during the First World War in the Context of Four Centuries: Blue-Water versus Continental Commitment," in *Naval History: The Sixth Symposium of the U.S. Naval Academy,* ed. Daniel M. Masterton (Wilmington, Del.: Scholarly Resources, 1987), 85–110; idem, "Why Did Britain Lose Command of the Sea during the War for America?" in *The British Navy and the Use of Naval Power in the Eighteenth Century,* ed. Jeremy Black and Philip Woodfine (Leicester, U.K.: Leicester University Press, 1988), 149–69; and idem, "Great Britain's 'Blue-Water' Policy, 1689–1815," *International History Review* (February 1988) 33–58.

14. David French, *The British Way in Warfare, 1688–2000* (London: Unwin Hyman, 1990), 232.

Maritime Strategy attested to noteworthy deficiencies in American strategic thought. The quality of strategic studies conducted in connection with the U.S. defense effort since the early 1950s notwithstanding, there are no modern classics (if that is not a contradiction in terms) of strategic thought that explain the lines of reciprocal influence connecting the land and the sea, let alone the land, the sea, the air, space, the electromagnetic spectrum, and the strategic nuclear realm. Proof of that judgment abounds in the texts and footnotes of the embattled contenders in the public debate over the Maritime Strategy. When Robert Komer argued, trivially, that "were the United States to command all seven seas and use them with impunity, we could not thereby seriously injure the Soviet Union,"[15] or when Edward N. Luttwak suggested that "the ground-forces divisions are the basic currency of East-West strategy,"[16] they neglected the strength of an all-embracing point made by Charles Callwell nearly a century ago: "The effect of sea-power upon land campaigns is in the main strategical."[17]

The predictable terms of hypothetical battle in Europe, or indeed anywhere else around the geopoliticians' "world-island" of Eurasia-Africa,[18] must depend critically on the exercise of sea power. To argue, in 1980s terms, that Soviet tank armies seeking to irrupt into Germany probably could not be stopped by the direct action of Western sea power—even sea power equipped with *Tomahawk* cruise missiles—shows a severe lack of grasp of the structure of the subject under debate. Major land powers can be overthrown only by action on land directly against the bases of their strength, or through their internal political collapse under the stress and strain of protracted unsuccessful war. To notice that the ambitions of Louis XIV were thwarted in good part by the Duke of Marlborough in land campaigns, or that Napoleon was beaten on land at Leipzig and finally at Waterloo, rather than at Trafalgar, is to notice only the obvious. To focus heavily on the consequences of battle on land is to risk failing to comprehend how, and

15. Robert W. Komer, "Strategy and Military Reform," in *The Defense Reform Debate: Issues and Analysis*, ed. Asa A. Clark et al. (Baltimore: Johns Hopkins University Press, 1984), 12.

16. Edward N. Luttwak, *The Pentagon and the Art of War: The Question of Military Reform* (New York: Simon & Schuster, 1984), 120.

17. Callwell, *Effect of Maritime Command on Land Campaigns*, 29.

18. "The joint continent of Europe, Asia, and Africa, is now effectively, and not merely theoretically, an island. Now and again, lest we forget, let us call it the World-Island in what follows." Halford J. Mackinder, *Democratic Ideals and Reality* (New York: W. W. Norton, 1962; first pub. 1942), 62.

by what means, the strategic conditions were established for defeat on the ground.

It is no endorsement of ancient blue-water fallacies or navalist conceits to argue that the tide of historical and strategic theoretical opinion in the West over the past several decades has overemphasized the limitations of sea power. Whether in the form of evaluation of Byzantine or Elizabethan grand strategy, the shaping of the course of the two world wars of this century, or the role of maritime strategy for the United States and NATO in a possible war with a then-Soviet continental superpower, balanced appreciation of the strategic utility of sea power has been rare.

In a book remarkable for its attempt to provide a theoretical framework encompassing the whole of warfare, Admiral J. C. Wylie advises that maritime theory "consists, briefly, of two major parts: the establishment of control of the sea, and the exploitation of the control of the sea toward establishment of control on land. . . . Prior to the middle of the twentieth century no one had set forth in writing the second half of the maritime theory of warfare, toward the establishment of control on the land."[19]

Wylie was too kind to the theorists of maritime power. He intimated that the second part of the maritime theory had had to await the development of vehicles for sea-to-land campaigning on board which theory could take safe flight. Amphibious operations, whether to seize, hold, and exploit, or merely to raid and ravage, were indeed notoriously difficult to conduct prior to World War II, their popularity through all of recorded history notwithstanding.[20] However, "descents on a hostile shore," in a phrase from yesteryear, comprise but a small, if ever more critically important,[21] element of the subject matter here. Public debate and the scholarly literature are not studded with references to "strategic" sea power, but by its very nature sea power is strategic in its working. There is everything to recommend the

19. J. C. Wylie, *Military Strategy: A General Theory of Power Control* (Annapolis, Md : Naval Institute Press, 1989; first pub. 1967), 33, 34. In this excellent book Wylie gives no indication that he is aware of the existence of Callwell, *Military Operations and Maritime Preponderance*.

20. "It was only during the Second World War that men had at hand the means they needed for the direct intrusion of their soldiery from the sea into combat ashore." Wylie, *Military Strategy*, 35. There were exceptions, however. On what justly could be called D-Day, July 13, 960, the Byzantine navy projected heavy cavalry against the shore (Crete) from ships specially configured for amphibious assault. See Gustave Schlumberger, *Un Emperor Byzantin au Dixième Siècle, Nicéphore Phocas* (Paris: Librairie de Firmin-Didot, 1890), chap. 2

21. At least according to Sean O'Keefe, Frank Kelso, and C. E. Mundy Jr., *From the Sea: Preparing the Naval Service for the 21st Century* (Washington, D.C.: Department of the Navy, September 1992).

sense in these words by a German general: "The strategic nature of forces and weapon systems is not determined by their range, accuracy or destructive power, but by the political objectives they are able to achieve."[22]

When NATO-European governments worried in the 1980s about the implications for regional security of radical reductions in theater and so-called strategic nuclear weapon systems, they were worrying about the strategic value of Soviet conventional forces that might not be balanced in kind, or otherwise prudently offset. Concerning crisis control, deterrence, and the prospective conduct of war, the U.S. Navy has said that it is in the business of "making a strategic difference."[23] In this book I examine the strategic difference that sea power can make to the course and outcome of armed conflict and discuss the likely strategic demand for naval forces in the future.

A STRATEGIC MISSION

In my cumulative argument, chapter by chapter, I construct a coherent understanding of the strategic utility of sea power. Four major contributing themes are the significance of strategic culture as expressed in national "ways in warfare," which emphasize the sea (plus air and space) or the land (plus air and space); the fundamental importance of geography for national orientation in style of defense preparation and way in warfare; the ultimate meaning of technological change for practicable choices in strategy and policy; and the broad trend in the relative strategic utility of sea power and land power.

I attack some persistent and plausible fallacies. By historical example and logical argument, in chapter after chapter, I criticize the views that in this century sea power has been locked into strategic decline vis-à-vis some mixture of land power, air power, nuclear-missile power, and space power; that history offers little of contemporary value for strategic education; that navies are best employed defensively; that weapons win wars; and that

---

22 Franz-Joseph Schulze, "SDI and the Conventional Defense of Europe," *International Defense Review* 19, no. 9 (1986): 1225.

23. See the U.S. Navy's basic "600 Ship Navy" briefing, presented by the chief of naval operations, Admiral James D. Watkins, on June 24, 1985, in U S. House of Representatives, Committee on Armed Services, Seapower and Strategic and Critical Materials Subcommittee, *The 600-Ship Navy and the Maritime Strategy, Hearings,* 99th Cong., 1st sess., 1985, 37.

general alleged strategic truths hold with tolerable reliability for particular historical cases. Let that last point serve as a note of caution for those who would proceed glibly from the classroom of general theory to the battlefield of specific application. Sea power and land power are not autonomous, free-floating forces; instead they are anchored critically by such adjectives as Roman, Russian, or U.S., and those qualifying adjectives matter profoundly.

In addition to probing the value of sea power in the future, it is an important purpose of this book to explore the strategic character of the relations between one geographically specific form of power—the maritime—and the rest, by and large, though not exclusively, continental in form. Albeit with a substantial foray into the realm of the nexus between sea power and space power, this book is designed to focus as much as practicable on the geophysically two-dimensional relations between the sea and the land. Although in this text I provide probing overlapping analyses of the sea power–land power tie, the method and spirit of these explorations could be applied to the nexuses between the land and the air, the air and the sea, and so forth.

2

Sea Power: The Great Enabler

In modern times there has been a clearly discernible pattern of rivalry between the leading land power and the leading sea power. That repeated antagonism has had to cope with the political and strategic fact that continental and maritime (and aerial) strength have a complementary relationship. The distinctive pattern of sea power–land power rivalry has produced a no less distinctive pattern of maritime success. Command at sea, or at least a sufficiency of control, has enabled maritime powers to wage war as a whole more effectively than has command on land for continental states. Time and again, superior strength at sea allowed first Britain, then the United States, so to structure a conflict by acquiring and subsidizing continental allies and—when expedient—by protracting hostilities, to realize and exploit systemic cumulative advantages. As a general rule, the leading sea power understood clearly enough that maritime excellence enables, but does not decide, victory. Frequently, soldiers and certainly continental allies fail to appreciate the inherently strategic value of "enabling" sea power.

THE DOMAIN OF COMMAND

What is the strategic relationship between sea power and land power? I consider two propositions here. First, I suggest that command of the sea tends to yield a more absolute and extensive superiority at sea than command on land does on the land. Second, I consider the idea that command at sea yields possibilities for influence on land superior to the influence at sea that can flow from command on land. By "command" I mean a working functional control, not absolute or literally exclusive, let alone ubiquitous, control. An effectively absolute control can be achieved, however. For example, in 1810 the Royal Navy's close blockade of French and major French-allied ports was so rigorous that not a single French naval squadron put to sea.[1] For a further instance, U.S. and other coalition naval forces enjoyed so absolute a control of the waters of the Persian Gulf in 1991 that the Mahanian term "command" was not inappropriate.

Command of the sea, for all its suggestion of an improbable literal exclusivity, expresses an enduring truth about the conditions for success in maritime endeavor in wartime. Since the time of Oliver Cromwell's statecraft in the 1640s and 1650s, sea power and command of the sea have been appreciated in the terms explained and popularized (very much later) by Mahan. Command of the sea may be in dispute; it will rarely deny the enemy use of the sea entirely; and it might be enjoyed only by night or by day (the situation in the "slot" in the Southern Solomons off Guadalcanal from August to November 1942). But by definition it cannot be shared. Command is exclusive in one place and one time; and because "the sea is one," with only coastal or closed-sea exceptions, it has the potential to be extensive in domain. The ubiquity of command at sea was more true in the days of totally Eurocentric international struggles than has been the case since the 1920s, however. U.S. and Japanese naval power could not be contained by the same accident of physical geography that placed Britain in a barrier position vis-à-vis aspiring naval powers in continental Europe.

It is important that maritime theology should not impede understanding or affront common sense. "Command of the sea" simply refers to an extreme quality of control of the sea. Save in a few uniquely hazardous areas—the enemy's coast, for example—a condition of command means that friendly maritime forces can proceed about their business confident that enemy

1. See William James, *The Naval History of Great Britain*, 6 vols. (London: Richard Bentley, 1847), 5:215. Even this close a blockade did not preclude the sailing of individual ships.

forces will be unable to impede them. Command can be *local*—as exercised by Germany in the Baltic in the two world wars. It can be *general* (or all but so)—as exercised by Britain after the Peace of Amiens (1802–3) in her war with imperial France. Or it can be thoroughly in dispute and shift with the movements of the fleets—as during the American War of Independence.

Prior to the early 1900s, Britain's command of Europe's narrow seas translated into control of global maritime communications. Indeed, after 1807 Britain explicitly sought to achieve a monopoly of Europe's seaborne commerce as a means both to survive in the face of Napoleon's continental blockade and to pressure his fragile continental empire. The complex European naval competition of the early 1900s, however, required Britain to concentrate her battle fleet in home waters at the very time when Japanese and U.S. naval power was on the rise. Britain no longer enjoyed global maritime command. The 5:5:3 Washington Treaty (1922) ratio in capital ship tonnage among Britain, the United States, and Japan made strategic sense for the Royal Navy only if there was no pressing need to concentrate naval force in European waters. But by the mid-1930s it was apparent that the security of the British Empire in Asia rested upon nothing more tangible than the hopes that the Japanese Empire would confine her predatory activities to the East Asian mainland, that the United States would defend British interests in the region in addition to her own, and that dangers in Europe somehow could be avoided. In the face of potentially hostile Italian naval power in the central Mediterranean and of German naval and air rearmament, there were no plausible circumstances in which the main British fleet could be dispatched half a world away to concentrate at the intended fortress of Singapore. The 1902 solution, of defensive alliance with a rising regional naval power in the Pacific, was not available in the mid 1930s. The Anglo-German Naval Agreement of 1935 was an ill-considered attempt to address the real problem of an excess of likely foes and a shortage of national or allied means and proved to be a case of a wrong measure taken for the right reasons.

In the wars with France the key to British maritime command had been a flexible concentration of naval force, with the principal center of gravity off Ushant in the western approaches to the Channel (weather and the fleet logistic train permitting), with complementary assembly areas off Cape Finisterre, Cape St. Vincent, or Gibraltar. With variations, this central idea for fleet deployment was applicable as late as the Second World War. In that war, as in 1914–18, the Royal Navy's Home Fleet substituted Scapa Flow for Plymouth and Torbay as the principal base, a position that provided flexibility in the provision of more or less distant cover by capital ships against the German surface raiders that menaced the North Atlantic, and later northern Russian, convoy routes. The Home Fleet's Force H at Gibraltar functioned in a manner reminiscent of the operational flexibility that a fleet based on the Bosporus permitted the Byzantine and Ottoman empires; it made a two-sea fleet from a single concentration of naval power. In 1941–42, Force H operated both in distant support of operations in the North Atlantic and on behalf of the convoys to and from the Middle and Far East via the Cape as well as in the Mediterranean, where it provided cover for the Malta convoys against Italy's fleet-in-being.

The strategic geography of the Cold War Soviet Union denied her foes even the possibility of adopting a single-theater focus in their maritime plans and deployments. The Trafalgar of World War III probably would have been waged in the Norwegian Sea, but the largest concentration of Soviet naval force was in the Far East. It should be recalled that despite its popular name, the key maritime theater in the Crimean War was the Baltic and not the Black Sea.[2] Given adequate notice, maritime assets could be transferred from region to region. The degree of global maritime command in war that an alliance against the Soviet Union would have required, although it would have been facilitated by the substantial eradication of the Soviet naval strength based on the Kola peninsula, could not have been secure unless the Soviet Pacific Fleet were also destroyed or otherwise reliably neutralized.

The geographical and political barriers that divide the land necessarily limit sharply the reach even of very superior land power. Mountains, wide rivers, deserts, and inconveniently located neutral states, can all hinder the momentum and grasp of powerful armies. Even when such internal continental hurdles are not a grave problem, all-conquering armies can be frustrated at the water's edge. Even with the benefit of a powerful air adjunct, superior land power, if not assisted by superior sea power, is essentially only of insular benefit (large though the "island" in question may be). First-rate land power, supported ably by no-less first-rate air power, is simply denied by geography the possibility of functioning as the basis for global strategy. However, this is far from the whole story, as I shall show.

THEORY AND PRACTICE

Although the military reach of superior sea (-air) power is greater than is the reach of land (-air) power, that judgment must not encourage any discount-

2. Basıl Greenhill and Ann Gifford, *The British Naval Assault on Finland, 1854–1855:*

ing of the strategic relations of interdependence that characterize land, sea, air, and now space operations. It is true that maritime command effectively places the military frontier on the enemy's coast. In principle, this point needs to be modified to accommodate the threat posed by land- and sea-based air power. But, in practice since 1939, maritime command has been understood to subsume the necessity for achieving air superiority over the fleet. One does not command the sea if one cannot command the air. The British defeats in Norway in April 1940, in Crete in May 1941, and most dramatically off Kuantan in Malaya in December 1941 with the sinking of the *Repulse* and the *Prince of Wales* were early signals of the interdependence of air and sea that was to be the cornerstone of military operations in the conflicts in Europe and the Pacific. The specific historical strengths of particular combatants is what is most important, not some abstract posited relationship between air power and sea power (and now space power). Following Desert Storm, a strategic theorist could write plausibly, if incompletely, that "air power had finally done it."[3] "Done it" in this context implies air power as the dominant agent for success in war. As the Gulf War demonstrated, there will be specific historical situations wherein land power and sea power will be largely adjunct to an air power that is itself about far more than the protection of the fleet or the acceleration of military progress on the ground.

The axiom that ships cannot successfully engage fortified shore batteries in gunnery duels has been superseded by the proposition that land-based air power has decisive advantages over sea-based air power. Both of these canons had considerable merit in their day. But they could always be invalidated if the strength of the particular opposing forces were sufficiently disproportionate. The Dardanelles might have been forced in February, March, or even April 1915 by naval power alone, had Anglo-French gunnery been properly directed.[4] As with the Byzantine Empire, which it superseded forcibly in

---

A *Forgotten Naval War* (London: Conway Maritime Press, 1988), is a major corrective to Crimocentric analysis.

3. Edward N. Luttwak, "Air Power in U.S. Military Strategy," in *The Future of Air Power in the Aftermath of the Gulf War*, ed. Richard H. Schultz Jr., and Robert L. Pfaltzgraff Jr. (Maxwell Air Force Base, Ala.: Air University Press, July 1992), 19. Also see Richard P. Hallion, *Storm over Iraq: Air Power in the Gulf War* (Washington, D.C.: Smithsonian Institution Press, 1992), and John F Jones, "Giulio Douhet Vindicated. Desert Storm 1991," *Naval War College Review* 45 (Autumn 1992)· 97–101.

4. This controversial thesis is argued in detail in Arthur J Marder, "The Dardanelles Revisited: Further Thoughts on the Naval Prelude," in *From the Dardanelles to Oran: Studies of the Royal Navy in War and Peace, 1915–1940* (London: Oxford University Press, 1974), 1–32.

1453, Turkey was uniquely vulnerable to pressure from the sea against her capital city, Constantinople/Istanbul. The notion that an Allied fleet acting alone against the Bosporus might effect Turkey's withdrawal from alliance with the Central Powers is by no means as fanciful as most commentators subsequently claimed. Lord Kitchener certainly did not find the idea absurd. "Kitchener told the Commander in Chief of the Dardanelles expedition, Sir Ian Hamilton, that 'if the fleet got through the Turks would make terms. He explained to me that the fleet would command the railways which feed Constantinople, and that although he hoped it would not happen so, they could blow a large part of the city to bits.' "[5]

In the Pacific in late 1943 and 1944, the U.S. Navy deployed so overwhelming a fast carrier strength that the nominal relation of advantage as between land- and sea-based air power simply was overturned by the great and growing disproportion in material resources against Japan. Military rules of thumb, such as the favorable 3:1 ratio deemed advisable for an attacker on land, are falsified so often that they should be accorded little respect. Brute force can never be despised, but success in war rarely reduces neatly and arithmetically to sheer quantities of military input.

The sea is a great highway or a barrier, depending on military relations in and over that medium. There has always been a strategic asymmetry favoring superior sea power over superior land power—when the sea power is geostrategically insular by nature or engineering artifice. The dominant sea power necessarily enjoys access to the territorial basis of the continental country's strength, whereas the dominant land power must either cross an uncommanded sea in order to enjoy reciprocal access or somehow wrest maritime command in preparation for invasion.

Since command at sea and on land is never absolute (well, hardly ever, with acknowledgment to Gilbert and Sullivan), sea powers and land powers can raid each other's realms. Historians and strategic theorists impressed by the access to hostile territory enabled by maritime command need to recognize that raiding at sea by a land power is likely to be more significant strategically than is amphibious raiding by a sea power. Time after time in modern history, *guerre de course* has been the preferred strategy for a second-class naval power obliged to disperse its fighting strength at sea.

STRATEGIC UTILITY

The traditional strategic advantages conferred by sea mobility have not been thoroughly negated by the technological and economic changes of this

5 Ibid , 30.

century. In their defense application those changes include new economies of force in rapid deployment for peripheral defense on land permitted by the development of the railroad and the internal combustion engine; a vastly increased scale of military power that can be maintained by modern economies; and the revolution in wide-area surveillance and the range of land-based firepower effected by aircraft and spacecraft. Still, only command at sea enables a country or coalition to implement a global strategy. Herbert Rosinski expressed a lasting truth in 1944 when he wrote that "in global war, merchant shipping is the ultimate key to strategy."[6]

There is no question about the feasibility of penetration of the sea environment by the country superior on land, or of the land by the country in a commanding position at sea. The important question, rather, is what can be achieved by such penetration, by the landward reach of sea power and the seaward reach of land power? There can be no generally valid answer because specific historical circumstances must determine what reciprocal land-sea access permits. Discussion of the relative value of sea and land power for securing access to the hostile environment is a debate about the ease with which either maritime power can generate strength on land or vice versa. This, truly, is the crux of the matter. Failure to understand that war cannot be waged to a successful conclusion by action in one environment alone is a persistent theme in the history of statecraft.

Napoleon's continental imperium was unable to concentrate a naval force of adequate fighting quality to cover an invasion of Britain or to wage a *guerre de course* sufficiently damaging to remove British ability to organize and finance sea-land coalitions. Imperial Germany was so burdened with military commitments on land that she was unable to build her "risk fleet" into a force that could challenge Britain's Grand Fleet for command in a general fleet action.[7] Germany's conduct of an unrestricted *guerre de course* in 1915, 1916, and again in 1917–18 lacked the numbers, the operational intelligence, and the technical-tactical proficiency to drive Allied merchant shipping from the high seas, formidable though that threat was in 1917. Nazi Germany, like imperial Germany before her, entered into war with a naval doctrine ill-suited to the scale of her naval assets.[8] However, Halford

6. Herbert Rosinski, *The Development of Naval Thought* (Newport, R.I.: Naval War College Press, 1977), 45.

7. See Holger H. Herwig, *"Luxury Fleet". The Imperial German Navy, 1888–1918* (London: George Allen & Unwin, 1980), and Ivo Nicolai Lambi, *The Navy and German Power Politics, 1862–1914* (Boston· George Allen & Unwin, 1984)

8 In 1914, the German navy shared with Britain's Royal Navy doctrinal fidelity to a notion of battle-fleet command of the sea. In 1939, pending the availability of a balanced fleet capable of challenging the Royal Navy for command of the sea, the German navy was committed to the

Mackinder's grim analysis of what a continental scale of political and military organization could imply for the seaward reach of the land, might have applied in the 1940s,[9] *if* Hitler had been willing to delay his timetable of military aggression to permit the development of a large and balanced navy, *if* the Luftwaffe had made sensible technical choices over aircraft, and *if* the war against the Soviet Union and the United States had been postponed. The reasons for the German errors in grand strategy lurked systematically in Hitler's personality, in the character and dynamics of his political regime, and in what may be called the German "way of war."

The wars of the French Revolution and Empire and the world wars of the twentieth century demonstrate clearly the strategic and operational utility of sea power. But maritime command is more a facilitator than a concluding executor; vital though sea power has been, alone it can rarely serve to bring a conflict to a satisfactory conclusion. One could argue that British sea power eventually wrought the destruction of the continental empires of Napoleon, Kaiser Wilhelm II, and Adolf Hitler, but such an expansive claim would be only partially true. It would be more accurate to claim that superior sea power created the strategic conditions wherein the continental enemy would be likely to be defeated. British and later American sea power were vital for the defeat of Hitler's Germany, but that sea power and the land and air power it both thrust ashore and (including the Soviet case) helped equip and feed were expressions of a fundamental economic strength for the conduct of war that dwarfed the defense economies of the Axis powers. Therefore, although the wars with France and Germany illustrate the landward and, in the latter case, "airward" strength of sea power, those struggles also demonstrate how victory finally goes to the side able to field, and keep fielding, the larger battalions; a matter of relative financial and economic strength mobilized by politics.

SEA POWER AND LAND POWER: COOPERATION AND ANTAGONISM

That sea power and land power are complementary is as obvious as the political rivalry between the leading sea power and the principal land power

---

waging of a "tonnage war" against merchant shipping to be conducted both by very powerful surface raiders and by submarines.

9. Halford J. Mackinder, *Democratic Ideals and Reality* (New York: W. W. Norton, 1962; first pub. 1942). "What if the Great Continent, the whole World-Island [Europe, Asia, and Africa] or a

is (or seems to be) perennial. In the essays published as *The Problem of Asia*, his most extensive commentary on the strategic relationship between the sea and the land, Mahan wrote:

> The struggle [for the future of Asia] as arrayed will be between land power and sea power. The recognition that these two are the primary contestants does not ignore the fact that neither is a pure factor, but that each side will need and will avail itself, in degree, of the services of the other element; that is, the land power will try to reach the sea and to utilize it for its own ends, while the sea power must obtain support on land, through the motives it can bring to bear upon the inhabitants.[10]

The leading sea power and the principal land power long have sought both an effective monopoly of power in the environment most important to it, as well as some distractive power in the environment most natural to the other. The leading sea power is obliged to treat the greatest land power or coalition of land powers as a potentially deadly threat. The creation of what would amount to a single security community in continental Europe threatens the insular power with an enemy unfavorably disproportionate in resources. That continental realm could apply those resources to the creation of power at, and now beneath and over, sea. In addition, great naval strength based on Eurasia would be geostrategically configured for the global exercise of sea power. As Wolfgang Wegener, among other frustrated German navalists, came to recognize, sea power was a function of strategic geography, or position, as well as possession of a fleet.[11]

Following the theoretical path laid out by Mahan, Mackinder, and Nicholas Spykman,[12] not to mention four centuries of British, and later American, statecraft, George Liska has suggested persuasively that "the specific configuration of the Euro-Asian spectrum of types and sizes of territorial powers has given particular shape to a recurring pattern of rivalry

---

large part of it, were at some future time to become a single and united base of sea-power? Would not the other insular bases be outbuilt as regards ships and outmanned as regards seamen?" (70).

10. Alfred T Mahan, *The Problem of Asia and Its Effect upon International Policies* (Boston: Little, Brown, 1905), 62–63.

11. Wolfgang Wegener, *The Naval Strategy of the World War* (Annapolis, Md.: Naval Institute Press, 1989).

12. Nicholas J. Spykman, *America's Strategy in World Politics: The United States and the Balance of Power* (Hamden, Conn.. Archon Books, 1970) and *The Geography of the Peace* (New York: Harcourt, Brace, 1944).

of which the U.S.-Soviet conflict is but the latest manifestation. Each pitted insular against continental powers and each outcome contained the seeds of new conflict."[13]

Liska pointed to an ever eastward shift in the location of the "rear-continental" state whose mission in (perhaps serendipitous) support of the sea power is both to provide distraction on land and, occasionally, the weight of land power necessary for victory against an aspiring land-power hegemon. In Anglo-American perspective, the principal rear-continental distractor-ally, successively, has been Burgundy (against France), Austria (against France), Prussia (against France), Russia (against Germany), and in the 1970s and 1980s, China (against Russia). In the future, the distractor-ally may be Russia (against China), or China (against a Greater Europe that includes Russia). The possibilities are not in short supply.

The threats posed by the leading sea power to the leading land power have typically been nowhere close to as severe as those the leading land power has posed in return. By its maritime mastery Britain and, later, the United States threatened the financial and economic feasibility of schemes for continental imperium. Maritime blockade for financial effect was practicable and frequently effective from the late sixteenth century until Napoleon demonstrated in the early 1800s how to make war on land pay for itself. The continental powers of preindustrial Europe, however, could not be menaced in their centers of strategic gravity by British sea power. This was not crippling given that British policy in the eighteenth century did not seek the definitive ruin of continental foes. England's centuries'-long bid for continental empire died with the close of the Hundred Years' War with France (1337–1457). Britain's great-power status in the classical age of sail rested initially on the financial strength accrued from overseas commerce and advanced institutions of public finance, and later on her long lead in domestic manufacturing excellence and scientific agriculture. At the peak, or peaks perhaps, of her international standing—which is to say in the late 1700s and the 1810s—Britain aspired to be the decisive arbiter of European quarrels, the critical weight in the balance of power. Britain did not herself seek to be both dominant sea power and major land power. British resources in manpower would not allow for preeminence at sea to be complemented by land forces on the continental scale triggered by the new nationalism of the era of the French Revolution. Moreover, British political culture would not tolerate such an ambition, and the ruling class in the Britain of the

13. George Liska, "From Containment to Concert," *Foreign Policy*, no. 62 (Spring 1986): 9.

Napoleonic Wars did not trust the masses sufficiently as to be willing to risk the potential consequences of a "nation in arms."

In the twentieth century, the continental balance-of-power system failed so thoroughly that traditional British statecraft for the conduct of war was obliged to reverse its historical course. Britain adopted conscription in 1916 and herself undertook to bear the heaviest burden of land fighting against the continental enemy. The first major British continental offensive in four centuries was launched on the Somme on July 1, 1916. The grand-strategic novelty of the Somme was that it was the first British military effort in modern times intended, almost wholly by British arms, to defeat the main body of the army of the land-power enemy. France and Russia certainly wore down the German army, but the British army, from mid 1916 until November 1918, was more than just an important complement to the fighting power of continental allies. Similarly in World War II, although the German army was defeated by attrition and maneuver in the East, the Anglo-American-Canadian *(inter alia)* continental penetrations into Italy and then France were launched on a scale intended to achieve decision on land.

This century has witnessed a good measure of that growth in the relative power of large continental states forecast by J. R. Seeley and Halford Mackinder.[14] From being the more or less agile "balancer" of the balance-of-power system, the leading Western sea power—Britain early in this century, the United States thereafter—has been compelled to become a permanent, indeed even principal, player committed fixedly to one side of the balance.

A navy or an army can sustain the reality behind a tradition of excellence over several generations, but long periods of peace typically see the demise of expertise in land-sea (and air and space) combined arms planning, both in the small, at the level of conjunct amphibious raiding operations, and in the large, at the level of operational art and strategy. The problem can stem from far more than just the effect of a long peace. More to the point can be the harmful influence of past victory. As Arthur Marder notes, "Armies and navies rarely learn from success."[15] The long-run reactions to the defeat of

14. Mackinder, *Democratic Ideals*, 259–62. Writing in 1883, J. R. Seeley was fearful for maritime Britain's ability to compete with the rising land power of the United States and imperial Russia. "Between them [the United States and Russia], equally vast but not continuous, with the ocean flowing through it in every direction, lies like a world-Venice, with the sea for streets, Greater Britain." *The Expansion of England* (Chicago: University of Chicago Press, 1971), 227, and 231–43.

15. Arthur J. Marder, "The Influence of History on Sea Power: The Royal Navy and the Lessons of 1914–1918," in *From the Dardanelles to Oran*, 57.

policy and grand strategy in Vietnam contributed massively to the operational, and hence strategic, effectiveness of the U.S. armed forces in the 1990s. Every war is different in its details, but war, *qua* war, is an activity apart and has a unity across time, technology, and opponents.

AN ENABLING AGENT

Because of strategic geography, the U.S. Army can engage in Eurasian or African (or South American!) continental campaigns only in the logistically expensive and inconvenient form of expeditionary warfare *overseas* (more or less eased by the prior presence of some now rapidly diminishing U.S. garrisons and prepositioned equipment and supplies). The contribution that offensive action by naval power could make to a large ground war can be difficult for the soldier to grasp. As a supremely strategic instrument, sea power provides benefit that may seem unduly remote to soldiers in immediate need of eminently tactical assistance. Action at sea, from Salamis, to Syracuse, to the Solomons, to the blockade of the Axis maritime supply route between Tunis and Sicily, can have immediate consequences for land warfare by so isolating enemy forces that they are compelled to withdraw if they are able or surrender if they are not. But more often, naval action out of sight of friendly land forces provides only indirect, *enabling* benefits to soldiers. Enemy initiatives by sea on a large scale are thereby precluded; friendly expeditions by sea become feasible; and enemy land and air deployments are dispersed to cover threats from the sea. But the final decision generally has to be enforced by the soldier on the ground.

A "law of the instrument" applies in warfare as in other human activities. A country whose long suit in defense is either land or sea power (with suitable air complements) is likely to seek such success as it can with that preferred instrument, even to the detriment of its overall performance in war. Although there were some significant exceptions—her performance in the War of Spanish Succession (1701–13), in the Seven Years' War (1756–63), and in the Iberian Peninsular Campaign (1809–14)—Britain was wont to mishandle her army. Similarly, in her second hundred-year struggle with Britain, France repeatedly misused her often formidable naval power. This is not a sweeping endorsement of Mahan's blistering criticism of the French navy for not seeking military command at sea. As a general rule, the French navy had no prudent alternative other than to adopt the maritime-defensive stance indicated by its second-class standing vis-à-vis fleet engagements. The question is whether or not France made proper use of such naval power as she had. Whenever France laid up her battle fleet in wartime in order to concentrate on the *guerre de course* and Britain recognized the fact, the principal result was the liberation of the Royal Navy for the much more active pursuit of global strategic objectives.

Statesmen frustrated in a search for political answers to pressing problems can be unduly credulous over the prospective efficacy of military solutions. Also, statesmen whose military instrument of excellence is either maritime, territorial, or aerial have been known to exaggerate its power of decision. At the level of grand strategy, the pervasiveness of a continental or maritime cast to national strategic culture can promote serious misassessments of the quality of menace that the one kind of power ultimately poses to the other. For example, the misassessment can take the form of exaggeration of the power of decision in war of national or coalition land power over hostile land power; witness German optimism in 1914 and 1941. Also, the danger posed by unfinished military business on land together with an undefeated enemy across the sea tends to be underappreciated. Parallel misassessments can bedevil a dominant sea power. That victory at sea is necessary but not sufficient for victory in war as a whole can evade notice.

The pattern of rivalry in modern times between sea power and land power to which Mahan, Mackinder, and Liska have referred has been a pattern of antagonism linking the leading sea power and the leading land power. Understood more broadly, however, the natural relationship between sea and land power is more one of cooperation than of antagonism. Sea-power and land-power rivals need to be effective in the environment in which the principal rival is, or has been, supreme. In the struggles with Spain, France, and Germany, Britain and Britain's major contemporary rival sought in their distinctive ways to evade the necessity of facing the principal fighting strength of the enemy on that enemy's preferred terms, while still waging war to military advantage.

A U.S. sea power that has co-opted and exploited the air and space medium is a great, perhaps the great, enabler for global policy and strategy. That sea power connects the islands of the world, binds together and sustains coalitions, and enables land power and short-range air power to achieve the reach to engage distant foes.

3

History for Strategists:
British Sea Power as a Relevant Past

Historians and strategic theorists have much to learn from each other, but there is little doubt that the two express different cultures and seek distinctive truths. Historians are apt to find uniqueness where strategic theorists will seek out, and almost certainly find, pattern. A study of the British experience with sea power over the past four centuries yields a rich haul of strategic history for careful exploitation by theorists. Provided strategic theorists do not fail to recognize that the applicability of general propositions about the land and sea, and later the air, are always governed by local detail, strategic theorists and historians can cooperate to mutual advantage. Viewed in the context of statecraft and conflict as a whole, British sea power over several centuries is a treasure trove of historical evidence that positively beckons for broad-gauged interpretation.

For a familiar refrain, the continuities in the structure and terms of statecraft and strategy from period to period are deeply impressive. The details of technology and political forms certainly have altered massively, but in the fields of strategic ideas, key features of geography—and broadly of geopolitical relationships—and the general warp and woof of the politics of strategy and security among states, continuities dominate discontinuities. For example, the significance of the Bosporous and the Dardanelles as a critical geostrategic chokepoint can be traced at least from the fifth century B.C. to the late 1980s and the end of the U.S.-Soviet rivalry.

Although most naval engagements throughout history have occurred close to shore, it is also true that galley warfare in the narrow waters of the Mediterranean comprised a distinct, even unified, historical experience. It is not true, however, that the geography and technology of ancient and medieval sea warfare was so distinctive in its tactical and logistic details that it has no operational or strategic value as a long case study (or series of case studies) for the strategic theorist. Closely dependent though galleys were on sustenance from the shore, land power did not eclipse sea power in strategic value. Rather, geophysical conditions in the Mediterranean prior to the modern era meant that continental powers were able to extract more strategic value for their sea power than could their successors in modern times. A related fallacy is the notion that the maturing of air power has, or will, render (surface) navies obsolete. All things are possible, but to date air power has had the paradoxical net effect of making great navies greater still.

It is unmistakable that in quite sharp general contrast with the ancient and medieval eras, in modern times continental states and coalitions have persistently failed to solve the strategic problems posed by great maritime foes. The geographical and political cultural differences between Britain and the United States are many and profound, but nonetheless the practical continuities in statecraft and strategy are vastly impressive. Of course it matters that the United States is a continental-size power an ocean away from Europe (and Asia), and not a small offshore island, but the theme of a balance-of-power policy vis-à-vis would-be hegemons in Eurasia dominates the Anglo-American experience in its entirety. The U.S. practice of superior sea power as a vital enabler for a forward continental policy has been thoroughly reminiscent of its British predecessor, even when the complications of air power and nuclear weapons are added to the stew.

There is much that strategic theorists and contemporary U.S. defense planners could learn from the four-centuries-long British practice of using sea power as the principal agency to support its statecraft. Above all else, perhaps, they could allow British strategic history to remind them of the hard cases when continental allies, as well as British expeditionary forces, failed in the field. Unfortunately, U.S. defense planning is usually based on a short-term perspective and conducted in support of shifting policy goals. History can remind only those who are willing to be reminded that bad times aiways return and that every peace lies between two wars. Finally, on a more positive note, both the British experience with sea power and the now-current U.S. practice speak to what dominant maritime power can contribute to help build, protect, and advance an international order characterized by respect for humane values.

HISTORY AND STRATEGY

After the fall of the great Russian naval fortress of Sebastopol on September 8–9, 1855, the realization gradually dawned in the Allied capitals that their combined arms had failed to wreak sufficient harm to the Russian state to cause the czar to accede to a peace of surrender.[1] The technological conditions of the mid 1850s were, of course, unique. Partially steam-driven naval power and superior armaments on the Allied side confronted a great continental state prior to its acquisition of strategic railroads. The tactical and operational feasibility of the Anglo-French (and Turkish) strategic designs of 1854–56 have nothing to say in detail to any other period. But the structure of the grand-strategic problems faced by sea-based and continental power in those years are of permanent interest.

Contemporary strategic studies is respectful but wary of history. Between them lies a disciplinary-cultural divide of no small significance. On the one hand, strategic theorists tend to be unduly interested in the general at the potential expense of the particular for the professional comfort of historians. On the other hand, historians are overly prone to retreat into the rich singularity of detail at the possible expense of a general wisdom for the professional comfort of strategists. In this chapter I seek to bridge the disciplinary-cultural divide by examining the validity of cross-historical theory and understanding, with particular reference to the British experience with sea power.

The British case virtually selects itself as the repository in modern times of strategic experience with the limits and possibilities of typically superior

1. See Andrew D Lambert, *The Crimean War. British Grand Strategy Against Russia, 1853–56* (Manchester, U.K . Manchester University Press, 1990), chap. 24. The Russian side is handled admirably in John Shelton Curtiss, *Russia's Crimean War* (Durham, N.C.: Duke University Press, 1979).

sea-based power. By no means is it my thesis that a theory explaining the strategic value of sea power can be based on three and a half centuries of British history. Nonetheless, the British record in managing sea power–land power relations is so instructive that it warrants unusual attention. It may be objected that Britain as a sea power was not so much an exemplar as an extraordinary phenomenon. Further, the objection might be registered that there is as much to be learnt about the theory and practice of strategy and statecraft from the experience of Britain's foes seeking to conduct conflict with the aid of generally second-rate naval instruments. The first objection is probably well founded, but is beside the point. Extraordinary or not, the British experience with sea power (and hence that of their foes) is an unusually rich vein to be mined and refined. The second objection is no more sound. British performance as a maritime state can be studied properly only in a context that has to include the strategic options, cultures, and styles that opposed her over the centuries. On this topic Britain is not by any means the only modern polity worth studying.

Geoffrey Till advises that "the chief utility of history for the analysis of present and future lies in its ability not to point out lessons, but to isolate things that need thinking about."[2] The British experience with the strategic value of sea power is of interest for the purpose of this chapter precisely because, as Till advises, the study of history has the ability "to isolate things that need thinking about." In his seminal examination of galley warfare in the Mediterranean in the sixteenth century, John Guilmartin Jr. warns strongly against seeking to derive a general theory of sea power from the British experience with "fighting sail" in the period bounded by the First Dutch War (1652–54) and the fall of Napoleon.[3] Of course he is right. It is natural enough that an Anglo-American author looking ultimately to explain the strategic utility of sea power for the United States in the 1990s and beyond should have the perspective provided by a tradition of dominant and open-ocean sea power. However, one can focus on the British experience and remain sensitive to the strategic-cultural and other differences between first- and second-rate sea powers, between conflict in confined waters and on the open ocean, and to differences among eras wherein marine propulsion was by oar and wind, by wind alone, by coal and oil generated steam, and—in small measure, overall—by nuclear reaction. The protracted British

2. Geoffrey Till, *Maritime Strategy and the Nuclear Age* (London: Macmillan, 1982), 224–25.

3. John Francis Guilmartin Jr. "The Mahanians' Fallacy," in *Gunpowder and Galleys: Changing Technology and Mediterranean Warfare at Sea in the Sixteenth Century* (Cambridge: Cambridge University Press, 1974).

case in the strategic value of sea power is useful for the scope and variety of experience it encompasses, including the experience of Britain's foes over the centuries, not necessarily for any model it might provide for the future, and certainly not as a mold for navies for all time.

Few students of strategy would agree with Henry Ford's dismissal of history as bunk, but few of those students are comfortable with analyses and theories that straddle the nuclear divide of 1945. It is easy to recognize an unchanging human nature, an unchanging physical geography, and unchanging impulses to compete for security. It is less easy to determine either the meaning of changing economic and technological conditions for the choices open to statesmen, or the salience of the choices exercised in one technological era for those in another.

History is a storehouse that lends itself to abuse by raiding parties on behalf of almost any persuasion among strategic theorists. Alfred Thayer Mahan was determined to put "maritime interests in the foreground" of his writing and to correct or balance the "tendency [among "historians generally"] to slight the bearing of maritime power upon events."[4] So far did he succeed that he overcorrected for the tendency that he may well have perceived accurately. So abundant is the historical record, yet so uncertain are causal relationships and so many are the levels of analysis—policy, grand-strategic, strategic, operational, and tactical—that the determined raider is unlucky indeed if he cannot locate examples to illustrate the plausibility of virtually any argument.

Analysis based on history is vulnerable to the biasing effect of the necessarily selective treatment of often uncertain data, conducted honestly or otherwise, by scholars who cannot help but have points of view. Moreover, it is all very well to assert the permanence of strategic principles, but many a general, admiral, and government has seen strategic enterprises founder on the rocks of logistic and tactical infeasibility. For example, galleys, because they needed to sustain large crews while remaining lightly burdened, had few navigational aids, were generally unseaworthy, and were obliged to operate both close to land and close to a thoroughly reliable (friendly) water supply on shore.[5] Plainly, naval squadrons whose cruising radius was limited by their ability to carry drinking water only for two or three weeks, and which could not venture out of the shelter of land onto the open sea save at

4. Alfred Thayer Mahan, *The Influence of Sea Power upon History, 1660–1783* (London: Methuen, 1965; first pub. 1890), viii and v.

5 See John H. Pryor, *Geography, Technology, and War: Studies in the Maritime History of the Mediterranean, 649–1571* (Cambridge: Cambridge University Press, 1988), 57–86.

major hazard, were operational and strategic instruments of distinctly limited value. For a further example of the critical importance of logistic details, it was not until Sir Edward Hawke organized the contemporary equivalent of the fleet train in 1759 that the British Royal Navy was operationally and tactically capable of imposing an effective close blockade of the French Biscay and Breton ports—weather permitting (another nontrivial factor in the age of fighting sail, as always).[6] Prior to 1759, it had been British naval policy to blockade Brest via distant observation from the western Channel ports. This traditional practice of distant observation had failed to provide an effective grip on the French battle fleet in 1756–58; its repetition in the War of American Independence was to have disastrous consequences for the balance of naval power off the American coast.

For a landward example, the strategic problem posed between 1914 and 1918 by the need to invest the continental "fortress" of Germany and Austria-Hungary was obvious even to a dim intelligence. The German army, the mainstay—in Clausewitzian terms the "center of gravity"—of the Central Powers, had to be beaten or at least worn down in the field, and the only logistically feasible field for the principal British effort on land was Belgium and northern France.[7] After allied setbacks in the spring and summer of 1915, and certainly after the launching of the German offensive against the French army at Verdun in February 1916, Britain had no practicable choice but to bear an ever heavier burden of the fighting on the western front. It is worth noting that the United States proved to be exceedingly suspicious of the fluctuating interest of its European cobelligerents in pursuing the defeat of the Central Powers in secondary (other than French) theaters of war. It was made very plain indeed in 1917 that a continuation of the principal concentration of allied effort on the western front would be a condition for the dispatch and employment of a large American Expeditionary Force.[8]

6. Geoffrey Marcus, *Quiberon Bay: The Campaign in Home Waters, 1759* (London: Hollis & Carter, 1960), 66. In another work, Marcus called the close blockade of Brest "a revolution in naval strategy." *Heart of Oak: A Survey of British Sea Power in the Georgian Era* (London: Oxford University Press, 1975), 20.

7. J.F.C. Fuller argued that "the main bases and the main theatre of war were fixed by geography and logistics, and no juggling with fronts could alter this." *The Conduct of War, 1789–1961: A Study of the Impact of the French, Industrial, and Russian Revolutions on War and Its Conduct* (London: Eyre & Spottiswoode, 1961), 162 Also see John Terraine, *The Western Front, 1914–1918* (London: Hutchinson, 1964), 90–113.

8 See David F. Trask, *The United States in the Supreme War Council: American War Aims and Inter-Allied Strategy, 1917–1918* (Middletown, Conn. Wesleyan University Press, 1961), 13, 146.

Notions of the strategically desirable are relatively unchanging, but feasibility is ruled by the details of supply, influenced by technology, and generally dominated by the quality and quantity of the military instrument to hand. The relationships among policy, grand strategy, strategy, operations, and tactics are all interactive. It does not suffice to say that forces and their tactics must be able to implement a strategy that relates military power effectively to the ends of policy. The policymaker and the strategist, no matter how wise their chosen policy and strategy, always must have an eye to the practicality of their designs. The first duty of the statesman vis-à-vis his armed forces in, or toward, war is so to set the political stage for the conflict that those forces stand a reasonable prospect of success. The forces should not depend for victory on some deus ex machina: "wonder weapons" introduced at the eleventh hour; the break-up of a hostile coalition; repeated gross military errors on the part of the enemy; or even the working of cunning deception plans to achieve tactical surprise.

A historically wide-ranging work of analysis and theory can founder on tactical and logistic details that have changed dramatically from period to period, but the opposite peril also applies. Works of theory may ascend to so high a plateau of generality that although secure against tactical invalidation, the "lessons" derived from historical study are stupefyingly obvious and practically useless. It has been a hallmark of successful statesmen and military leaders that they knew when to break the rules (divide the fleet, engage in a melee battle via "general chase" rather than rigidly forming in line-of-battle as required by the Permanent Fighting Instructions, and so on). Knowledge of how to apply general precepts is much more important than the precepts themselves.

It is not enlightening or helpful to be advised by careful historical study to have a genius in command. Genius by definition is rare and is difficult to identify prior to its unmistakable demonstration in action. There is much to be said for the advice that "the best strategy is always to *be very strong* . . . at the decisive point" (obedient to the principles of concentration and economy of force).[9] Admiral Yamamoto's violation of this precept (among others, to include the principle of simplicity in operations) helped critically to lead to defeat at Midway in June 1942. But since the location of the decisive point is determined by interaction between rival military machines, the ability to identify at will and enforce the location and timing of the decisive point is unlikely to be wholly reliable.

---

9 Carl von Clausewitz, *On War*, ed and trans. Michael Howard and Peter Paret (Princeton, N.J.: Princeton University Press, 1976; first pub. 1832), 204. Emphasis in original.

The strategic significance of particular features of physical geography has varied greatly as the identity, and hence location, of the major players in the politics of international security has altered, as technologies of many kinds have increased or decreased the cruising range of ships, and as economic, political, and military intercourse has expanded from the eastern Mediterranean to encompass the entire world. To cite a case of continuity in importance, the maritime defiles connecting the Aegean and the Black Seas, the Bosporus and the Dardanelles, retained a strategic significance that defied time, technology, and changing polities. Those defiles were critical to Greek security against Persia; vital for Athens's food supply from the Crimea;[10] provided refuge for the fleet of the Byzantine Empire and served as the protected central hub (interior lines, à la Jomini) from which the Byzantines, and later the Ottoman Turks, flexibly could choose to concentrate in the Aegean or the Black Sea (a two-sea fleet on the cheap, courtesy of control of the Bosporus and Dardanelles chokepoints); promoted the security of Venetian and Genoese trade with Asia; and in more recent times were the key to keeping Russian sea power out of the Mediterranean, keeping Anglo-French sea power out of the Black Sea for the succor of a hard-pressed Russian ally (1915), and in the Cold War were critical for the confinement of the Soviet Black Sea Fleet. Only the advent of air power modified the geostrategic significance of the Bosporus and the Dardanelles. In recent decades neither NATO nor the Soviet Union could be optimistic over the wartime survivability of surface fleets in the confined waters of the Aegean and the eastern Mediterranean. Since the early 1940s the air balance has been critical for the determination of permissible risk-taking in forward deployment in restricted waters. Eric Grove makes an essential point when he asserts that "sea power and air power are indivisible."[11]

The relevance of sea power to the rivalries and wars of particular states and coalitions has depended far more on geostrategic context than on contemporary level of technological development. The parable of the whale and the elephant or, if one prefers, the tiger and the shark, who each have enormous difficulty forcing a decision on the other, is as relevant for U.S.-Soviet rivalry as it was for Greece in the fifth century B.C. The contrasts in basic transportation and other technologies between the fifth century B.C. and the twentieth century A.D. notwithstanding, for many decades continental Sparta could not effectively oppose the system of war devised by maritime

10. See Josiah Ober, *Fortress Attica: Defense of the Athenian Land Frontier, 404–332 B C.* (Leiden: E. J. Brill, 1985), 36–37.
11. Eric Grove, *The Future of Sea Power* (Annapolis, Md.: Naval Institute Press, 1990), 138.

Athens while the land-power Germany of the Third Reich was strategically baffled by the Straits of Dover and an insular, sea-power enemy on the flanks of its continental empire. Unlike Germany, Sparta was able to solve its strategic problems after Athens had overreached itself with its Sicilian expedition (415–413 B.C.). The Athenian disaster in Sicily emboldened Persia to assist the Spartans and Corinthians in assembling sufficient sea power to challenge Athens in its own realm of strategic excellence. Nazi Germany, far from solving its problems of bringing superior land power to grips with a maritime enemy, fatally compounded its difficulties by undertaking a great adventure in the East for which, again, its system of war (particularly its logistic reach) was thoroughly unsuited. To press the analogy further, both maritime Athens and continental Germany had to ruin themselves by overextension in their own mediums of general excellence before they were weak enough to be liable to definitive defeat, which is say defeat in the war as opposed to the loss of a battle or even a campaign. Persia did not dare subsidize Sparta's maritime war against Athens prior to the Athenian catastrophe at Syracuse in 415–413 B.C. The sea-based power of the Western members of the Grand Alliance against Nazi Germany became competitive in land warfare only following Germany's gross continental overextension in the war in the East and with the achievement of air superiority early in 1944.

Far from being eclipsed in strategic importance as a result of the maturing of air, missile, and other space technologies, some of the ideas of maritime strategy, in addition to retaining their value for operations on earth, are applicable to military operations in space. The marine ocean and the space ocean—admittedly with the important exception of weather, which does not exist (save for the consequences of variations in solar activity, and the problems that terrestrial weather can pose for space launch activity) in the latter—as well as the desert on earth, have some geostrategic features in common. There is more to learn about military space operations from Julian Corbett's 1911 book, *Some Principles of Maritime Strategy*,[12] than from any number of much more recent tracts on air power, let alone on the geophysically mysterious, hybrid concept of aerospace power.

Technological change necessarily modifies the tactical and operational application of sea power. But the case for affirming continuity in the relevance of the sea-land nexus in crisis and war from the time of Themis-

---

12. Julian S. Corbett, *Some Principles of Maritime Strategy* (Annapolis, Md.: Naval Institute Press, 1988; first pub. 1911).

tocles to the present day is far stronger than any claim for bounding the terms of reference in accordance with one or another technological or political great divide. There are many candidate fences for the bounding of the historical experience relevant to the future.

First, there was the shift from a preponderance of oar power to virtually all wind power in the late fifteenth and sixteenth centuries, married both to revolutionary advances in the science of navigation and to the adaptation of gunpowder artillery for shipboard use. Naval tactics altered dramatically as ships became artillery platforms rather than merely platforms for infantry combat at sea. Second, in Western perspective, there is a great divide between ancient/medieval and modern times, with the reorientation of the most important lines of conflict in European security politics from those states that bordered the closed sea of the Mediterranean to those on the shores of the open Atlantic.

Third, one might employ as a breakpoint for historical evidence the wholesale change from sail to steam power in the third quarter of the nineteenth century, as marine and naval science applied the fruits of the industrial revolution. Fourth, there is a case for fencing-out allegedly irrelevant historical experience by focusing on the change in the economies of transportation effected by the rise of the railroads and the internal combustion engine. Speaking in 1904, the British geographer and occasional geopolitical theorist Halford J. Mackinder concluded that the internal unification of the continents by the railroad was effecting the end of a four-hundred-year-long Columbian Era characterized by the preponderance of sea power over land power.[13]

Fifth, it is possible to argue for the exclusion of historical evidence prior to the maturing of air power. In its strategic significance, air power came of age during World War II. Air power, as well as sea power, helps shape the course and outcome of war. When air power in its many forms is interrogated for its meaning, no problems of substance arise. As a general rule air power has functioned as an adjunct to land and sea power; it has been an expression of and has expanded the nature and effectiveness of each. Even in some cases wherein air power appeared to be strategic in operation, in the particular sense of being independently decisive, it transpires on closer investigation that the air campaign in question was conducted from advanced

13. Halford J. Mackinder, *Democratic Ideals and Reality* (New York: W. W. Norton, 1962; first pub. 1942), 241ff. See W. H Parker, *Mackinder: Geography as an Aid to Statecraft* (Oxford: Clarendon Press, 1982), chap. 6, and Geoffrey Parker, *Western Geopolitical Thought in the Twentieth Century* (New York: St. Martin's Press, 1985), chap. 3.

bases seized and held by some mixture of sea and land power. The argument
I develop here is sensitive to the possibility that the maturing of air power
either has invalidated, or is about to invalidate, analysis framed in a
traditional sea-land framework.

Sixth, the clearest and probably most popular and defensible criterion for
inclusion or exclusion of historical experience is that provided by the nuclear
revolution heralded in 1945.[14] Seventh, and typically rather vaguely related
to the sixth suggestion, the emergence after World War II of a bipolar U.S.-
Soviet standoff could be taken to herald the beginning of prudently usable
historical experience. Eighth and finally, there is the view that the conclusion of the Cold War in 1989–90 and the demise of the Soviet Union itself
in December 1991 ushered in a new era, which will, or might, function in
the security realm with terms of reference very different even from those of
the 1970s and 1980s, let alone from distant centuries.

These suggestions comprise only a sample of the breakpoints that could
be selected for the fencing-out of arguably irrelevant historical experience.
The importance of the historical changes just cited is not seriously in doubt.
But none of those changes, *including the nuclear revolution*, has so far
changed the missions statesmen endorse for their sea power so profoundly
that previous wars and insecurity conditions hold only an antiquarian
fascination. Mackinder's thesis that the twentieth century would see a closed
world that must favor land power over sea power did not point to a change
with boundary-for-evidence implications for examination of the sea-land
strategic nexus. Mackinder predicted that every shoreline would be held by
organized security communities increasingly better able to move people and
material efficiently and rapidly by land.[15]

Mackinder's closed-world argument was correct and strategically important, but it did not imply the eclipse of sea power that he predicted and
feared. The twentieth century to date has seen the critical influence of sea
power in *grande guerre* demonstrated twice, and the world war that might
have been, between East and West, bore much promise of being structured
in part by familiar sea power–land power factors. Furthermore, the influence
of land power on sea power is at least as significant and interesting as is the
influence of sea power on land power. The Persians, the Spartans, the
Macedonians, above all others—to date—the Romans, and in nontrivial
measure the Germans sought to command the sea *from the land*. It was,

14. The clearest exposition is Robert Jervis, *The Meaning of the Nuclear Revolution· Statecraft and the Prospect of Armageddon* (Ithaca, N Y. Cornell University Press, 1989), chap 1.
15. Mackinder, *Democratic Ideals and Reality*, 242.

however, in the thousand-year struggle between Christian and Moslem sea power in the narrow waters of the Mediterranean that the significance of land power for sea power was demonstrated most persuasively. In the Mediterranean of late antique, medieval, and early modern times, the high road to superior sea power was the control of coasts and therefore of naval bases. This contrast with modern navalist beliefs was dictated by the weather and physical geography of the Mediterranean, as well as by the marine and navigational technologies of the long period in question.

Sea power is a direct product of the resources of the land—people for crews, wood or iron and steel (and other metals) for construction, food and water for shipboard supplies, and so forth.[16] If rival states are deprived of coastline from which sea power can be projected, they can pose no maritime threat. Despite its definitive naval victory in the first war with Carthage (over the control of Sicily), Roman strategic culture remained thoroughly land-minded. Apart from periodic difficulties with piracy, prior to the final time of troubles of the Western Empire Rome had scant need of a large navy of dedicated warships because the Mediterranean was *mare nostrum* for Rome, a sea totally bordered by Roman territory. Nonetheless, the leading modern historian of the imperial Roman navy has pointed out that "we are dealing with the Romans, so generally and with some justice considered a landbound folk, but these same Romans developed the control and organs of sea power to their highest refinement in antiquity."[17]

Roman statesmen had the precedent of Alexander the Great (ruler of another land-minded empire, Macedon) solving the problem of the Persian maritime threat to his lines of communication by eliminating that threat, at its source, from the land. Of more recent vintage, Adolf Hitler briefly was intrigued in the fall of 1940 with a landward project against Gibraltar (Operation Felix), but Francisco Franco declined to cooperate.[18] A powerful strategic incentive behind the British offensive in Flanders in 1917 (Third Ypres, or Passchendaele) was the Royal Navy's insistence that the German

16. Writing of his British fellow countrymen in the nineteenth century, Mackinder said: "They knew what it was to enjoy sea-power, the freedom of the ocean, but they forgot that sea-power is, in large measure, dependent on the production of the base on which it rests, and that East Europe and the Heartland would make a mighty sea base." Ibid., 138.

17. Chester G. Starr Jr., *The Roman Imperial Navy, 31 B.C.–A D 324* (Westport, Conn.: Greenwood Press, 1975; first pub. 1941), 167. For two centuries the Roman Navy kept the principal commercial routes in the Mediterranean clear of what had been the perennial scourge of piracy (173). Not until the nineteenth century was the Mediterranean again to be as free of pirates as it was in the first two centuries of the Christian era.

18. See Ronald Lewin, *Hitler's Mistakes* (London: Leo Cooper, 1984), 113–19.

U-boat bases in Flanders had to be seized from the land. As early as January 1, 1915, Winston Churchill, then First Lord of the Admiralty, informed the commander in chief of the British Expeditionary Force (B.E.F.) as follows: "The battleship *Formidable* was sunk this morning by a submarine in the Channel. Information from all quarters shows that the Germans are steadily developing an important submarine base at Zeebrugge. *Unless an operation can be undertaken to clear the coast,* and particularly to capture this place, it must be recognized that the whole transportation of troops across the Channel will be seriously and increasingly compromised."[19]

During the Cold War, U.S. defense planners considered the influence of a NATO preponderant at sea on an effectively landlocked, continental Soviet enemy. But U.S. grand and military strategy also had to consider what a Soviet victory on land in Western Europe would have meant for Soviet sea-air power (Soviet submarine bases at Brest, Lorient, La Rochelle, La Rota?); what such a victory would have meant for U.S. access to European and North African waters, territory, and airspace; and how Soviet sea power could have had direct and indirect influence over the military effectiveness of NATO land power.

Although there is some historical support for the proposition that "it is easier for landpower to take to the sea than for sea power to take to the land,"[20] this notion warrants the judgment that it is a persuasive fallacy. Certainly one should not be blinded by the British experience into believing that thalassocracies enjoy inherent and abiding competitive advantages over continental empires. There is considerable potential for misunderstanding in this much-quoted judgment by Field Marshal Montgomery: "From the days when humans first began to use the seas, the great lesson of history is that the enemy who is confined to a land strategy is in the end defeated."[21] The field marshal was not claiming that land powers have always been beaten by sea powers. Rather did he mean that land powers confined to a continental strategy always have been beaten *eventually*. Furthermore, there are some abiding reasons why the plainly discernible advantage in modern times (post 1500) of sea power over land power is likely to continue. Significantly, Martin Wight noted that "Mackinder's most cogent examples

19. Quoted in John Terraine, *The Road to Passchendaele: The Flanders Offensive of 1917—A Study in Inevitability* (London: Leo Cooper, 1984; first pub. 1977), 10. Emphasis added.
20. Martin Wight, *Power Politics* (New York: Holmes & Meier, 1978), 78. Wight is simply interpreting Mackinder; he is not endorsing the proposition.
21. Quoted in Peter Gretton, *Maritime Strategy: A Study of Defense Problems* (New York: Praeger, 1965), 43.

of the ultimate superiority of land power are drawn from classical history. Perhaps he did not sufficiently consider that the states-system of classical antiquity grew up round a sea enclosed by land, while the modern states-system has grown up on a continent surrounded by the ocean."[22]

Mahan and Mackinder, though they adopted contrasting geostrategic perspectives, nonetheless agreed on the dependence of sea power on the resources of the land. In his essay "The Elements of Sea Power" Mahan gave pride of place to geographical position. His first sentence under that heading proceeded as follows: "It may be pointed out, in the first place, that if a nation be so situated that it is neither forced to defend itself by land nor induced to seek extension of its territory by way of the land, it has, by the very unity of its aim directed upon the sea, an advantage as compared with a people one of whose boundaries is continental."[23]

The reasoning in this point was the principal motive force impelling Elizabeth I to expend scarce English assets in direct support of the revolt of the Spanish Netherlands against Madrid. Elizabeth reluctantly dispatched a modest body of soldiers for continental campaigning and initiated the policy of subsidizing continental allies, practices that were to be hallmarks of British statecraft for nearly four centuries. It would be an error to believe that there are land powers as contrasted with sea powers in some thoroughly exclusive sense. In practice, strategic geography and economic necessity or opportunity indeed have inclined states in one or the other direction, but great naval strength can be accumulated by a traditional land power, just as a formidable army can be raised by a sea power. It was Mackinder's great fear in the early decades of this century that a land power, or a continental coalition inadequately distracted on its landward frontiers, would have the economic resources for the development of overwhelming sea power.[24] Mackinder, in company with many commentators before and since, was prone to overestimate the ease with which great naval power could be developed from nominally adequate resources. The infrastructure for a first-class navy takes decades to construct.

Mahan drew the wrong lesson from the Roman strategy in the Second

---

22. Wight, *Power Politics*, 77.
23. Mahan, *Influence of Sea Power upon History*, 29.
24. "What if the Great Continent, the Whole World-Island or a large part of it, were at some future time to become a single and united base of sea-power? Would not the other insular bases be outbuilt as regards ships and outmanned as regards seamen? . . . [M]ust we not still reckon with the possibility that a large part of the Great Continent might some day be united under a single sway, and that an invincible sea-power might be based upon it?" Mackinder, *Democratic Ideals and Reality*, 70.

Punic War. The Roman conduct of that war does indeed demonstrate the utility of command of the sea. But no less important was the example provided of how strategic necessity can drive a well-founded, land-minded state to seek at sea a vital complement to its traditional orientation toward continental campaigning. To a lesser degree, Sparta had done the same (one should recall the seemingly definitive eclipse of Athenian naval power at Aegospotami in 405 B.C. by Lysander), as had Alexander the Great when he created Macedonian naval strength out of the landward defeat of the base structure of the Persian fleet on the Mediterranean littoral (333–332 B.C.). The sources of Roman, Spartan, and Macedonian sea power were scarcely at all those specified canonically by Mahan, with his emphasis on the links in the chain among domestic production, colonies, maritime trade, and, inevitably, a fighting fleet. Rome, Sparta, and Macedon became *naval powers*, but were not true or "natural" sea powers. A maritime focus for strategic analysis can incline scholars to wax unduly lyrical about the natural inclination to the sea, and hence the organic and enduring character of the sea power of such thalassocratic states as Athens, Carthage, arguably Byzantium and Genoa, Venice, and Britain. But important though the distinction may be between a "merely military" naval power and a natural sea power,[25] the potential of the former to threaten the latter should not be despised. It so happens that the greatest naval power of the 1990s, the United States, is far from being a natural sea power.

Geostrategically, the United States is all but insular, because of the weakness of the countries on its borders, but its sheer size has imposed a continentalist strategic outlook, albeit an outlook somewhat modified in recent decades by a preference for air power. Americans are a very air-minded people. Nonetheless, the United States is the world's largest trading nation, and by volume by far the larger part of that trade comes by sea. It is true that most of the more than 850 million tons of U.S. exports and imports each year is carried in the merchant ships flagged to other states, but that fact is not of great importance. What does matter is that the overwhelming bulk of U.S. trade, like world trade in general, is necessarily maritime. The security of maritime trade routes is of the most vital importance to U.S., and world, prosperity. The American people have little direct and obvious connection with ships and have less and less personal experience of maritime travel on the social dimension to strategy; that continuing trend is not helpful to public understanding of the importance of their stake in order at sea.

---

25. The idea of a "natural," as contrasted with an artificial, sea power, was developed in Herbert Richmond, *Sea Power in the Modern World* (London: G Bell & Sons, 1934), chap 1.

Virtually all the elements necessary for understanding sea power–land power nexuses can be gleaned from the British experience over four hundred years in modern history. Nonetheless, there are strategic cautionary points of value to learn from ancient and medieval times, wherein maritime Athens, Carthage, Persia,[26] and—much later—Byzantium lost to continentalist Sparta, Rome, Macedon, and Ottoman Turkey. These cases do not illustrate anything as simple as the superiority of land power over sea power. On the contrary, perhaps, they show how land powers can, and have, taken to the sea—or have bribed or intimidated maritime allies—in order to neutralize and then defeat the strategy of a true sea power. Strategic history is not a repetitive tale of sea power versus land power, but rather the saga of how each can be exploited to generate strength for decision against the other in a medium where there is a common unit of campaign account.

In the remainder of this chapter I treat the question of the relevance of historical experience for the present and the future with the argument focused, with an important caveat, on the British experience from the Elizabethan period to the 1940s. The caveat is that it is easy to forget that bodies of water can be either barriers or highways, depending on who, if anyone, "commands" them. Britain did not win its first world war (the Seven Years' War, 1756–63) or its twenty-two-year-long struggle with revolutionary and later imperial France because it was a true sea power or because a sea power somehow is beyond the strategic grasp of a land power. Britain won those wars because it made fewer significant errors in grand strategy than France did. There are linked formulas, perhaps broad principles, for grand and national military strategy that go far to explain British success. When pursued competently, those principles tended to produce performance in the conduct of war superior to that by a France that lacked a suitable policy-strategy system. In the first three years of the Seven Years' War, again in its maritime war with France (and Spain, from 1779) from 1778 to 1783, and arguably yet again in the 1790s, Britain showed that it was at least as capable as France of pursuing faulty strategy.

THE BRITISH EXPERIENCE

One should resist any temptation to read the modern British experience in statecraft and strategy as all-purpose validation of allegedly eternal precepts

26. The Persian Empire was a great naval power, not a natural sea power in Richmond's sense.

concerning sea power–land power relationships. Like the United States in the early campaigns in the Pacific in World War II, the British worked for, and generally deserved, the luck that was theirs. The incompetence of the enemy, nonetheless, was frequently critical for national success. This is not to deny that in modern times continental powers have tended to find insuperable difficulty understanding either how to transmute land power into sea power, or otherwise how to offset hostile sea power. Overall, continental statesmen have proved unequal to the problem of composing and executing military strategy suitable for assault on the strategy of an essentially maritime enemy. The Spaniards, the French, and the Germans failed in both grand and military strategy to solve their British problems. But, as noted already, the Spartans, the Macedonians, the Romans, periodically the Arabs, and certainly the Turks did succeed in resolving their maritime difficulties, albeit through that excellent education which painful experience provides.

The relevance of the protracted British historical example to the American situation is in good part a function of the geography of the Western alliance that the United States has led. Too much can be made of the idea that Columbia has inherited Britannia's trident. Geopolitics is about possibilities, not about geographically determined policies and policy outcomes. Soviet maritime power could have been forcibly confined to Eurasian coastal waters not by U.S. naval strength per se, but rather by U.S. naval strength applied to chokepoints or zones that would be chokepoints precisely because the relevant landforms were in friendly hands. Operating unilaterally at transoceanic range, the U.S. Navy and Air Force probably could have rendered hazardous Soviet naval passage into the Atlantic from the Barents Sea, the Baltic, and the Mediterranean, as well as passage into the Pacific and the Yellow Sea. However, the potential for the landlocking of Soviet naval power was at least as much a result of political, as of physical, geography. Should a few among Norway, Denmark, Iceland, Britain, Turkey, Spain, Portugal, and Japan have ceased to be active and reliable allies of the United States, then the four-centuries-long British analogy for U.S. maritime strategy in the Cold War would have lost some of its relevance.

Geostrategically appreciated, Britain itself is a breakwater, physically located to canalize the seaborne trade of southern Europe with northern Europe and well placed to interdict at will, subject to capability, the maritime traffic of the great *entrepôts* of northern and western Europe with their transoceanic sources of supply and their markets.[27] The measure of

27. See Halford J. Mackinder, *Britain and the British Seas* (Oxford: Clarendon Pres, 1915; first pub. 1906), chaps. 1, 18

safety that reposes in mere distance, subject to the caveat already provided concerning the balance of maritime strength, poses the enemies of the United States a difficult logistic problem. But U.S. policymakers cannot forget that their country, although strategically advantaged by oceanic separation from Eurasia, is also handicapped in comparison with its functional British predecessor by the geopolitical fact that U.S. territory is not itself a barrier against bids for maritime *Weltpolitik* stemming from continental Eurasia. Although we should recognize the geopolitical and geostrategic dissimilarities between the Britain of the alleged Columbian Era and the United States of the 1990s, the relevance of the British experience to the structure of the U.S. security context remains impressive.

Periodically, Britain has been threatened by the possible emergence of a dominant power or coalition on the continent at least nominally able to use a large fraction of its economic assets to support a great maritime challenge. Speaking in 1911, the British Foreign Secretary, Sir Edward Grey, warned that a Britain aloof from European balance-of-power politics could find itself challenged by the need to meet what would amount to a five-power standard in naval strength.[28] In part, though only in part, to arrest the maturing of this recurring danger, it was British policy to seek alliance with the second strongest power or coalition in Europe. The purpose was to tip the balance of power against the aspiring hegemon and keep it occupied in an expensive ground war. Britain would contribute as little by way of direct land power as its allies could tolerate, consistent with satisfactory conduct of the continental contest. British statecraft typically was indifferent to the political complexion of allied states. Alliance ties were made and unmade expediently for management of the balance of power. Britain's interest in the balance of power in Europe did not focus narrowly on the idea that landward distraction would fatally inhibit a continental foe from building a truly first-class navy. Particularly with reference to France in the eighteenth century, Britain understood very well that the hindrances to French sea power were much more numerous and substantial than just the periodic fact of continental military distraction.[29]

In the eighteenth century, following a useful period of alliance with

---

28. Cited in Norman Gibbs, "British Strategic Doctrine, 1918–1939," in *The Theory and Practice of War*, ed. Michael Howard (London: Cassell, 1965), 190.

29. An outstanding recent discussion is N. A. M. Rodger, "The Continental Commitment in the Eighteenth Century," in *War, Strategy, and International Politics: Essays in Honour of Sir Michael Howard*, ed. Lawrence Freedman, Paul Hayes, and Robert O'Neill (Oxford: Clarendon Press, 1992), 39–53

France after the Peace of Utrecht in 1713 (in which period Britain used France to accelerate forcibly the decline of Spanish sea power, much as it had sought to use France against the Dutch in the 1670s), Britain successively allied, again, with Austria in the 1740s in the War of Austrian Succession (1740–48), and with Prussia in the Seven Years' War (1756–63). In the period 1815–1914, following the war with France (1793–1815, with brief pauses in 1802–3 and 1814–15), Britain generally eschewed formal alliance entanglements. In the nineteenth century the principal foe was France—in the 1890s it was the Franco-Russian Alliance—a status transferred to Germany in the First Morocco Crisis of 1905. (Even while Britain and France were allied against Russia in the Crimean War, Britain's Royal Navy was building major warships in competition with the French navy.) In the words of Winston Churchill:

> For four hundred years the foreign policy of England has been to oppose the strongest, most aggressive, most dominating Power on the Continent, and particularly to prevent the Low Countries falling into the hands of such a Power. . . . Observe that the policy of England takes no account of which nation it is that seeks the overlordship of Europe. The question is not whether it is Spain, or the French Monarchy, or the French Empire, or the German Empire, or the Hitler regime. It has nothing to do with rulers or nations; it is concerned solely with whoever is the strongest or the potentially dominant tyrant.[30]

It should be recalled that the United States intervened in the First World War as a cobelligerent in 1917 and was enthusiastic in its alliance with the totalitarian Soviet Union, as well as with democratic, but imperial, Britain, from 1941 until 1945. Similarly, the American colonies had no terrible crisis of conscience over accepting military assistance from monarchical France and Spain in 1778 and 1779. Notwithstanding the ideological cast to American political culture, U.S. policymakers have obeyed in practice the ancient precept that "the enemy of my enemy is my friend." In support of a rather dim vision of some "new world order," the United States of the early 1990s embraced the "terrorist" state of Syria as an ally of temporary convenience and deemed it expedient not to dwell on China's record of

---

30. Winston S. Churchill, *The Second World War*, vol. 1, *The Gathering Storm* (London: Guild Publishing, 1985; first pub. 1948), 186, 187.

domestic oppression. *Plus ça change* . . . In the twentieth century the
United States has acted to restore or sustain a balance of power in Eurasia
when the British weight in the scales, for the same purpose, was manifestly
inadequate (1917, 1941, 1947).

British statesmen had to resolve the grand and military strategic conun-
drum of how much effort to allocate directly to continental power balancing
(from sending British soldiers, to hiring [German or Portuguese] mercenaries, to simply subsidizing allies), and how much to allocate to maritime
endeavors. British naval historian Piers Mackesy notes that in the Great War
with France from 1793 to 1815 Britain "ranked as a great power not because
of its army but because of its wealth, which it used to keep the armies of the
other great powers in the war."[31]

Over the past hundred years too much has been made of the proposition
that there is a traditional British way in warfare. As expounded by Julian
Corbett and Basil Liddell-Hart, and revived recently by Daniel A. Baugh,[32]
this "British way" allegedly entails the blockade of continental ports, distant
"blue water" maritime operations (to acquire the colonies and overseas trade
of continental powers cut off by the Royal Navy from access to the world
beyond Europe), subsidies to allies, symbolic ground-forces' commitment to
the continent, and peripheral raiding around the continental littoral to
exploit the flexibility of sea power for surprise maneuver.[33] Corbett and
Liddell-Hart, for example, confuse necessity with strategic grand design.
Those theorists neglect to appreciate the extent to which geostrategic circumstances alter, if not priorities, then at least the operational application of
priorities in defense planning.

The British way in warfare that approached a navalist's ideal was rarely
attained or sustained in practice, and the repeated exceptions to its exercise
are at least as instructive as its occasional reality. Britain was a small, if

31. Piers Mackesy, "Problems of an Amphibious Power: Britain against France, 1793–1815," in
Assault from the Sea· Essays on the History of Amphibious Warfare, ed. Merrill L. Bartlett
(Annapolis, Md.: Naval Institute Press), 61.

32. Daniel A. Baugh, "British Strategy during the First World War in the Context of Four
Centuries: Blue-Water versus Continental Commitment," in *Naval History: The Sixth Symposium
of the U S. Naval Academy*, ed. Daniel M. Masterton (Wilmington, Del.: Scholarly Resources,
1987), 85–110.

33. Corbett, *Some Principles of Maritime Strategy*, chaps. 3–6, and Basil Liddell-Hart, *The
British Way in Warfare* (London: Faber & Faber, 1932). For a powerful critique of "the British
[limited, maritime] way in warfare" thesis, see Michael Howard, "The British Way in Warfare: A
Reappraisal," in *The Causes of Wars and Other Essays* (London: Unwin Paperbacks, 1984; first pub
1983), 189–207. David French, *The British Way in Warfare, 1688–2000* (London: Unwin Hyman,
1990), is workmanlike.

increasingly wealthy, country during the course of the most virulent century-plus of Anglo-French antagonism in modern times, from the 1680s until 1815. Since for reasons of domestic politics Britain could not introduce conscription for the army, it simply could not maintain a first-class navy, plus adequate garrisons for the growing empire overseas, plus a large army of occupation in Ireland (and, until the 1750s, in the heavily Jacobite-loyal parts of Scotland also), as well as an army sufficiently large for continental campaigns. Variations on this theme of manpower shortage applied even with conscription (1916 and 1939) to the two world wars of this century, as well as to the wars of the French Revolution and Empire.

The British military commitment in the Iberian peninsula, first under Sir John Moore and later under the Duke of Wellington, was close to comprising the maximum feasible British land-power effort. British imperial forces under Sir Douglas Haig's command in 1918 totaled fifty-nine divisions. Although there is ample ground for questioning the massive dispersal of Imperial Army assets to "Eastern" and colonial theaters throughout the First World War (East Africa, Gallipoli, Mesopotamia, Palestine, Salonika), there is little doubt that having borne the brunt of the fighting on the western front from mid 1916 until the end of hostilities, the well of British manpower was running dry in 1918.[34] The case of World War II is even plainer.

The principal British military effort in that war, as it had been in the rearmament program of the 1930s, was devoted to the Royal Air Force, not to the army or the navy. For a variety of reasons, including prestige and longer-term imperial security as well as immediate strategic advantage, by late 1944 Britain, supported by its empire, was waging three massive continental campaigns; in France and the Low Countries, Italy, and Burma. Field Marshal Bernard Montgomery was obliged to direct his 21st Army Group from Normandy to the Elbe in the knowledge that it comprised, quite literally, Britain's last army; there were no British reserve divisions. John Terraine makes the telling point that in the First World War the British Empire suffered 38,834 fatalities among officers, a loss of the nation's elite that contributed strongly to the interwar determination in Britain that "never again" must it wage large-scale continental warfare. However, in the Second World War the RAF suffered 55,573 aircrew (largely officer) fatalities.[35]

---

34. For Haig's manpower problems on the eve of the German spring offensive of 1918, see John Terraine, *Douglas Haig: The Educated Soldier* (London: Hutchinson, 1963), chap. 11; but see Tim Travers, *How the War Was Won: Command and Technology in the British Army on the Western Front, 1917–1918* (London: Routledge, 1992), 36, for a much less sympathetic opinion.

35. John Terraine, *A Time for Courage: The Royal Air Force in the European War, 1938–1945* (New York: Macmillan, 1985), 682.

Dependence on air power had been touted misleadingly as a way to avoid the slaughter of continental warfare à la 1914–18.

Time after time, maritime Britain was obliged to make a maximum feasible continental effort. Because Britain never prepared ahead of time for continental campaigning on a large scale, its army, typically pared to the bone in peacetime, was never as effective as it should have been in continental warfare. Indeed, Britain's peacetime neglect of its army drove its grand and military strategy toward heavy dependence on continental allies. Britain's greatest ever commitment to continuous and very large scale continental warfare, from 1914 to 1918, stands as a classic illustration of how not to raise and employ a mass army. This is not to demean the monumental achievement of the British army in utterly transforming its character in the course of two years and then beating through attrition (that is to say, hard fighting) the finest, or at least what had been the finest, army in the world.

Repeatedly, British statesmen have been attracted to a fairly pure form of maritime warfare. Provided the enemy of the day had an important overseas economic network, as was true of Spain, the Netherlands, and France (though to differing degrees), it is not difficult to see why Britain preferred to have land war waged on the continent, the dying performed by allies (or by German mercenaries), the commercial profits of war accrue to London (some of which could be invested in the bribery of continental allies), and permanent colonial advantage follow from the success of British naval arms.

Britain's recurring strategic problem was that continental allies failed to play their part adequately in occupying the attention of the aspiring hegemonic power on the Continent. Allies either went down in defeat or were in serious danger of so doing. The British army that was eventually to triumph over a somewhat dispirited enemy in the hundred-days' campaign of fall 1918, had its origins in a mere six-division commitment in August 1914, one division of which was withheld in Britain against a nonexistent German invasion menace. Until the era of long-range bombardment by aircraft and ballistic missiles, offshore Britain had to design its grand strategy so that some suitable weight of land power could threaten the would-be hegemonic foe of the day. In principle there should have been a fairly direct inverse relationship between the scale of danger to Britain's vital interests and the quantity and quality of continental distraction provided successively to the Spaniards, the Dutch, the French, and the Germans. Frequently, however, there was the danger that the enemy would succeed on land, despite substantial British and British-allied effort, or that the enemy might decide to resolve its continental problems by dealing a fatal maritime stroke at the British paymaster of the antihegemonic coalition.

In common with ancient Athens and, with suitable provision for a robust nuclear deterrence, the United States of the Cold War, British statesmen of the Columbian Age knew that if they maintained the ability to command the seas of most interest to them, the scale of peril to Britain was limited. The first principle of British strategy was to maintain command of the Channel. This principle first found systematic operational expression in the War of Austrian Succession (1740–48), and thereafter (following precedents from the time of the defeat of the Great Armada in 1588) in the form of a concentration of superior force by a Western Squadron off the island of Ushant, or in Plymouth and Torbay. If the wind blew strongly from the West, the Royal Navy could not safely maintain station on a lee shore for the close blockade of the French Navy in Brest, but neither could the French beat out to sea. Looking to the eastern approach to the Channel and the Thames, British statesmen were extremely sensitive to the issue of who controlled the Scheldt estuary. Prior to the development of Cherbourg, Antwerp was the only continental port on the Channel and southern North Sea capable of hosting a mass of hostile shipping of deep draught. Antwerp was close to Britain, and—unlike Brest and the other Biscay ports of France—when an east wind blew an invasion fleet could sail to Britain, but the British fleet could not put to sea from the Thames or beat up the Channel. In the late 1850s, however, the France of the Second Empire invested in both a deep-water Channel harbor in Cherbourg and a steam-driven fleet capable of ignoring the vagaries of the wind.

A great continental foe undistracted militarily on land would not necessarily be able to construct a first-class fleet, but the possibility was a repeated attention-getter in London. Critically important though it was that a continental balance of power be maintained, Britain had an absolute need for maritime superiority in its home waters. Security against invasion was the first strategic priority, just as an effective working command of the Atlantic approaches to continental Europe was the sine qua non for all overseas military efforts.

Loss of, or a condition of temporarily alternating, local maritime command can be dangerous, as the U.S. Marine Corps learned in August and September 1942 on Guadalcanal, and—if not retrieved—even locally fatal, as the Athenians learned in their great expedition to Sicily in 415–413 B.C. and the French discovered in Egypt in 1798–1801. But disasters or near disasters can be survived, always provided command of the center of gravity of national strength is not lost. Athens was obliged to fight *à outrance* for the security of its grain supply route to the Black Sea and eventually lost through incompetence. Britain occasionally and briefly (for example, in 1779) lost command of the Channel, but the French never succeeded in exploiting that fact. Imperial Japan lacked the strategic reach and weight ever to place the United States in a position from which it would have been obliged to withdraw from the contest. Had Japan identified the U.S. fleet carriers as the operational center of gravity of U.S. resistance in the Pacific, and had it seized Hawaii and Ceylon (and perhaps Madagascar) early in 1942, the course of World War II and not simply of the Pacific War, might have been very different. However, contemporary naval doctrine, the continentalist outlook and ambitions of the Army-dominated Japanese government, and the firm determination of Tokyo to wage a limited war render this case not just hypothetical but distinctly fanciful.[36]

The British experience in the balancing of maritime effort with direct continental endeavor speaks to recent U.S. strategic problems also. There is an obvious geostrategic parallel with the NATO commitment; there is the question of the priority to be accorded protection against the worst eventuality (then invasion, more recently nuclear assault on the homeland); and there is the residual issue of what to do should a major part of grand strategy collapse. Modern British history provides several partial parallels for the hypothetical defeat of NATO on what used to be its central front in Europe. The question of continental commitment by sea-based power is a hardy perennial topic. Throughout most of the twenty-two years of the last of its military struggles with France, Britain, like the United States of recent decades, was as supportive of a coalition strategy as military and diplomatic circumstances permitted. Britain did not delete from choice a sustained commitment to continental warfare after 1795. The strategic problem was that France made a habit of rapidly defeating the European powers whose armies British forces might join in the field, if they could reach them, that is. After the French conquest of the Netherlands in 1795, the British army had a problem of access to European battlefields, not to mention logistic difficulty operating far from the coast. With the collapse in 1807 of British hopes in Russia, Britain could only wage war at sea, or more or less immediately from the sea and readily sustainable by sea power, as in Portugal, for example.[37] As in June 1940, the defeat of continental allies left

36. See Herbert Rosinski's brilliant 1946 essay "The Strategy of Japan," in *The Development of Naval Thought* (Newport, R.I.: Naval War College Press, 1977).

37. See Piers Mackesy, *The War in the Mediterranean, 1803–1810* (Westport, Conn.: Greenwood Press, 1981; first pub. 1957); Donald D. Horward, "British Seapower and Its Influence upon the

a Britain deficient in ground forces with no practical option but for a time to foreswear major continental campaigns against the principal strength of the enemy.

VALUABLE HINDSIGHT

Students of contemporary strategy who look backward are often content simply to repeat obvious, if important, generalities about the sea power–land power connection. The beginning of wisdom is to appreciate the merit in Paul Kennedy's judgment that "the conflict with France also confirmed the limitations of sea power, the necessity of watching carefully the European equilibrium, the desirability of having strong military allies in wartime, the need to blend a 'maritime' strategy with the 'continental' one."[38] So far certainly so good. But beyond these bland desiderata for prudent statecraft lies a set of quasi-permanent problems. How much national effort should be devoted to the direct, local bolstering of continental allies? What forms should that direct effort assume? What if the continental allies decline to make what British, or U.S., statesmen and attentive publics regard as a sufficient defense effort? Could a forward continental military commitment be so substantial that its potential loss in combat would actually imperil either the nation's survival or at least some values of critical importance later in the conflict? In the event of a victory in Europe for hostile land power, how would or could a United States preponderant over most of the world's oceans and possessing a thoroughly convincing nuclear counterdeterrent conduct war thereafter? How would the United States reach the enemy's center of gravity (with long-range air and missile power, perhaps, or from space)? Where would a continental enemy's power be reached, grasped, and overcome?

The relevance of the British experience for U.S. policy and strategy in the 1990s extends beyond the hard-eyed world of geostrategy and realpolitik to considerations of ideology and ethics. Albeit imperfectly, Britain pioneered and practiced, while her sea power protected, humane values in political

Peninsular War (1808–1814)," *Naval War College Review* 31 (Fall 1978): 54–71; and David Syrett, "The Role of the Royal Navy in the Napoleonic Wars after Trafalgar, 1805–1814," *Naval War College Review* 32 (September–October 1979): 71–84.

38. Paul M. Kennedy, *The Rise and Fall of British Naval Mastery* (New York: Charles Scribner's Sons, 1976), 147.

intercourse. However amoral and ruthless British statesmen and admirals may have been, it is simply fact that British grand-strategic success in peace and war tended to support the preservation and advancement of individualistic, democratic values. This is neither to deny that the "balancer" in a fluid balance of power system sometimes had to be agile in its affiliations, nor to fail to register that the Japanese actions against Port Arthur (February 8, 1904) and Pearl Harbor (December 7, 1941) had distinguished precedents in the British surprise attacks on Copenhagen (April 2, 1801, and September 2–7, 1807), not to mention the preventive action taken forcibly to neutralize the French fleet at Oran (July 3–4, 1940).

Naturally, Britain served herself in pursuing a generally consistent antihegemonic, balance-of-power policy toward continental Europe. Moreover, of course the British economy prospered as a result of the protection offered overseas trade by a superior Royal Navy. Nonetheless, the *Pax Britannica*, like its far antecedent *Pax Athenica* (but unlike the very genuine *Pax Romana*), and its successor *Pax Americana*, the disciplinary writ of all of which tend to be exaggerated,[39] served interests far more extensive than those of the home superstate only. Athenian and British wealth, influence, and arrogance were resented widely in their time, as have been those facets of American performance since World War II. Tracts on the arrogance of power have been drafted against each of these three great sea powers. The charge has been valid, yet dwarfed in significance by the fact that each helped forge in its own self-interest an international order that advanced a general peace and prosperity. Furthermore, these states have stood for an idea of individual human worth that has proved both exceedingly precious and in need of much muscular support.

Historical parallels must always be imperfect, because history, unlike historians, does not repeat itself in detail. Not to belabor an argument advanced most appropriately in Chapter 8, the fact remains that the contemporary U.S. context for statecraft and strategic maritime matters is more than casually reminiscent of the British condition from 1815 to 1853. The argument today about the obligations of the international primacy, even hegemony, of the United States, to protect or advance humane values, is a resounding echo of forward-looking liberal opinion in Britain in the first half of the nineteenth century. Moreover, the strategic challenge to prudent

39. See Gerald S. Graham, *The Politics of Naval Supremacy: Studies in British Maritime Ascendancy* (Cambridge: Cambridge University Press, 1963), 96–125, and C. J. Bartlett, "Statecraft, Power and Influence," in *Britain Pre-eminent: Studies of British World Influence in the Nineteenth Century* (New York: St. Martin's Press, 1969), 172–93

yet economical defense planning today that is posed by the absence of plausible immediate superpower-level perils abroad, finds more than a distant echo from the 1820s, 1830s, and 1840s, for Britain's Royal Navy. One could go on, and on. . . . The point is that the need to cope responsibly with a sudden, and then long-lasting, peace, was faced by Britain and her navy for forty years after Waterloo. With due allowance for the differences between the eras and the state-principals, still there are insights for the 1990s that might be gleaned from a careful study of the decades between Waterloo and the Alma.[40]

Cause and effect are often difficult to trace, but it is worth noting the judgment of a biographer of Mackinder. Writing of the continuing validity of Mackinder's geopolitical concepts after nearly half a century, W. H. Parker claims, persuasively: "But the great geographical realities remained: land power versus sea power, heartland versus rimland, centre versus periphery, an individualistic Western philosophy versus a collective Eastern doctrine rooted in a communal past. Mackinder died [March 1947] but his ideas lived on."[41] It is easy to be cynical about British, Athenian, or U.S. policy motives. It is less easy to be cynical about the consequences for political and other humane values of British, as contrasted say with German, success in statecraft. The United States can learn both positive and negative lessons from the British way in statecraft and strategy vis-à-vis the dangers of unchecked, continental-based power. Also, Washington can recognize that while it is balancing power for the sake of U.S. national security, it happens also to be the contemporary torchbearer and first cohort of the praetorian guard for a concept of human dignity that has always been under assault. More often than not that assault has come from states and empires whose political philosophies have been the products of distinctively continental experience. Writing of the British way with coalition warfare, John Terraine judged that "the ultimate strength of a coalition is not to be measured by the number of its members, but by the strength of its strongest member."[42] The Persian Gulf in 1990–91 attested to the wisdom in Terraine's point.

The long and full British experience in managing strategic relations between sea power and land power invites extensive attention by strategic theorists. Objectively speaking, few of the strategic concepts or classes of

40. C. J. Bartlett, *Great Britain and Sea Power, 1815–1853* (Oxford: Clarendon Press, 1963), is the outstanding study.

41. Parker, *Mackinder*, 175.

42. John Terraine, "Lessons of Coalition Warfare: 1914 and 1939," *RUSI Journal* 134 (Summer 1989): 62.

activity of interest fail to apply to British strategic history. Subjectively viewed, that British experience is recent, readily accessible, familiar to most strategic theorists and commentators, and characterized in its essentials by continuity to the present.

Part II
SEA POWER
AND
LAND POWER

4

Continental or Maritime Power? The Necessity for Combined Arms

Conceptually, it could hardly be more self-evident that sea power, land power, and now air power are complementary. Land power and sea power should work synergistically for combined-arms success, together with the benefits that can accrue from superior air and space power. So much for high principles and pious nostrums. In practice, land power and sea power are rarely wielded skillfully for synergistic effect, and the story deteriorates further when the air element is introduced. It is a common error to believe that many single-environment battles were "decisive." Few land battles warrant ascription as decisive, let alone sea or air battles, which, by their very nature, can only be enabling or disabling, rather than conclusive. It may be needless to add that defeat in battle at sea is near certain to be potentially of decisive strategic significance only for the sea power (e.g., Jutland, had Britain lost), whereas defeat on land is unlikely itself to have strategically terminal consequences for an effectively insular sea power (Waterloo, had France won).

Simultaneous military preeminence on land and sea is an extremely rare condition. The only historically indisputable cases of such true super power were the Rome of the early empire and Byzantium in the first quarter of the eleventh century. The United States in the 1990s is the third legitimate candidate for this exclusive strategic hall of fame. Indeed, the contemporary United States can claim superiority not only on land and sea, but also in the air, in space, in nuclear systems, and in electronic warfare. Vastly impressive though the U.S. claims must be acknowledged to be, the presence of other nuclear-capable states, and particularly a heavily nuclear-armed and politically unstable Russia, points to a plausible source of neutralization of U.S. military power that had no parallels for Rome or Byzantium.

Few polities have been confused or uncertain over the key issue of whether, in the last resort, they were more continental or more maritime in the structure of their security. The Byzantines were a lonely and frequently unhappy exception to the rule that statesmen who are the heirs to a geographically particular culture have little trouble recognizing their strategic orientation. In modern times both France and Germany have bid seriously, but not persistently, for truly first-class naval strength. In both cases continental distractions obliged them to discard the fantasy that they were strong enough to be supreme on land and sea simultaneously. For Britain, the quintessential sea power of recent centuries, dominant continental land power was deemed a potentially deadly menace because it was judged likely to breed a policy demand and strategic need for a continentally based first-class navy. Such a navy was probably not attainable by a dominant continental power, but the British anxiety was both understandable and prudent.

A sensible combined-arms approach to strategic problems does not exaggerate the enabling value of sea power and air power. An important reason why the strategic utility even of quite well combined arms can fall far short of the sum of their parts lies in the possibility of political and strategic incompetence. Superior sea and air power enabled the Allies to invade Italy in 1943: whether or not that invasion was wise and whether or not the subsequent land campaign was well conducted are issues that bear not at all on the value of sea power or air power.

The contrasting worldviews among military professionals are an enduring problem for the planning, conduct, and exploitation of combined-arms operations in war. The "battlefield," campaigning area, and war zone for a sailor (and some airmen) is global in nature. The sailor, like the soldier and the airman, has his strategic mentality shaped decisively by the geographical medium in which he functions and, with the partial exception of the soldier, by the tactical possibilities of the vehicles specialized for each environment. No environmental military specialization—land, sea, air, or space—is inherently superior in its characteristic reasoning, but the maritime, air, and space viewpoints are certain to be geographically more inclusive than is the approach from the land. To offset that point, the view of the soldier is the view of the person who most typically must orchestrate the final act of a war, on land, where the enemy has his politically organized territory.

PERSPECTIVE

It is more common to assert than to explain or explore the complementary nature of the relationship between sea power and land power, with air power and space power adjuncts today. Furthermore, the relationship often is understood to mean little other than the navy enables the army to fight as an expeditionary force overseas by providing security for sea lines of communication.[1] A narrowly theater-operational frame of reference for appreciating the value of sea power cannot advance public understanding very far. Rather, such a narrow focus would tend to reduce what should be debated as national or coalition military strategy to a debate over means and methods for naval impact on an individual continental campaign. Because of the different worldviews, which stem from their different geographical foci, the distinctive skills and duties of soldiers and sailors are seldom well coordinated. More often than not war at sea and war on land, though intimately connected in their outcomes, have been conducted with scant relation one to the other. An absence of overarching strategic direction has been particularly prevalent in modern times, as combat forms and technologies had become more specialized.

Air power, space power, and the power of "strategic" nuclear forces are, by and large, subsumed in the land/sea classification. Save in exceptional circumstances, it is in the geophysical nature of the air and space mediums of operation that the forces specialized to function there should work as

1. For the other side of the coin, the dependence of sea power on the ability of the army to take and hold naval bases, see the interesting study by R. B. Pargiter and H. G. Eady, *The Army and Sea Power: A Historical Outline* (London: Ernest Benn, 1927). This book about "the contribution of the Army to sea power" (11) was written by two staff officers from the Royal Artillery and the Royal Engineers.

adjuncts to land and sea power. The United States might fairly be described as an air power and a space power (and a nuclear power), but most of the traditional meaning and value of the binary distinction between sea powers and land powers endures. Writing in 1947, W. D. Puleston advised that "only when the bulk of the freight now carried by merchant ships is airborne can the term 'air power' be used in a sense that compared to 'sea power.' "[2] His criterion directs the same answer for the 1990s as it did for the 1940s.

In this analysis I seek to explain how and why countries differ in choosing and adhering to a maritime or a continental frame of strategic reference. There are important distinctions between seaward and landward foci of strategic attention, between the strategic cultures of sailors and soldiers, between the objectives sought at sea or on land, and between the lead times necessary to prepare a first-class navy as contrasted with a superior army. Overall, however, in this chapter and the next one I develop as their central theme how sea and land power complement each other at the strategic level.

COMBINED ARMS AND MILITARY DECISION

Preoccupation with the technical aspects of armed forces, like undue fascination with the delights of arms control regimes, discourages disciplined speculation on strategy. Technical challenge can be so formidable and exciting that a military establishment may scarcely notice that it has no strategy worthy of the description. That establishment may even lack operational plans beyond those for mobilization and wartime deployment. For example, neither the Royal Navy nor the navy of imperial Germany had an overall strategy at the outbreak of the First World War. British endeavors in the Dreadnought and super-Dreadnought building race, the redeployment of the Royal Navy's capital ships to home waters, its eschewal of close blockade and refusal to hazard itself by offering battle in the Heligoland Bight, all left Germany's High Seas Fleet desperately short of important and feasible wartime missions.[3] As for the Royal Navy, Arthur J.

2. W. D. Puleston, *The Influence of Sea Power in World War II* (New Haven, Conn.: Yale University Press, 1947), 16.
3. See Herbert Rosinski, *The Development of Naval Thought* (Newport, R.I.: Naval War College Press, 1977), 77–81, and Paul Kennedy, "Fisher and Tirpitz Compared" and "Strategic Aspects of the Anglo–German Naval Race," in *Strategy and Diplomacy, 1870–1945: Eight Studies* (London: George Allen & Unwin, 1983), 111–26 and 129–60.

Marder notes that "the Navy of the early twentieth century was wrapped up in the revolutionary advances in *matériel*. The study of strategy and tactics was bound to suffer."[4]

Military strategies that truly combine arms are the exception rather than the rule. The strategic connections for synergistic success between sea power and land power (accommodating air and space power today) may be obvious to the student of statecraft and military affairs, particularly in retrospect, but the practice of war shows no easy marriage between ocean and continent. The traditional rarity of strategic thinking in the United States needs to be appreciated with reference to sea power's principal function at the level of strategic effect, on the maintenance of peace or the course of crisis and war. It is scarcely cause for wonder that the contribution of sea power to national security can be uniquely difficult to grasp for many people who are otherwise deeply knowledgeable about defense.

Democracies are not in the habit of thinking strategically. Traditionally, they have viewed their military instruments of policy with distaste as the *ultima ratio* to solve a problem in short, and therefore necessarily very violent, order. The armed forces are committed forcibly to exorcise some evil ("Kaiserism" or Prussian militarism, Nazism, communist tyranny, or, more recently, the beast of Baghdad), not to provide pressure and influence in peace and crisis as well as in war. Navies cannot be instruments for rapid decision against continental powers. Victory or defeat in battle at sea can be important for the subsequent terms and course of conflict in that environment, and for the landward ventures enabled or precluded as a consequence, but only in special circumstances can the outcome of a sea battle be in any strategic sense "decisive."

Trafalgar was not decisive because maritime command was not, and was unlikely ever to be, in question. Had Nelson lost, even in the unlikely form of near annihilation, the fleet he would have lost could have been replaced rapidly through redeployment from distant stations. Jutland was a different matter altogether. Jellicoe was leading Britain's only battle fleet on May 31, 1916: there was no replacement available. Correlli Barnett has advanced the foolish argument that even a Britain beaten badly at Jutland could have waged a defensive naval war from its geostrategically advantageous—that is, European "breakwater"—home base.[5] Even if Britain could have resorted to

4. Arthur J. Marder, *From the Dreadnought to Scapa Flow, The Royal Navy in the Fisher Era, 1904–1919*, vol. 3, *Jutland and After (May 1916–December 1916)* (London: Oxford University Press, 1966), 4.

5. Correlli Barnett, *The Swordbearers: Studies in Supreme Command in the First World War* (London: Eyre & Spottiswoode, 1963), 125–26.

the defensive naval strategy of a second-class sea power, the definitive loss of surface command in home waters would have compelled London to sue for peace in a matter of weeks. The threat of starvation, the cessation of raw material imports, the absence of outgoing manufactured trade goods required critically to help finance the British war effort, and the menace to the cross-Channel lines of communication of the B.E.F. would have mandated British withdrawal from the coalition.[6] It is true that a High Seas Fleet victorious in the North Sea would still have lacked strategic position, the geography that Mahan so correctly emphasized. Also, it would have had very short legs; it was, after all, constructed to wage battle within one hundred miles of its home base. Nonetheless, to argue that an unchallengeable High Seas Fleet could have accomplished nothing of great importance—as did interwar German naval theorist Wolfgang Wegener—is thoroughly unpersuasive. A sophisticated disdain for battle per se easily slips into a wholesale discounting of the strategic utility of success in battle, or disutility of defeat, which verges on the absurd.[7]

A naval battle or campaign can have a near-term decisive impact on the course and outcome of a war only in very restricted circumstances. One of the fleets must belong to a country able to conduct war only if it enjoys maritime command. Sea transportation must be critically important, to feed the population, sustain war industries, and as a source of national income. Furthermore, the use of the sea must be vitally important for securing access to continental theaters of operations. Also, strategic decision should be at stake if the fleet hazarded in battle by a sea power is the only, or last, fleet of the country; a fleet irreplaceable by redeployment from other stations, by rapid new construction, or by substitution by allies. This case, the "Jutland model," allows the possibility of decision only for the land power with the large fleet, not for the sea power that enjoys a workable maritime command already. Decision is possible if the theater of war is wholly or largely maritime. Examples include the Falklands in 1982, the Pacific in World War II, or for a distant and imperfect case, Sicily and coastal North Africa in the Punic wars. Moreover, neither combatant must be able or willing to wage war in such a way that the conflict can be decided other than through

6. For a contrary view, see Holger H. Herwig, "Wolfgang Wegener and German Naval Strategy from Tirpitz to Raeder," in *The Naval Strategy of the World War*, by Wolfgang Wegener (Annapolis, Md : Naval Institute Press, 1989; first pub. 1929), xl.

7. Some genuine and a few spurious illusions of decision by battle are assailed energetically in Jan S. Breemer, *The Burden of Trafalgar: Decisive Battle and Naval Strategic Expectations on the Eve of the First World War*, Newport Paper no. 6 (Newport, R.I.: Naval War College, October 1993).

combat for control of sea lines of communication. Finally, a dominant land power undefeated in land warfare can find further prosecution of landward designs frustrated by the consequences of defeat at sea. The defeat of Xerxes I at sea at Salamis (480 B.C.) and off Cape Mycale (479 B.C.) rendered further land operations in Europe all but impracticable for the Persian army. Nelson's victory at the Nile (August 1–2, 1798) had strategic meaning for Napoleon's ambition to conquer an empire in the East, but was only an important tactical incident when viewed in the total context of the wars of 1793–1815.

Tactical defeat on a grand scale in battle at sea is far more likely to have an immediate and decisively negative strategic effect on a sea power than on a continental land power. Nonetheless, sea powers can often suffer considerable naval losses before they confront a tactical situation that might cost them a war. The naval battle of the Aegates Islands in 241 B.C. made further Carthaginian resistance in Sicily impossible and led directly to the conclusion of the First Punic War on terms advantageous to Rome. The final act in the Peloponnesian War was the Athenian naval rout at Aegospotami in 405 B.C., which led directly to Athens (Piraeus) being blockaded by sea and besieged by land for six months. By the terms of peace, Athens's fortifications were leveled and its fleet limited to twelve ships. It should be remembered, however, that these naval defeats with immediate strategic consequences occurred after twenty-three years of conflict in the Carthaginian case, and twenty-eight years (with pauses) in the Athenian. (I treat the question of decision in war in more detail in Chapter 6.)

CONTINENTAL OR MARITIME POWER?

It is highly unusual, though not unknown, for a state to be preeminent on both land and sea. The mid and late Roman Republic and then Empire is the leading such case. The restored (Eastern) Roman Empire of the middle decades of the sixth century A.D. of Justinian I is also a candidate for this exclusive class of land-sea superstates, but the later decades of that century showed that the restored empire could not be a continental, as well as a maritime superpower.[8] But Byzantium in the tenth and early eleventh

8. See John W. Barker, *Justinian and the Later Roman Empire* (Madison: University of Wisconsin Press, 1966), and George Ostrogorsky, *History of the Byzantine State* (New Brunswick, N.J.: Rutgers University Press, 1969; first pub. 1940), 68–86.

centuries again showed that some facsimile of continental and maritime superpower could be achieved briefly. Preeminence in one or the other environment alone usually has sufficed to stir sufficient anxiety or envy on the part of foreign powers to catalyze a defensive antihegemonic coalition. The threats posed by that coalition compel the superstate to choose between maximum effort by land or by sea. Without obvious historical exception to the rule, every superstate that appeared first class on both land and sea, in reality, when pressed hard, was either a sea power with a large and competent army or a land power with a large and competent navy. Rare indeed is the country that in time of desperate and protracted conflict, has not been obliged by stark necessity to slight its commitment to one or the other combat environment. That stark necessity manifests as a scarcity of resources and a differential in the intensity of the dangers on land and at sea. Furthermore, it is equally rare to find a country that has been in serious doubt whether its more pressing dangers were maritime or continental.

In the First Punic War, republican Rome became the preeminent naval, as well as land, power in the central Mediterranean. Following the Punic wars, and later the civil wars of the first century B.C. (84–82, 49–44, 43–31 B.C.), Rome was first the preponderant then the only naval power in the Mediterranean; as a consequence it had no large-scale need for a permanent fighting fleet. There were, of course, residual problems with piracy and periodic military revolts in distant provinces. The empire founded by Augustus, though not challenged by foreign naval power until the end of the fourth century, nonetheless had learned from the time of troubles of the late republic that control of sea passage was vital for security and as a deterrent to revolt. In their appreciation of Roman roads and the landward mentality of the Romans, commentators have been wont to forget that the empire comprised a continental rimland encircling the Mediterranean. Romans used their naval power for campaign support on inland waterways— the Danube, the Rhine, the Rhône—and to provide literally critical imperial communications. Rome was not, and did not think of itself, as a maritime empire. But it is noteworthy that that continental superstate, the only power bordering the Mediterranean for four centuries, retained the services of a fighting fleet.

The Byzantine Empire, with its economically critical heartland in Anatolia, never quite decided whether its principal instrument of security should be sea power or land power.[9] This uncertainty was understandable, given

---

9 Sharply contrasting opinions on whether Byzantium was primarily a maritime or a continental power are offered in Archibald R. Lewis, *Naval Power and Trade in the Mediterranean*, A D

the landward pressure to which Byzantium repeatedly was subject in both Asia and in Europe, but ultimately it proved fatal. Notwithstanding the vast scale of its territorial holdings prior to the disastrous defeat by the Seljuk Turks at Manzikert in 1071, Byzantium was a maritime, perhaps more than it was a continental, empire. Defeat on land could be serious, since it denied the empire manpower for defense and tax revenues for the hiring of military professionals and the bribing of barbarians, but only weakness at sea could prove terminal. Like Athens and Tyre of classical times, the Constantinople of the Byzantine Empire could be assaulted successfully only by combined land-sea operations. The first great Arab siege of Constantinople (A.D. 674–78) was finally broken decisively by a Byzantine naval victory that restored maritime command in home waters. The fall of the city in 1204 to the Latin powers of the West and in 1453 to the Turks was in both cases due to the absence of Byzantine naval strength.[10] So long as Byzantine or allied ships could reach Constantinople, and particularly if they could help defend the sea walls of the city facing the protected anchorage of the Golden Horn, the great triple land walls of Theodosius II could be trusted to defy even a quite extraordinary weight of assault. Those impregnable walls, the military wonder of medieval times, worked synergistically with the superbly maritime site of the city to pose would-be besiegers a major problem in the combined use of land and naval power.

In modern times, two great continental powers briefly acquired a naval strength that appeared to be within reach of first-class status. France in the 1670s and 1680s and imperial Germany after 1900 both built fleets that on a good day, might fight broadside-to-broadside with the dominant sea power of the period and make a respectable or better showing. Strategically considered, had France in the 1680s or Germany in the 1900s been able to continue naval building, the superior economic resources of those countries ought to have enabled them to challenge successfully for command of Britain's coastal waters. General command of the sea should have followed in the French, though not the German, case. The strategic geography of an international security system that in the seventeenth and eighteenth centuries focused almost exclusively on Europe, contrasted sharply with the

---

500–1100 (Princeton, N.J.. Princeton University Press, 1951), and Warren Treadgold, *The Byzantine Revival, 780–842* (Stanford, Calif · Stanford University Press, 1988), esp 260.

10 Edwin Pears, *The Fall of Constantinople: Being the Story of the Fourth Crusade* (New York: Harper & Brothers, 1886), and Steven Runciman, *The Fall of Constantinople, 1453* (Cambridge: Cambridge University Press, 1965), remain the best studies Donald M Nicol, *The Immortal Emperor: The Life and Legend of Constantine Palaiologos, Last Emperor of the Romans* (Cambridge· Cambridge University Press, 1992), also is helpful.

geostrategic context of the 1900s. In the latter period, Japanese and U.S. naval power could not be negated via command of the sea approaches to Western Europe.[11]

Britain transferred the status of principal enemy from the Dutch to the French in the 1680s, and from the French (and Russians) to the Germans in the 1900s, for the same leading reason, the expansion of the continental country's navy. As always, Britain had a host of other reasons for identifying a particular state as the principal enemy. In the earlier of these two cases the reasons included dynastic politics, William of Orange's distinctively Dutch view of the French threat on land, colonial irritants in America, and religious bigotry on both sides of the Channel.[12] In the later case the British army in the early 1900s needed a new role once it had decided that the defense of India's northwest frontier against Russia was infeasible. Nonetheless, perception of a naval challenge was sufficient to set Britain on a course of rivalry and eventual enmity. British statesmen in the 1680s and the 1900s did not require great discernment to appreciate that the French, and German, navies were intended—partially in the former case, wholly in the latter—to challenge British maritime command. One must say partially in the case of the France of Louis XIV, because in the years leading up to 1688 Britain typically was considered an ally rather than a rival of France. For different reasons, in the 1670s both London and Paris viewed the Dutch as the enemy of the hour. There has been a notable exception in the twentieth century to the generalization that a perceived naval challenge leads Britain to define a country as an enemy. That exception was the Anglo-American naval rivalry, which emerged apparently full blown following Germany's defeat in 1918. For political, geostrategic, financial, and cultural reasons, the genuine commercial and naval rivalry between the two great democracies could not escalate into a real danger of war between them. As a point of pride, some British opinion was not happy to concede parity in

11. See Holger H. Herwig, *Politics of Frustration: The United States in German Naval Planning, 1889–1941* (Boston Little, Brown, 1976), and Holger H. Herwig and D. F. Trask, "Naval Operations Plans between Germany and the USA, 1898–1913: A Study of Strategic Planning in the Age of Imperialism," in *The War Plans of the Great Powers, 1880–1914*, ed. Paul M. Kennedy (London: George Allen & Unwin, 1979), 39–76.

12. William's principal motive in seizing the English crown in 1688 from James II (by Parliamentary invitation) was to enlist English resources for his lifelong cause of defending the independence of the Netherlands. The change in religion of the occupant of the crown in 1688, from the Catholic James to the militantly Protestant and vigorously francophobe William, guaranteed that France would fight Britain.

capital ships to the United States with the Washington treaty of 1922, but war was politically and culturally unthinkable.[13]

Britain could choose to tolerate the growth of a great continental power, as in the cases of France in the early decades of the reign of Louis XIV and imperial Germany after 1871. Indeed, Britain could survive and even prosper in the face of such a power achieving close to continent-wide hegemony; as happened when Napoleon negotiated the Treaty of Amiens with Britain (March 27, 1802), imposed the Treaties of Tilsit on Russia and Prussia (July 7–9, 1807), and the Treaty of Schönbrunn (October 14, 1809) on Austria following the battle of Wagram. But the imminent reality of continental-based naval power on a major scale always eventually called forth offsetting measures, diplomatic and military, even if sometimes they were more than a little belated. Britain traditionally was not indifferent to the growth in potentially hegemonic land power, but the quality of threat posed by such power was critically less than that posed by naval strength. The problem with continental hegemony would be the inevitability of its complement with naval power. Adolf Hitler believed for many years that by choosing to expand with farmland rather than sea power, he could avoid the cardinal grand-strategic error committed by Wilhelmine Germany; the arousal of Britain's enmity.[14] He was wrong. British statesmen believed that sea power tends to grow from unbalanced land power. In a sense they saw excessive land power as sea power delayed. This is not to exaggerate the fungibility of great land power and great sea power, but neither is it to understate the risks of continentally based sea power.

Throughout its second hundred years of struggle with France and most of its half-century-long contest with Germany, Britain endeavored to help maintain a balance of power *on* the continent rather than the general impossibility of a balance of power *with* the continent. A forward continental diplomacy typically has been preferred to strictly unilateral force-building as the most effective and economical approach to the deterrence and conduct of war. Britain never seriously doubted that continental disasters and set-

13. See Stephen Roskill, *Naval Policy Between the Wars*, vol. 1, *The Period of Anglo-American Antagonism, 1919–1929* (London: Collins, 1968); David F Trask, *Captains and Cabinets: Anglo-American Naval Relations, 1917–1918* (Columbia: University of Missouri Press, 1972); Christopher Hall, *Britain, America, and Arms Control, 1921–37* (New York: St. Martin's Press, 1987); and John B. Hattendorf and Robert S. Jordan, eds., *Maritime Strategy and the Balance of Power* (New York: St. Martin's Press, 1989), part 3.

14. See Eberhard Jäckel, *Hitler's World View* (Cambridge: Harvard University Press, 1981; first pub. 1969), chap. 2.

backs, even those involving British land forces, would be disasters and setbacks of a survivable kind—always provided the country's last line of defense, in those days the Royal Navy, could retain command in home waters. In the optimistic but realistic words of John Jervis, Lord St. Vincent, in 1803: "I do not say, my Lords, that the French will not come. I only say they will not come by sea."[15]

RELATIONS OF DEPENDENCE

In theory the maritime component of the national military strategy of a sea power is not in an adversary relationship with the land-power component. In practice, however, the need to decide on the allocation of scarce resources produces tension between them. Also, the timescales of strategic effect can be different as the consequences of combat at sea and on land. The terms of dependence between sea power and land power are always specific to the geostrategic condition of the adversaries and the political character of the war as defined by the objectives of the belligerents.

Following Antoine-Henri de Jomini rather than Carl von Clausewitz, Alfred Thayer Mahan developed what he intended to be a general theory of the influence of sea power on history. But both he and Julian Corbett rested their analyses too narrowly for the scope of their theoretical ambitions, or the authority of their conclusions, on the British experience in the heavily maritime conflicts of less than two centuries of warfare in the age of sail. More balanced inquiry demands that the scope of historical reference be sufficiently broad to encompass the history of great maritime empires, which, unlike the British, fell to land powers who learned to perform *well enough* at sea. The Athenians, the Carthaginians, and the Byzantines are prominent cases in point of peoples who failed, ultimately, to perform adequately at sea. Mahan appreciated very well the basic dependence of sea power on land power.[16] Sea power depends on the quantity and quality of assets on land; it has strategic meaning only with reference to conflict among territorially organized polities; and, as he went to great pains to develop, sea

15. Quoted in G. J. Marcus, *The Age of Nelson. The Royal Navy, 1793–1815* (New York. Viking, 1971), 229

16. See Alfred Thayer Mahan, *The Influence of Sea Power upon History, 1660–1783* (London: Methuen, 1965; first pub. 1890), chap. 1, and *The Problem of Asia and Its Effect upon International Conditions* (Boston Little, Brown, 1905)

power is a supremely strategic instrument of state policy.[17] Unfortunately, Mahan was unduly reticent on the influence of landward concerns on freedom of strategic and tactical operations at sea.

Few states have enjoyed a robust insularity that rendered them substantially immune to damage by an enemy dominant on land. Examples include Athens, whose continuous fortifications embracing the city and the corridor to the port of Piraeus enabled the maritime-commercial empire to function despite threats on land;[18] Rome in the Second Punic War, whose city walls as well as the fortifications of the port of Ostia were too formidable for Hannibal's military resources or skill to overcome;[19] Byzantium, whose great triple walls, more than 100 feet high (measured from the bottom of the moat) and 190 to 270 feet in depth, gave Constantinople an insular character; Venice, set on offshore islands and protected by marshes;[20] Britain, insular physically (and politically once the Scottish "backdoor" was closed in the eighteenth century with the defeat of the Jacobite cause); imperial Japan, which had inappropriate continental ambitions and was unable to develop sufficient sea-air power to provide security either for the maritime flank of its continental operations or, ultimately and fatally, for the strategic security of its insular home base; and, finally, a United States rendered effectively insular by the good fortune of having extremely weak continental neighbors.

Loss of maritime command by a sea power or a sea-dependent coalition invariably leads to defeat in war. Continental policymakers from Philip II of Spain in the 1580s and 1590s to Adolf Hitler failed to understand that there was only one sound and reliable way to defeat Britain. The British battle fleet had to be reduced to impotence; that could be effected by defeat at sea, by neutralization through blockade, or in the 1940s, by assault from the air. Had Spain, France, or later Germany wrested command of European waters from the Royal Navy, invasion would have been unnecessary.

Many amphibious operations have been conducted over an uncom-

17 A point that does not appear in Carl von Clausewitz, On War, ed. and trans. Michael Howard and Peter Paret (Princeton, N.J . Princeton University Press, 1976; first pub. 1832).

18. See D. M. Lewis, "Mainland Greece, 479–451 B.C.," in The Cambridge Ancient History, 2d ed , ed D. M. Lewis et al., vol. 5, The Fifth Century B C (Cambridge: Cambridge University Press, 1992), 113. Also see Donald Kagan, Pericles of Athens and the Birth of Democracy. The Triumph of Vision in Leadership (New York. Touchstone, 1991), chap. 12.

19. See Brian Caven, The Punic Wars (London: Weidenfeld & Nicolson, 1980), 148–49, 173–74.

20. See Frederick C. Lane, Venice: A Maritime Republic (Baltimore· Johns Hopkins University Press, 1973), 1–5

manded sea, Corbett's sensible excoriation of such ventures notwithstanding, but they risked disaster. Examples of such operations include Napoleon's expedition to Egypt in 1798, Hitler's Norwegian stroke in April 1940, the Japanese expedition to seize Midway and force a major sea battle for command of the central Pacific, and the U.S. amphibious thrust in the southern Solomons into Guadalcanal in August 1942. Fortunately for sea powers, continental strategists typically have been unwilling to assume great risks with the bulwark of their national security, the army, by throwing it over an uncommanded sea. But such strategists have speculated that prompt success ashore against the land base of hostile sea power would erase the meaning of the temporary loss of control of the maritime lines of communications of the expedition. Twice in this century, in the fall of 1914 and the summer of 1940, a sufficiently courageous German leadership might have succeeded with the gamble of a hastily improvised invasion of Britain. Jehuda Wallach argues persuasively that

> a consistent attitude toward England runs through every part of German military thinking, from the planning phase of the First World War right up to the last desperate offensives in spring and summer 1918. Its most striking feature is the complete lack of a maritime outlook. It was, of course, the first time in centuries that German strategists had to deal with a hostile Great Britain, and were also compelled to think in terms of a major war outside the continental boundaries.[21]

All of which was just as well, since, as Correlli Barnett has noted, "the retirement of the Grand Fleet to Scapa [in the Orkneys] meant that Britain no longer controlled the North Sea. Throughout the war it was a disputed zone, where the Germans were always free to make dangerous sallies."[22]

The proposition "that sea power, in the last analysis, required the possession of some land power, in a way in which the reverse was not true,"[23] is a definitional truth, albeit an important one. It is extremely unusual for war to be concluded as a result strictly of action at sea. Spartan hoplites could ravage Athenian farmland in Attica and German panzer crews could sunbathe on the sand at Dunkirk, but neither could grip the

21. Jehuda L. Wallach, *The Dogma of the Battle of Annihilation: The Theories of Clausewitz and Schlieffen and Their Impact on the German Conduct of Two World Wars* (Westport, Conn.: Greenwood Press, 1986), 148.

22. Barnett, *Swordbearers*, 117

23. Martin Wight, *Power Politics* (New York: Holmes & Meier, 1978), 71.

strength of the hostile sea power, either at sea or in its shore bases, to compel
a favorable outcome. To compare the relative need of sea power for land
power with the need of land power for sea power requires specific detail on
the purposes and character of a conflict. Of course one must bear in mind
that those purposes and character are likely to be in dispute between the
belligerents. Arthur J. Marder was correct to affirm as a principle of war the
axiom that "tactics are governed by strategy,"[24] but strategic feasibility is not
just a matter of political or strategic choice, it too may be tactically
vulnerable to an enemy strongly motivated to change the terms of combat.

Great sea powers generally have been able to oblige the continental
enemy of the day to settle for a compromise peace rather than wage a long
struggle of attrition, attempt a landward end run to frustrate the sea
power's policy of assembling a potentially overwhelming land-sea coalition
(Napoleon's invasion of Russia in 1812, Hitler's repeat of the same cardinal
error in 1941), or rent or acquire sufficient sea power itself in order to
contest maritime command (Sparta, Rome, the Arabs, the Ottoman Turks).
A sea power can lose a war by defeat abroad on land only if it chooses to
regard such defeat as signaling the need to terminate a conflict on unfavor-
able terms. Hitler waited in vain in the summer of 1940 for the British
Government to sue for peace.

THE HORIZONS OF STRATEGY

The pervasive influence of physical geography on human affairs is nowhere
more clearly evident than in the contrasting worldviews of the sailor and the
soldier. In the words of Rear Admiral J. C. Wylie:

> Where the sailor or airman thinks in terms of an entire world, the
> soldier at work thinks in terms of theaters, in terms of campaigns, or
> in terms of battles. And the three concepts are not too markedly
> different from each other.

> Where the sailor and the airman are almost forced, by the nature of
> the sea and the air, to think in terms of a total world or, at the least,

24. Marder, *From the Dreadnought to Scapa Flow*, 3:185.

to look outside the physical limits of their immediate concerns, the soldier is almost literally hemmed in by his terrain.[25]

In contrast to terrain, the featureless indivisibility and all but global continuity of the sea provides an ease of worldwide maritime movement that is without parallel on land, with the limited exception of desert conditions. Maritime command cannot always be readily exploited to influence events ashore, but its possession is the sine qua non for the exercise of global strategy. Superior sea power has been the critical source of overall military advantage in many wars, ranging in time from the three-act struggle between Rome and Carthage to the Second World War and beyond. This is not to claim that mastery at sea inevitably must lead to success in war. Command or working control at sea enables a state to wage distant expeditionary conflicts. That command or mastery carries no guarantee either that policy-makers will pick the right wars to wage, or that they will wage them ashore in a strategically intelligent manner; witness the U.S. military effort in Vietnam. Above all else, sea power is an enabling agent, rarely is it a direct, let alone the sole, agent of victory. In the apposite words of Robert Leckie, "Although great wars are usually fought and won on land, they are often decided at sea."[26]

The proposition that sailors tend to take a broader strategic view than do soldiers has a way of being forgotten in the heat of defense debate. Furthermore, this distinction between military cultures can have an under-recognized influence on the strategic reasoning of statesmen who are heirs to broadly continentalist or maritime cultures. The broader strategic view of the sailor is no more likely to be correct than the narrower, terrain-bounded view of the soldier, but the broader framework necessarily has a logical and strategic priority over the narrower. As a strategic instrument of high policy, sea power does more than complement the land power of a geostrategically insular United States. Sea power is not simply a valuable adjunct to U.S. land power; more important, as noted, it is an essential enabler. Without secure sea routes, whatever the naval strategy selected to safeguard them, the United States cannot function save in a token fashion as a land power in Eurasia.

Sailors often appear to soldiers to be overimpressed with the strategic

25. J. C. Wylie, *Military Strategy: A General Theory of Power Control* (Annapolis, Md.: Naval Institute Press, 1989; first pub. 1967), 42.

26. Robert Leckie, *The Wars of America* (New York: HarperCollins, 1992), 603.

dexterity permitted and facilitated by preponderance at sea and underimpressed with the adverse consequences of military setbacks on land. Global strategic thinking, no matter how important, can be seen as a luxury by soldiers whose perspective on war is narrowed by the exigencies of terrain and problems of tactical mobility influenced critically by an enemy with whom near-permanent contact is established. In a physical sense, it is as usual for land forces to be in contact with their enemy as it is unusual for sea forces to be in contact with theirs.

A soldier worries about the outcome of his war on a particular piece of ground. Such a perspective does not encourage appreciation of the extent to which deterrence and defense in the region in question rests on the global reach of a maritime power able to unite the world strategically. Operation Desert Storm of 1991 provided an awesome illustration of the potency of state-of-the-art air power. But observers could not fail to notice that to wage large-scale war half a world away from home was scarcely less awesome a demonstration of sea power. Writing of Field Marshal Count Alfred von Schlieffen, Jehuda L. Wallach argues that

> despite the widespread assumption that the ignorance of the problems presented by Great Britain and British sea power was Schlieffen's fault—which is, in fact, true—the roots of the failure are much deeper. There can be no doubt that the full weight of responsibility must be put on Clausewitz' shoulders. Indeed, unawareness of that vital sphere of sea power in global military relations (although an explanation may be found in Germany's history) is the principal deficiency of Clausewitz' almost faultless theoretical edifice. Against this background one ought to be more lenient in judging Schlieffen on that point.[27]

---

27. Wallach, *Dogma of the Battle of Annihilation*, 148.

5

The Search for Advantage

Diverse though its parts may be, a conflict constitutes a single entity. The enterprise is war, not war at sea, on land, in the air, or in space. By fire and maneuver in several geographical environments, belligerents seek strategic advantage. Whatever the primary orientation of a state or coalition, maritime or continental, the instrumental purpose is the same; to reach and grasp the enemy's center of strategic gravity. If the coalition-leading rivals are a land power and a sea power, the central challenge to statecraft and strategy is to translate advantage at sea into advantage on land, or vice versa, perhaps with air power as a critical "equalizer" (as for the Allies in Normandy in the summer of 1944).

Great land powers have sought sea-power allies, and great sea powers have sought land-power allies. In modern times sea powers have found it easier to team with continental allies than land powers have found it to team with maritime allies. One must hesitate before imposing a pattern on a broad outline of the strategic events of several centuries, but still it appears to have been the case that dominant land powers have posed much greater threats to other land powers than leading sea powers have posed to other sea powers. The Netherlands, Britain, and the United States organized mixed maritime-continental coalitions to which their land-power foes—Spain, France, Germany, and even the Soviet Union—signally failed to respond in kind. Germany might have succeeded in the 1930s and 1940s, but the Italian navy was too weak to be other than a serious nuisance to Britain (whereas, geopolitically, the Italian empire yielded Britain a feasible campaigning ground, pending the restoration of her continental fortunes), and the imperial Japanese navy was too distant and eventually overmatched by U.S. sea-air power.

A notable problem with general theories is that they can fail to hold for any individual case. Theoretically, it is not difficult to explain how an off-Eurasian-shore Britain, or the United States, "set up" continental foes for eventual destruction by superior maritime-continental coalitions. It is always possible, however, for general truths about great continental-maritime rivalries to be falsified in a particular instance. It is a fact that no continental state in modern times has succeeded in reaching and grasping a maritime's foe's center of strategic gravity at sea (its seaborne trade) on a scale sufficient to deliver victory in war. Nonetheless, 1917 and 1941–43 might have seen a land power perform well enough with a distinctly second-class navy to drive the sea-power enemy out of the conflict.

It is commonplace to note the vulnerability of continental powers to damage or defeat on land. It is less commonplace to recognize that sea powers too have homelands vulnerable to damage or seizure by the enemy. The record of maritime-power success in the great wars of recent centuries notwithstanding, it is well to remember that prominent among the contrasts between armies and navies is the *relatively* small number of major combat vehicles that comprise the latter and hence, in principle, the fragility of an advantage in fleet size. In the twentieth century, even the greatest of sea powers have deployed their "capital ships" in numbers only rarely higher than a few dozen, if that.[1] The scale of SSN (nuclear powered attack

1. First employed in 1652, at least as far as history records, the term "capital ship" has meant simply a battleship, which is to say a ship capable of being in the line of battle (another concept traceable to the First Anglo-Dutch War). The outstanding discussion is Michael Vlahos, "A Crack in the Shield. The Capital Ship Concept Under Attack," *The Journal of Strategic Studies* 2 (May 1979): 47–82. Even when a great sea power maintained more than a hundred capital ships in commission—as Britain did during the Napoleonic Wars—the increments by which the fighting power of the fleet might be attrited were very distinctly larger than was true for the army. This argument is even more true for the twentieth century, wherein capital ship numbers in a fleet

submarine) deployment has been the clearest exception to this twentieth-century rule, but the SSN is also the least flexible of the ship types ranked informally as "capital" in this century, though that flexibility is greater than is widely appreciated (its mere "presence" can literally paralyze enemy shipping, for example).

The differences between armies and navies typically are not well understood. Although a navy takes much longer to construct and train than does an army, even an army cannot be improvised hastily, thrust into combat against a first-class foe, and be expected to hold its own. In World War II the hastily assembled U.S. Army eventually became almost combat competitive with a much weakened German army, but in the interim it relied heavily on comprehensive air support to make up the difference in combat effectiveness.

That the land is the final gameboard in war is reflected in the history of maritime conflict. In part because war at sea ultimately is about securing advantage on land, most sea warfare, in all periods, has been conducted in coastal waters and close to maritime chokepoints. The land and the sea are very different combat environments, but both armies and navies have been able to retire to fortified sanctuaries. Also, even though command at sea is about the freedom of passage of friendly ships, whereas "command" on land is about the control of territory, the focus on reaching and grasping enemy forces is common to warfare in all environments.

It is an arresting paradox that although a balanced navy is more difficult to build than is a comparably capable army, second-class navies pursuing properly second-class strategies (though first-class for them) are far more effective than are second-class armies, no matter what strategies the latter pursue. The qualification, *pursuing properly second-class strategies*, is vital. If a second-class navy finds expression as a second-rate battle fleet seeking an opportunity for success in fleet battle, it will be worse than strategically useless; its opportunity costs could be on a war-losing scale. A sea power has to exert more effort on land to secure the defeat of a land power, than a land power needs to exert afloat to defeat a sea power. This fact renders impressive indeed the persistent success in modern times of maritime powers and maritime-led coalitions.

There have been few true duels between sea powers and land powers; coalition warfare has been the historical norm. As sea power and land

---

typically have fallen to less than one fifth the range just cited for the Royal Navy of the 1800s and 1810s.

power, and later air power and space power, complement each other, so the strategic benefits of synergisms among their several forms of prowess depend critically on the ability of each to understand the nature and the strengths and limitations of the other (or others). The history of conflict is the history of success and failure in combined arms.

TO REACH AND TO GRASP

How can sea powers and land powers grapple for strategic advantage? Success on land may not compensate for failure at sea; success at sea may not offset failure on land. Sea powers would like to perform so well at sea that they can cash that advantage in continental clout. Similarly, land powers wish to translate continental preponderance into maritime influence. These long-standing aspirations can prove difficult to realize. Many wars between states and coalitions headed by antagonistic sea and land powers have been terminated by a compromise peace or interrupted by a compromise armistice. Such compromises recognize stalemate between a sea power unable to challenge a land power on land and a land power unable to challenge a sea power at sea.

Sea power can be used to extend a conflict in time and space, but no iron law of strategic history requires that time must work to the advantage of maritime states. Of recent centuries, the dominant land power of the day invariably has been distracted from the sea power–land power standoff on the coasts of Europe by unfinished continental business. That distraction can even be welcome, since continental problems are problems a land power believes it can resolve in short order. For example, Napoleon's Austrian difficulties obliged him to break up the invasion camp at Boulogne in August 1805, and the methods adopted in forcibly resolving those difficulties led directly to the necessity of solving new difficulties with Prussia. In its turn, the brief conflict with Prussia again brought French land power face to face with Russian land power. The long-term consequences of that confrontation were fatal to Napoleon's bid for a lasting dynastic Bonapartist hegemony over Europe.

For a more recent example of the frustration of superior land power at the water's edge, Hitler knew all about the perils for Germany of a two-front war and was not at all ignorant of the fate of Napoleon's Grande Armée after it crossed the Niemen. Nonetheless, Hitler aspired to defeat Britain strategically by depriving it of hope of a Russian alliance in a potentially war-winning coalition of land power with sea power. In *Mein Kampf*, as throughout the 1920s and most of the 1930s, Hitler believed that he must, and would be able to, choose between a Russian or a British alliance. Ironically, he produced the very strategic condition that he feared might be fatal for Germany, a two-front war against great continental and maritime enemies. At best, Hitler's strategy could only be as good as the operational art and physical weight of the forces he unleashed in Operation Barbarossa on June 22, 1941. At worst, the strategy itself may have been flawed. Britain might have declined to sue for peace even had the Soviet Union been defeated definitively before the autumn mud arrested ground movement. It was hoped in Berlin in 1940–41 that a collapse of Soviet power would free Japanese military assets from their massive Soviet-oriented distraction in Manchuria to move into the central Pacific and Southeast Asia. Not unreasonably, Hitler believed that a Japan on the move in the Pacific would direct U.S. attention firmly away from Europe. As a map exercise Hitler's grand-strategic design was not implausible. In practice it foundered on operational misdirection, on inadequate force to space ratios, on insufficient mechanization (the German army in World War II functioned on a logistic shoestring), and in the mud; all of which precluded the test of its validity at the level of grand strategy. Britain was probably invasion-proof by the fall of 1941, but there can be little doubt that Britain alone, or even Britain and the United States, could not have defeated Germany. Truly, *Festung Europa* would have been an impregnable citadel. In order to win a war *à outrance* against continental Nazi Germany, Britain had to acquire a continental ally with an army capable of holding its own in the field, albeit with Allied material assistance, against the German army. Only with the faltering of the German drive on Moscow and the opening of the great Soviet winter offensive in the first week of December 1941 was it apparent that Britain had found such an ally.

The experience of the past two centuries has seen the protraction of major war between sea powers and land powers function strongly, and eventually conclusively, to the benefit of the former. One must beware, however, of generalizing too confidently from Britain's experience of conflict with France and Germany. It is true that Britain's inveterate opposition first to French, then to German, continental-hegemonic ambitions was critical to provision of the grand-strategic framework that enabled the eventual overthrow of the land-power enemy. But the lion's share of the actual combat against French, then German, land power was effected by Britain's continental allies.

One can argue that a continental power, no matter how successful in the short term, invariably will reach on land for more than it can grasp, or will grasp more than it can hold. If only it can sustain the struggle, the offshore sea power will eventually find powerful continental allies. Through its actual or threatened success on land, the dominant land power cannot help but arouse a continental opposition that is the natural ally of the sea power. This is a comforting analysis, but for it to be close to a reliable theory of success in statecraft and war it requires extraordinary fortitude and commitment on the part of the sea power. Furthermore, it could be wrong in any particular instance, with potentially fatal strategic implications for the sea power and its remaining allies. There is a mentally stimulating realm of nightmarish "what ifs." What if Nazi Germany had acquired the French fleet in 1940 and had eschewed invasion plans against the Soviet Union, pending achievement of decision in the West? Or, what if the Soviet Union in the 1970s or 1980s had defeated NATO in Europe, having first secured with Beijing the diplomatic and strategic triumph of the functional equivalent of the Molotov-Ribbentrop Pact (August 23, 1939)? In this speculative second instance, whose land power would have complemented the sea, air, and missile power of a distant, undefeated, yet presumably still belligerent United States?

Neither sea power nor land power is an intrinsic value that transcends precise circumstances of strategic geography, general economic strength, level of technology, or intensity of political purpose. Also, Sir Halford Mackinder's proposition that it is easier for land power to take to the sea than for sea power to come ashore,[2] is nonsense apart from exact historical context. One must beware of any strategic mysticism that seeks to impart to reified Sea Power, Land Power, or Air Power immanent properties for relative strategic advantage, regardless of the material and geostrategic circumstances of the actual rivals of the day. Other things being equal, a large economic advantage in a military rivalry should permit that much stronger side, whether it be traditionally land or sea oriented in its strategic culture and policy, eventually to gain the strategic advantage in any conflict environment.

OBJECTIVES ON LAND AND SEA

War at sea, or operations bearing directly on war at sea, is a struggle for freedom of maritime communications *for the passage of ships*. The purposes

2. Halford J. Mackinder, *Democratic Ideals and Reality* (New York: W. W. Norton, 1962; first pub. 1942), 111.

to which tolerably secure maritime communications are applied, and the methods by which those communications are secured, may be defensive or offensive, though typically will be a mix of both. Furthermore, control at sea is likely to be sought through action in all environments. Coastal control translates into air power over the sea, for example. War at sea is about the ability to use maritime highways, whereas war on land *de profundis* is about the control of territory, with the latter logically more important than the former.

States are territorial entities. References to thalassocracies, seaborne empires, maritime powers, sea powers, and the like should not blind us to the sensitivity of those polities to threats to their homelands. Athens, Rome, and Byzantium could suffer ravagement by enemy armies in their homelands yet still endure, but modern Britain has always feared prompt catastrophe if an enemy should invade. For centuries, British statesmen, admirals, and generals accepted the principle that the security of the home islands was the first strategic charge on their armed forces. Threats of invasion were a standard ploy applied by continental powers to throw Britain on the defensive and paralyze British offensive capability overseas.

For Britain, command of the sea did not mean freedom from anxiety over the danger of invasion. Every country has a strategic culture formed in good part by distinctive historical memories. Britain never forgot that the Great Armada of 1588 might have succeeded in providing naval coverage for the transport of the Duke of Parma's veteran soldiers from the Spanish Netherlands to the North Foreland of Kent. More poignantly, though objectively less dangerous since the enemy of the day had no ambition to invade and conquer, the memory lingered long and bitterly of Lieutenant-Admiral Michiel de Ruyter blockading the Thames estuary in June and July 1667, thereby ensuring England's defeat in the Second Anglo-Dutch War (1665–67).

The differences between war at sea and war on land are easily summarized, if frequently neglected in arguments over defense policy. At the most basic level of purpose, in the words of Roger Barnett: "States conduct war on land in order to achieve long-term political control over territory. Warfare at sea, on the other hand, is concerned with temporary control over selected maritime areas for the purpose of influencing what is taking place on the land."[3]

Man fights to use the sea but to occupy the land. Strategically, the sea is valuable as a highway for movement between landmasses and, in recent

3. Roger W. Barnett, "Are Naval Operations Unique?" *Naval Forces* 7, no. 5 (1986): 25.

times, as an environment in which long-range bombardment platforms can hide. It follows that combat at sea can also have strategic value if it harasses traffic on the maritime highway and denies sanctuaries to bombardment platforms. Outside an enemy's coastal waters, naval victories can have global implications for freedom of movement at sea. In his posture statement for Fiscal Year 1983, then chief of naval operations Admiral Thomas Hayward itemized what he regarded as the unique characteristics of naval operations in peace and war.[4] He pointed out the three-dimensional nature of war at sea (to which for the 1990s and beyond one should add the fourth dimension of space), the absence of geographical battle lines at sea, the global domain of the threat to maritime forces (there tend to be no safe rear areas), the shortness and mobility of the logistic tail of naval forces, and the difficulty of surveillance of ocean-sized space and further explained that all forces at sea are maneuver forces and the presence of nonbelligerents in the arena for war at sea can be a complication qualitatively different from the situation on land.

Differences abound between the land and the sea as environments for armed conflict. In addition to Hayward's points, the concentration of naval strength in a relatively few units contrasts sharply with the distribution of land power over vast numbers of personnel and machines. Also, the all but absolute options for the refusal of battle at sea have no close counterpart on land. Whether it was the French after the Battle of La Hogue-Barfleur in 1692, the Germans throughout the 1914–18 war—save what for them was the accidental fleet-scale encounter off Jutland on May 31, 1916—or, as a historical might-have-been, the Soviet Union in a Cold War turned hot, the second-class sea power can elect to operate much of its navy as a fleet-in-being, more or less secure behind coastal defenses.[5] Acquiescence to an enemy's maritime command, though not to that enemy's untroubled use of sea lines of communication, is a surrender of the strategic initiative at sea. For a land power such a surrender is not fatal. Indeed, a defensive strategy is almost inevitable for a land power at war with a preponderant sea power. That defensive strategy, aimed to secure the negative objective of denial of reliable use of the sea, requires an offensive style of operations in the form of air, surface, and subsurface raiding (in the future, space-supported).

Ground forces providing direct cover for national homelands cannot

4. Testimony of Admiral Thomas Hayward before the Senate Committee on Armed Services, February 25, 1982.

5. See Charles E. Callwell, *Military Operations and Maritime Preponderance: Their Relations and Interdependence* (Edinburgh: William Blackwood & Sons, 1905), 60–61, 77–80.

refuse combat without leaving open to enemy seizure some part of that which they are maintained to protect. An enemy fleet unchallenged on the high seas holds nothing of intrinsic value; it protects the ability to move, no more and no less. A hostile army left unchallenged can seize, hold, and exploit national resources, deny the logistic base of the defending force, and generally render the continuation of hostilities close to impossible, if not pointless.

One must beware of venturing too stark a comparison between land and sea warfare. Desert warfare in all ages, and certainly from the great Arab conquests of the seventh century, through the western desert in 1940, to the Arabian peninsula in the 1990s, has had some of the characteristics of war at sea: relatively featureless terrain, typically open flanks, high mobility, and great space. Similarly, warfare in the "sea of grass" that extends from Central Asia to the Carpathians has in certain important features also closely paralleled maritime conflict.[6] As late as 1941–42, the semimechanized legions of Nazi Germany lacked the logistic reach and overall mobility to grasp, hold, and defeat rapidly a Soviet army able to exploit the geographical depth of its homeland in order to refuse battle except on favorable terms. Autumn mud and an unusually severe winter functioned synergistically with sheer distance, the material inadequacies of the German army, and appalling errors in higher campaign direction to deny Hitler victory in the East in 1941.[7] It is true that there is no parallel at sea to the ramparts on land provided naturally by irregular landforms, incidentally by the urban areas of civilian society, and intentionally by military engineering, but sea power does not lack for defensible, fortifiable bastions. Given the inalienable dependence of sea power on the land, it is only to be expected that maritime conflict has been very much the history of struggle for the control of coastal waters. Such struggle has focused on those maritime chokepoints domination of which decides which party is at liberty to venture at tolerable risk on the high seas.

6. See René Grousset, *The Empire of the Steppes: A History of Central Asia* (New Brunswick, N.J.: Rutgers University Press, 1970; first pub. 1939); and William H. McNeill, *Europe's Steppe Frontier, 1500–1800: A Study of the Eastward Movement in Europe* (Chicago: University of Chicago Press, 1964).

7. Albert Seaton, writing of the succeeding years, judges as follows: "The causes of German failure during 1943 were identical to those which gave rise to the defeats in 1942, an inadequacy of resources, particularly motor vehicles and motor fuels, and the insistence by the Führer on a rigid defensive strategy." *The Russo-German War, 1941–45* (New York: Praeger, 1970), 404. But see R. H. S. Stolfi, *Hitler's Panzers East: World War II Reinterpreted* (Norman: University of Oklahoma Press, 1991).

In the age of sail, ships enjoyed powers of transoceanic endurance subject only to the sustenance and health of the crews. But throughout that age it was extraordinary for a major sea battle to be fought out of sight, or at least beyond fairly easy reach, of land. Struggles over maritime command, or for the launching of complex naval operations on a large scale while evading the battle fleet of the country that enjoyed such command, necessarily were undertakings about freedom of access to the high seas. Against a succession of continental naval powers, the British Royal Navy repeatedly gave the appearance of picketing the coast of Europe, though in such a way that a speedy and hopefully overwhelming concentration of force would always be feasible.[8]

The thin literature on the contrast between warfare at sea and on land is unduly essentialist in character. The valid contrast to be drawn between the featureless, if ever weather-variable, high seas, and the human-altered and natural variety of the land needs to be supplemented by recognition of significant modifying points. The character of sea and land power may differ, but the operational objectives need not differ as radically as might be expected. For example, fleets do not have physically continuous lines of communication after the fashion of roads or railroads, but they do have logistic trains that can be threatened and damaged and, functionally, lines of communication that can be harassed and severed. Moreover, where sea power meets the land, in coastal waters and in port, chokepoints exist that attract enemy action. It is true that sea warfare is about the ability to use an environment for transportation, whereas land warfare is about the defense or seizure of territory, but both forms of conflict require that attention be focused on the military forces of the enemy. As Herbert Rosinski explains it: "What we wish to command or control is not 'the sea,' but our opponent, or the neutrals; it is precisely because we cannot 'reduce' the sea 'into possession' that there is the difficulty and delicate problem of the neutral and his rights to be faced in naval warfare."[9] Just as the sea may be freely traversed once working control, let alone command, is established by battle or blockade, so enemy territory can be occupied and exploited once the hostile army is defeated, driven off, or effectively masked.

The sea is featureless and unpopulated, but it is not bereft of places of

8. Julian S. Corbett, *Some Principles of Maritime Strategy* (Annapolis, Md.: Naval Institute Press, 1988; first pub. 1911), 128–52, remains the outstanding explanation of what concentration of force means in terms of naval deployments.

9. Herbert Rosinski, *The Development of Naval Thought* (Newport, R.I.: Naval War College Press, 1977), 4

unusual military significance certain to attract the attention of both sides in war. The concept of the maritime chokepoint was as significant for the coast-hugging galleys of classical sea warfare, as it has been recently for navies that have vessels with a global cruising range. The Bosporus and the Dardanelles have been important in all eras; certainly they were as strategically critical for ancient Persia, Athens, Sparta, and Macedonia as the Greenland-Iceland-U.K. "gap" was for East and West during the Cold War.

Both fleets and armies can retire to fortified places.[10] The history of warfare is amply stocked with cases of fleets-in-being and armies-in-being. In principle, an army that falls back on some fortified position leaves some of its dependent territory open to seizure and ravagement. But in practice, an army-in-being tends to compel a concentration of enemy forces. That concentration to mask the enemy's army-in-being can severely restrict the invader's freedom of action to exploit a context where much of the hostile country no longer is directly defended. Whether or not an army-in-being can exert major influence on a campaign or the war as a whole depends on the relative strengths of the two sides. Troops in a fortress status—as, for example, were German soldiers in Memel, Königsberg, Breslau, and Budapest in 1944–45—simply may lack the numbers and mobility to influence significantly the course of a campaign. Fleets-in-being are not literally inaccessible; rather, they are inaccessible save at a price the besieger-blockader is unwilling to pay. Both on land and at sea one may oblige a reluctant enemy to come out and give battle if a sufficiently severe threat is posed to interests that he values highly. For example, the British Royal Navy would have been compelled to venture forth to give battle against an invasion fleet, regardless of the odds. But even for that navy, with its strong tradition of offensive action, there were occasions when the fleet-in-being strategy was prudent and effective. Admiral Lord Torrington, explaining his actions following the defeat of his Anglo-Dutch fleet off Beachy Head on July 10, 1690, wrote that "most men were in fear that the French would invade, but I was always of another opinion; for I always said that whilst we had a *fleet in being* they would not dare to make an attempt."[11] This was the origin of the phrase, though certainly not the concept.

The sea cannot be fortified after the manner of the land, but countries of all maritime degree provide protected places for their naval power. In the

10. Callwell, *Military Operations and Maritime Preponderance*, chap. 4.

11 Quoted in George Clark, "The Nine Years' War, 1688–97," in *The New Cambridge Modern History*, ed. J. S. Bromley, vol. 5, *The Rise of Great Britain and Russia, 1688–1715/25* (Cambridge: Cambridge University Press, 1970), 240. Emphasis added.

case of a commanding sea power prior to the advent of long-range aviation and missiles, the protected places could encompass virtually all of the world's oceans beyond the enemy's coastal waters. For example, consider the mine barrages that Britain and the United States laid in the First World War in the Straits of Dover in 1914 and 1916, between the Shetlands and Norway in 1918, and to block the narrow exit from the Adriatic in 1918. Given the strength of motivation for the leading sea power to pursue an offensive strategy, it is inevitable that enemy coastal bastions should serve as foci of attention. As the seaward reach of land-based weapons and instruments of reconnaissance expanded, along with the emergence and evolution of mines and of flotilla craft potentially lethal against capital ships, so too did the extent of what amount to maritime bastion areas. In the First World War the Heligoland Bight was a German bastion, as was the Baltic. The North Sea was a region of disputed command, with the local advantage depending on the relative proximity of the fleet bases of the two sides. For another example, in the early 1980s, according to Bryan Ranft and Geoffrey Till, "recent exercises suggest that the Soviet Navy is working to establish a 1,500-mile defence perimeter around Soviet territory, passing through the Greenland-Iceland-United Kingdom Gap, the Sicilian straits and enclosing a sizable chunk of the north-west Pacific."[12]

Closely adjunct to the problems of landward and seaward reach and grasp, and of the generally contrasting, though sometimes similar, natures of war on land and at sea, are the persisting differences between the time taken to build an army and to construct a navy. The differences in lead time for the achievement of excellence on land and at sea have implications for policy and strategy that continue to be profound. It is to this subject that the discussion now turns.

LEAD TIMES FOR NAVIES AND ARMIES

The British historian H. P. Willmott has observed that "sea power is a rational instrument of state power, and, moreover, it is a long-term phenomenon; ships, design teams, industries, and, above all, experience, cannot be improvised."[13] This has always been true to a degree, but it has never been

12   Bryan Ranft and Geoffrey Till, *The Sea in Soviet Strategy* (Annapolis, Md.: Naval Institute Press, 1983), 157.

13. H. P. Willmott, *Sea Warfare: Weapons, Tactics and Strategy* (Chichester, U K.: Antony Bird, 1981), 10.

more true than it is today. In the ancient world, compensation for lack of
nautical proficiency could be sought in the combination of technology,
superior numbers, and a choice of battle tactics that would enable the less
skillful navy to wage what amounted to an infantry fight at sea on favorable
terms of engagement. The Roman invention of the *corvus* (crow), a spiked
grappling device attached to boarding gangways intended to lock two ships
together, enabled an improvised navy to dispute the crucial sea lines of
communication of the Carthaginian maritime empire in the First Punic
War. The corvus was used to deadly effect in the Battle of Mylae in 260
B.C., barely a year after the Senate had decided that Rome was to build
naval power on a scale sufficient to challenge Carthage for command at
sea.[14] The transferability of military competence between land and sea
declined sharply as fighting ships evolved from floating platforms for infantry
combat into dedicated artillery platforms. The displacement of the galley by
the all-sailing ship, as maritime commerce and, inevitably, conflict shifted
its horizons from the narrow coastal waters of the Mediterranean to the
transoceanic sea routes to the East and the Americas, necessarily placed
seamanship and sea-keeping properties of all kinds at a premium.

Since the birth of distinctive navies in modern times in the seventeenth
century, the capital ship has been the largest and most complicated man-
machine system built and operated by a state. The ships that could stand in
the line of battle in the age of fighting sail were the most complex
and expensive machines produced by preindustrial economies. Little has
changed. The aircraft carrier, the nuclear submarine, and the antisubmarine
warfare (ASW) and air defense cruiser are the largest, most complex,
and inevitably most expensive, weapon systems produced by contemporary
science-based economies. At least modern navies do not have the timber
problem that periodically slowed naval shipbuilding in the age of sail.
Geoffrey Marcus notes that "an oak-tree took about one hundred years to
attain maturity. Nearly two-thousand oak-trees had to be felled for the
construction of a [line-of-battle ship with] 74 [guns]."[15]

The U.S. Navy that won the war in the Pacific was the product of a
rearmament surge that long antedated Pearl Harbor. Indeed, the U.S.

14. See William Ledyard Rodgers, *Greek and Roman Naval Warfare: A Study of Strategy,
Tactics and Ship Design from Salamis (480 B.C.) to Actium (31 B.C.)* (Annapolis, Md.: Naval
Institute Press, 1983; first pub. 1937), 275–76, and F. E. Adcock, *The Roman Art of War Under the
Republic* (Cambridge: Harvard University Press, 1940), 46.

15. G. J. Marcus, *A Naval History of England*, vol. 1, *The Formative Centuries* (Boston: Little,
Brown, 1961), 345.

Navy's construction program announced in June 1940 in the Two-Ocean
Naval Expansion Act probably had the effect of contributing critically to the
acceleration of Japan's timetable of seaward expansion.

> The Japanese were aware that after the U.S. Congress passed the
> Two-Ocean Naval Expansion Act of June 1940 they were in a
> quandary. The long-term prospects of a naval victory over the
> Americans would be ended by the 1940 measure. To have even
> matched the American program of June 1940 Japan would have had
> to double the proposed construction program of 1942 (the Fifth
> Replacement Program), and already in 1940 there were doubts
> about whether Japan could fulfill the provisions of the current
> Fourth Program.[16]

The benefits of U.S. naval rearmament were apparent in the large
numbers of new ships deployed with the fleet beginning in 1943.

Land power can be built, certainly improvised, more rapidly than can sea
power, but truly effective land power cannot be generated reliably in a hurry.
There is a difference in lead times in the construction and mobilization from
low peacetime levels of fleets and armies, but this distinction can be drawn
too sharply. The equipment for armies can be produced more rapidly than
can the equipment for navies, but hastily improvised armies are merely
militias or even rabbles in uniform and, save under exceptional circumstances, are no match for disciplined and seasoned professionals. Other
things being tolerably equal, enthusiasm and self-confidence neither substitute adequately for military skills nor long endure in the face of the defeat in
the field which is the fate of military incompetence.

With two important partial exceptions, sea powers in modern times have
improvised large, competent enough, though not truly first-class, armies,
but land powers have been unable to improvise naval power on a large and
effective scale. The notable exceptions to this generalization are the German
U-boat fleets of World Wars I and II. Certainly France, except possibly in
the 1680s and 1770s, and later Germany, were unable to invest suitably on
a long-term basis in naval infrastructure in order to be able to surge major
peacetime warship construction to a level sufficient to challenge for surface

---

16. H. P. Willmott, *Empires in the Balance: Japanese and Allied Pacific Strategies to April 1942*
(Annapolis, Md.: Naval Institute Press, 1982), 61. For an admirable recent history of the U.S. Navy
in this period, see Robert W. Love Jr , *History of the U.S Navy*, vol. 1, 1775–1941 (Harrisburg,
Pa.: Stackpole, 1992), chaps. 35–39.

maritime command. The aspiring hegemonic land powers of modern times have always had continental distractions that denied or helped deny them the resources necessary to build a convincing challenge for command at sea. Indeed, Mahan went so far as to claim that "history has conclusively demonstrated the inability of a state with even a single continental frontier to compete in naval development with one that is insular, although of smaller population and resources."[17] In the case of France in the eighteenth century, it would be a mistake to emphasize the malign significance for her navy of continental menace and ambition. French problems with naval power had more to do with a lack of sailors, uncertain access to vital naval stores, and a shortage of advanced gun foundries than with allegedly competing claims of land warfare.[18] The British close blockade prevented the sailors of Napoleonic France from maintaining or learning the skills necessary to operate and fight at sea on terms tolerably equal to the Royal Navy. The system of maritime command that worked efficiently for the Royal Navy after the late 1790s prevented France from restoring its naval competence to the level of rough equality achieved briefly in the war of 1778–83. Prolonged absence of exercise at sea causes fleets-in-being to lose efficiency in seamanship and consequently as fighting instruments.

Apart from the differences in lead time for the construction of equipment for fleets and for armies, differences that function to the net benefit of sea powers over land powers, it can be argued that armies may be turned into effective fighting instruments more rapidly than navies. The difficulty with this is that it may not rest soundly on balanced analysis of war as a whole. Maritime Britain, whose traditional leading military-strategic instrument was the battle fleet, did succeed in 1914–18 in raising a mass army that performed well enough in the field. However, that mass army did not reach a size considered respectable by continental standards until 1916; it was never as skillful as the German army at its best;[19] and the victory for which

17. Alfred Thayer Mahan, *Retrospect and Prospect: Studies in International Relations, Naval and Political* (London: Sampson, Low, Marston, 1902), 169.

18. The nonfungibility of French land power and sea power is strongly, perhaps excessively, argued in N.A.M. Rodger, "The Continental Commitment in the Eighteenth Century," in *War, Strategy, and International Politics: Essays in Honour of Sir Michael Howard*, ed. Lawrence Freedman, Paul Hayes, and Robert O'Neill (Oxford: Clarendon Press, 1992), 39–53.

19. The superiority of German military method at the tactical, even "grand tactical," level is well handled, though probably overstated, in Timothy T. Lupfer, *The Dynamics of Doctrine: The Changes in German Tactical Doctrine During the First World War*, Leavenworth Papers, no. 4 (Fort Leavenworth, Kans.: Combat Studies Institute, U.S. Army Command and General Staff College, July 1981). Also see Bruce I. Gudmundsson, *Stormtroop Tactics: Innovation in the German Army, 1914–1918* (New York: Praeger, 1989)

it was primarily responsible in 1918 was achieved against an enemy already greatly weakened by four years of war. Because of the strategic geography of Britain, the British army lacked a tradition of excellence in the conduct of warfare on a continental scale. Nonetheless, it is interesting to note that a careful scholar of the First World War has observed that "only autumn mud, broken roads, demolitions and the staunch rear-guard fighting of German machine gunners prevented the collapse of the German Army [in the fall of 1918]. The figures for prisoners taken in the final weeks indicate how close to disintegration it had come."[20]

The Anglo-American mass armies of World War II performed well enough, but they fought a German army already ruined on the eastern front between 1941 and 1943. In terms of the fighting power generated in relation to the resources committed, the German army in World War II, on the offensive or the defensive, was as superior to its British, American, and Russian opponents, as was the Confederate States of America's Army of Northern Virginia to the Union's Army of the Potomac.[21] A crucial difference in fighting power in these particular instances, of World War II and the American Civil War, lay in the character of military tradition and its implications. Military tradition is no guarantee of military success, however, as the Prussian experience in 1806 and the French experience in 1870 well attest. Superiority of military method, greater intensity of political

20. Dominick Graham, "*Sans Doctrine*: British Army Tactics in the First World War," in *Men at War: Politics, Technology and Innovation in the Twentieth Century*, ed. Timothy Travers and Christon Archer (Chicago: Precedent Publishing, 1982), 87. The Allies took nearly 400,000 prisoners on the western front between July 18 and November 11, 1918—of which number 188,700 surrendered to the British, 139,000 to the French, 43,000 to the Americans, and 14,500 to the Belgians. Obviously, though the instrument of a maritime power, the British army in World War I must have done something right. On the still-booming debate over British military competence in the First World War, see Brian Bond, ed., *The First World War and British Military History* (Oxford: Clarendon Press, 1991).

21. In the words of Trevor Dupuy. "On a man-for-man basis, the German ground soldiers consistently inflicted casualties at about a 50 percent higher rate than they incurred from the opposing British and American troops under all circumstances." *A Genius for War: The German Army and General Staff, 1807–1945* (London: Macdonald & Jane's, 1977), 253. Also see Martin van Creveld, *Fighting Power: German and U.S. Army Performance, 1939–1945* (Westport, Conn.: Greenwood Press, 1982), chap. 12. On the superior fighting power of Confederate soldiers, see Herman Hattaway and Archer Jones, *How the North Won: A Military History of the Civil War* (Urbana, Ill.: University of Illinois Press, 1983), 728. But see the iconoclastic study, Michael C. C. Adams, *Our Masters the Rebels: A Speculation on Union Military Failure in the East, 1861–1865* (Cambridge: Harvard University Press, 1978). One has to be careful to specify just which Confederate and Union armies are included in the judgment rendered. Confederate forces in the West, and particularly the Army of Tennessee, had a poor record of performance and contributed notably to the final defeat.

motivation,[22] and sheer weight of assets, severally or in combination, can more than offset the military value of an enemy's military tradition.

The outcome of war is the product of combined arms in the broadest of senses. States or coalitions earn an overall grade for performance in war. Superior performance strictly on land, or on the sea, or in the air in the context of failure in the other environments typically has not sufficed to produce a favorable outcome. At least to date in modern times, the leading land power has been insufficiently preponderant on land to create a secure continental base for the building of a first-class navy—if the building of such a navy is even feasible, that is. For the contrasting case, leading sea powers have achieved and sustained a measure of command afloat unmatched by continental enemies in their control ashore. But sea powers have had to wed strength at sea to land power of their own or to the land power of subsidized allies in order to achieve victory in war.

The jury is still out on the question of whether or not a dominant continental power, though fighting at a great disadvantage at sea, can improvise a navy capable of so negating the maritime command of a sea power that intolerable pressure is brought to bear on him. The concept of command of the sea was popularized and rendered canon law for many people by Alfred Mahan on the basis of detailed study only of the history of maritime conflict among Britain, Holland, France, Spain, and the United States over the course of one hundred and fifty years of the classic age of sail. Mahan's world was geographically one-dimensional, the surface of the sea, and was strategically one dimensional in that his chosen vantage point was that of the dominant sea power. Those facts are not fatal for the merit in his naval theory, because his strictures against fleets-in-being and commerce raiding were not in principle technology- or opponent-specific. Nonetheless, that *guerre de course* has yet to provide the leverage critical for success in war does not mean that it could not do so, even though Mahan's theory of the utility of battle-fleet command was not invalidated by the world wars of the twentieth century. In the inimitable words of the master: "The battle-fleet is the solid nucleus of power."[23] That theory was proved to be

22. A major study of the American Civil War concludes that it was Confederate deficiencies in morale and in the political will to resist that proved fatal. See Richard E. Beringer et al., *Why the South Lost the Civil War* (Athens: University of Georgia Press, 1986), chap. 17. I find this thesis unconvincing as argued Morale did slump, but as an understandable result of military failure in the field. Gabor S. Boritt, ed., *Why the Confederacy Lost* (New York: Oxford University Press, 1992), and Archer Jones, *Civil War Command and Strategy: The Process of Victory and Defeat* (New York: Free Press, 1992), are useful recent additions to the apparently unending debate.

23. Mahan, *Retrospect and Prospect*, 194.

incomplete rather than erroneous in the face of submarine and aircraft threats to surface shipping. In theory at least, and practice was not that far distant in the first half of 1917 or again in 1941–43, an antishipping campaign, married to success on land, could deny a sea power the ability to wage war effectively.[24] A continental naval power need not seek even a working control at sea, much less some facsimile of command. It would suffice to deny the maritime enemy the principal benefit that command at sea confers, the ability to use the oceans freely.

An interesting contrast looms. A balanced navy, capable of contesting command at sea, is much more difficult to build than is a capable army sufficient for the task of taking war to the enemy on land. But in large part because a second-class navy can, or could, hide (under the sea, in fortified ports), a "strategy of evasion" (of the need to contest military command) is considerably more effective at sea than are its parallels on land.[25] On the one hand, Germany might have driven Britain from the active list of enemies in both world wars by its exercise of the *guerre de course*. On the other hand, Britain could not possibly have wrought Germany's defeat on land by means of raids, guerrilla warfare by partisans in occupied countries, or even by sustained peripheral campaigns.

The relative difficulty of improvising effective sea power and effective land power has to be seen in the context of war considered as a whole. In theory, a sea power has to exert a lot more effort on land in order to defeat a land power than a land power needs to exert at sea in order to defeat a sea power.[26] German naval power in World War I was most menacing after it had abandoned hope of wresting military command in the North Sea from the Grand Fleet via strategems leading to ambush in detail of the Royal Navy's capital-ship strength; whereas in a World War II that occurred seven to nine years too soon for its building plans, the German navy could never even aspire to command at sea.

24. Richard Compton-Hall· *Submarines and the War at Sea, 1914–18* (London: Macmillan, 1991), and *The Underwater War, 1939–1945* (London: Blandford Press, 1982), are very much on target.

25. The pejorative phrase is in J.F.C. Fuller, *The Conduct of War 1789–1961: A Study of the Impact of the French, Industrial, and Russian Revolutions on War and Its Conduct* (London: Eyre & Spottiswoode, 1962), 160–65.

26. The human and material cost to Germany of the U-boat campaign was trivial when compared with the great land battles that were waged. In World War I Germany lost a total of 178 U-boats (5 in 1914, 19 in 1915, 22 in 1916, 63 in 1917 [the critical year], and 69 in 1918). See Robert H. Barnes, "German Submarine Action in World War I," U.S. Naval Institute *Proceedings* 68 (October 1942)· 1444, and John Terraine, *Business in Great Waters: The U-Boat Wars, 1916–1945* (London: Leo Cooper, 1989), 772.

The great difficulty and expense in acquiring and maintaining high-quality naval strength has repeatedly frustrated the policy and strategy of continental powers. The dominant land power of the day has had much less success in exploiting the maritime assets or potential of allies than has the leading sea power in finding allies on land who could field armies good enough to detain, distract, and attrit the continental enemy to a serious degree. Only once in modern times has the leading sea power been obliged itself to assume the major burden of continental warfare: Britain in 1917–18. This exception to the rule is reduced in its potential authority as a weathervane phenomenon by the fact that the French and Russian armies already had dulled the edge and reduced the depth of German fighting power by late 1916. The Second World War saw a return to the familiar pattern of the (Anglo-American) sea (-air) powers committing themselves to major ground combat as a late adjunct to the principal land campaign waged by a great continental ally.

Traditionally, sea powers evade the need to seek decision head-on with the center of military gravity of the enemy on land, his principal field army, by contriving to wage coalition warfare in consort with powerful continental allies. During the wars of the French Revolution and Empire, Britain sought always to have two, and preferably all three, of the great Eastern powers—Russia, Austria, Prussia—active as allies. The sea power has to mobilize sufficient land power of its own for the purposes of peripheral distraction, *tangible* token of continental commitment and steadiness of purpose, and often of vital makeweight to the local balance of forces on the ground. None of those purposes requires a sea power alone to improvise land power capable of defeating a continental enemy in its own sphere of excellence.

COLLEAGUES AND RIVALS

Sea power more often needs land power to conclude a war successfully than land power needs sea power. There are rare occasions when sea power alone can conclude, or can generate sufficient leverage to conclude, a campaign or war. Admittedly, those cases are rare. Furthermore, one has to beware of "truths" that are really only matters of definition. When does an amphibious raid or an invasion warrant identification as the exercise of land power rather than sea power? Sea power and land power in conflict cannot grip each other effectively to compel a military decision; some of each needs to be translated into the currency of the other. This is the heart of the matter. Failure to grasp the truth of this quintessentially strategic proposition has led to monumental errors in statecraft. However, understanding is one thing; the ability to act effectively on understanding is another. As often as not it is unclear whether the principal problem is lack of strategic insight or lack of material means.

Is it easier for a land power to acquire a major scale of sea power than for a sea power to acquire a major scale of land power? This question is included here to demonstrate the error in it. Which sea power? Which land power? Modern history has witnessed many bilateral rivalries—Anglo-French, Anglo-German, Soviet-American—but few actual duels. The Franco-Prussian (1870–71) and Russo-Japanese (1904–5) wars stand out as isolated exceptions to the generality of coalition warfare in modern times. The Franco-Prussian War was concluded so swiftly and decisively in its regular military essentials on land that superior French naval power was deprived of strategically important options.[27] As for the Russo-Japanese War, both of those countries were continental by strategic culture and policy ambition, though both had large navies. In practice in modern times, sea powers have fared better finding complementary land power, than have land powers in finding complementary sea power. There is a good reason why that should be so. Dominant land powers typically pose a threat to the potential continental allies of sea powers of an intensity that those sea powers do not even begin to approach and would have difficulty achieving under any circumstances. Furthermore, dominant sea power often has the ability physically to prevent other sea powers from performing usefully in a land-sea coalition. Herbert Rosinski advised that "it is the most peculiar and outstanding asset of 'Command of the Sea,' in contrast to war on land, where even the most conclusive superiority, as in the case of Napoleon, is utterly unable to affect the situation on the Sea, it confers not only absolute superiority within its own sphere, but with it the power of interfering most effectively on land as well."[28] Some of the more strategically acute of Germany's World War II generals noticed the same point.[29]

27. See Theodore Ropp, *The Development of a Modern Navy: French Naval Policy, 1871–1904* (Annapolis, Md.: Naval Institute Press, 1987), 22–25. Ironically, the French people were as impressed with the wartime devotion showed by their sailors *on land*, as they were unimpressed with the exploits of their navy at sea

28. Rosinski, *Development of Naval Thought*, 25.

29. For example, General Frido von Senger und Etterlin, *Neither Fear Nor Hope* (Novato, Calif : Presidio Press, 1989; first pub. 1960), 329-30.

This argument can be overstated; preeminence on land both in ancient-medieval and in modern times certainly has conferred major, even occasionally definitive, advantage in the struggle for control of sea routes. Rosinski was stating a general truth for the sailing-ship era and a distinctly ever-more-arguable proposition for each succeeding decade of this century. There is a strategic sense in which command at sea places the front line on the enemy's coast. But that truth became less axiomatic as the reach of land-based power expanded. Rosinski's argument was true for World War II against Germany once the Allies' surface command at sea had been secured via the defeat of the German subsurface and air threats. In general, so this point suggests, command at sea translates into sea *and* land power, whereas dominance on land—à la Napoleon—remains only dominance on land. The historical detail is critically important. Which era is under discussion? Is air power or nuclear capability a factor?

Sea power and land power may be strategic colleagues or strategic rivals. In the sage words of F. E. Adcock: "Not the least important element in the art of war is to be aware that naval power and land power may be friends and may be enemies, colleagues or rivals, as time and place may dictate, and to make the best use of both."[30] On balance, sea power and land power are strategic colleagues rather than rivals. The geopolitical perspective of British or U.S. security inevitably suggests some eternal truth to sea power–land power tension. Through most of recorded history, though, leading sea powers have sought land-power allies, just as leading land powers have sought allies with powerful navies.

Because of the global continuity of the oceans, as contrasted with the political and physical barriers to movement on land, the strategic view of the sailor tends to be far broader than that of the soldier. This point both indicates an enduring truth and suggests an important reason why national styles in the conduct of war differ so markedly. There is what may be called a rhythm to war, in Clausewitz's terms a "grammar"[31] of tactical and operational terms and objectives of conflict unique to each geographical environment. Combined arms are key to the successful conduct of war, but the variety of more or less available combinations can be wide indeed. For combined arms to be better than a superficial condition, soldiers, sailors, and airmen need to understand what each can contribute to a particular

30. F. E. Adcock, *The Greek and Macedonian Art of War* (Berkeley and Los Angeles: University of California Press, 1957), 46.
31. Carl von Clausewitz, *On War*, ed. and trans. Michael Howard and Peter Paret (Princeton, N.J.: Princeton University Press, 1976; first pub. 1832), 605.

case of conflict. For example, what can an air campaign, itself a range of possibilities, contribute to the course and outcome of a war?[32]

The operational object of war at sea is fundamentally different from the object of war on land. At sea the object is to control communications rather than to seize, occupy, and perhaps exploit particular territory. As always, there are exceptions. Bernard Lewis, writing of the Arabs in the seventh century, advises that "the strategy employed by the Arabs in the great campaigns of conquest was determined by the use of *desert power* on lines strikingly similar to the use of sea-power by modern Empires."[33]

Taken in the longest view, history does not demonstrate any consistent pattern of advantage to states or coalitions headed by a dominant sea power over states or coalitions headed by a dominant land power. The student of classical, medieval, and early modern statecraft and war would have to argue for the ultimate superiority of land power over sea power. The student of modern history, however, would have to argue the reverse. Both students would be seriously in error, because the history of international conflict is only superficially about sea power *versus* land power. Combat at sea, on land, in the air, or in space is important for statecraft as a contribution to the course and conclusion of war as a whole. The addition of air, space, and generically nuclear dimensions to what as late as 1914 really was only a land-sea context for war does not undermine the central argument advanced here. War is a whole, no matter how complex its structure, how varied its environments, or how rich the menu of military technologies for its conduct. Sea power may have become indivisible from air power, from space control, and from nuclear deterrence, but still it must function strategically to influence the course of war, which ultimately has meaning only for political values on land.

32. See John A Warden III, *The Air Campaign: Planning for Combat* (Washington, D.C.: Pergamon-Brassey's, 1989; first pub. 1988), for a pre–Gulf War (1991) perspective. Richard P. Hallion, *Storm over Iraq: Air Power in the Gulf War* (Washington, D.C.: Smithsonian Institution Press, 1992), offers a view that expertly advocates air power, whereas Lawrence Freedman and Efraim Karsh, *The Gulf Conflict, 1990–1991: Diplomacy and War in the New World Order* (Princeton, N.J.: Princeton University Press, 1993), chap. 23, provides balanced scholarly judgment (see the authors' overall conclusion on air power on 437).

33. Bernard Lewis, *The Arabs in History* (New York. Harper & Row, 1967, first pub. 1958), 55.

6

Influence and Its Uses

The key test of the quality of national military strategy is its adaptability in the face of setbacks; in strategy a principled flexibility is the stamp of excellence. Operational flexibility is not synonymous with strategic flexibility. In the 1980s, for example, the U.S. Army, and more generally the military reform movement, produced what then was called the doctrine of AirLand Battle, together with the associated desideratum of Overwhelming Force. The doctrine expressed a narrow focus on the continental menace of Soviet arms in Europe and tended to equate the defense of NATO-Europe with success or failure in war as a whole. There was no unified vision. The U.S. Navy provided much of that vision in its maritime strategy, but the fit was uncertain between that "strategy" and AirLand Battle (a doctrine rejected by the United States's NATO allies because of its operationally offensive requirements). What was noticeable through most of the 1980s was that although the Navy held to a unified global vision of war and its deterrence, the Army confined itself to a vision of land-air battle in one geographical theater only. At least in the 1950s the several core visions of future war among the armed services were unified into irrelevance by the nuclear strategy of the day.

For the United States the unity of strategic vision of the 1950s was atypical; however, it is normal for countries to design and blend (or force-fit) into a whole some unified conception of deterrence and war. Geostrategic asymmetry between adversaries is very usual, whereas the need to drive armies, navies, and air forces to wage tolerably compatible campaigns is also a familiar challenge. Each environmentally specific military instrument is wont to believe that its contribution to victory was the decisive one. Indeed, it is no great historical burden to reconstruct the course of events to demonstrate that victory would not have been possible without the (therefore) decisive part played by the favored forces. Unfortunately, the list of purportedly "decisive" factors or instruments can be as long as is the list of special pleaders.

The narrative histories that convey best the course of war at all levels, often do not—alas—have much to say beyond impressionistic judgments about the synergisms among land power, sea power, and air power. Too many historians are more concerned to tell the story in its rich complexity, rather than explain how the several elements in the story actually worked together. On the other hand, too many social scientists are too ignorant of history to be trusted with analytical tools, no matter how sharp in principle those tools may be. Suffice it to say that the central subject of this chapter, the respective, relative, and synergistic influence of sea power, land power, and air power, within a genuinely unified vision of conflict, is not well trafficked country.

One would not know this from reading the continentalist Carl von Clausewitz, but most of the great struggles of history have had an actual, or a significant potential, maritime dimension. (The Mongol conquests of the thirteenth century stand as an obvious exception.) The principal reason is not hard to uncover. Throughout history transportation by water has been easier and cheaper than transportation on land. It follows that societies have been attracted to water and to the access to other parts that water grants. Again, there are of course some important exceptions in the form of deeply continentalist cultures. But as a significant generalization, historically, most of the political, economic, social, religious, and strategic world has been accessible from the sea or by river. That is not to claim that most of the world has been maritime, and hence most likely commercial, in its culture.

Security communities differ widely in their cultures. But international security politics is a single game that has to be played according to common rules by maritime and commercially minded polities, as well as by continentalist and, say, agrarian states. The forms of state power and the balance preferred among the methods for influence will vary from time to time and from place to place, but it would be an error to emphasize uncritically the differences among communities. Great sea powers have functioned no less aggressively in their pursuit of power, profit, and glory than have great land powers. Some patriotic historical claims to the contrary notwithstanding, Britain no more acquired her global empire by accident than the United States filled the space from sea to shining sea as an exercise in manifest destiny free from brute strength, greed, and chicanery.

Fundamentally, the greatness of a country at sea or on land is an expression of its general strength. Geographical situation, particularly the absence of vulnerable continental frontiers and the location of the state, can augment sea power. But ultimately the sea power, land power, air power, and space power of a state is bounded by the relevant economic potential and political culture. Sea power, land power, or air power may be assessed for their relative strategic utilities, but there can be no escaping the fact that they must always be variables dependent on the conditions for their generation. For all his special pleading and unbalanced claims for sea power, Alfred Thayer Mahan was exactly correct when he emphasized the importance of the "General Conditions affecting Sea Power" in the first chapter of *The Influence of Sea Power upon History, 1660–1783*. Whether a great power is primarily maritime or continental in strategic orientation, its military strength must derive from its overall economic vitality and its international status must be won in competition with other actual, or would-be, great powers.

One dimension of its geography, that is to say *location*, has inclined the United States to be a sea power. However, other dimensions of its geography, physical size, and general economic productivity have enabled the United States to become the dominant sea power. Given its demonstrated ability to co-opt some land power, air power, and space power, the relative strategic utility of the U.S. Navy in this century has burgeoned in line with the general strength of the country that created it. Navies, and sea power much more broadly, have been able to merge with, while typically controlling, developments potentially challenging to their value. With the wisdom of hindsight, it is plainly apparent in these 1990s that the gloomy prognoses of the continental-focused geopoliticians a century ago who foresaw the end of the maritime Columbian Era were fundamentally unsound (as to probable, and actual, wartime outcomes, though not as to severity of strategic challenge). Sea power in all its aspects has seen successive waves of critics come and go.

A UNIFIED VISION

Public debate on great issues of national security policy tends to give short shrift to genuine complexity, fundamental indeterminacy, and nuance. This does not mean that truth necessarily is particularly difficult to find, but rather that it can be more complicated and beset with more qualifications than is convenient for political discourse. Some members of the military reform movement in the United States in the 1980s were fond of referring to "the discipline of strategy."[1] They emphasized sensibly the criticality of choice to strategy, but then proceeded from unarguable generalities to assert the specific strategy of their choice. That strategy, more often than not, was one that Venetian politicians in the fifteenth century, or British politicians recurringly from the 1580s to the 1940s, would have recognized as continental rather than maritime.

With a narrow focus on the more efficient conduct of war on land in Europe, some of the American military reformers of the 1980s were no less blinkered than were those British army officers who, from 1906 to 1914, with the acquiescence of the politicians, hitched the fate of a generation of British manhood to the wagon of French continental strategy. What is more, that turn toward Europe was not founded on a sophisticated analysis of how Britain could best deter war, let alone of how it could best apply its sea-based weight in war. Rather was it rooted in a recognition that the army's previous major mission, to defend India against Russia, was not practicable. The continentalist turn after 1906 flowed most powerfully from the need of the British army to find a task it believed it could perform. That task was defined not as it transpired in practice from 1916 to 1918, to conduct mass warfare in a protracted continental struggle, but instead to make a critical difference with relatively small forces in a land war between evenly balanced continental combatants. It so happened that from late August to mid

---

1. Edward N. Luttwak, *The Pentagon and the Art of War: The Question of Military Reform* (New York: Simon & Schuster, 1984), 60.

November 1914 the B.E.F. was in the right place, at the right time, with just enough force to make the kind of difference that had been intended.[2]

Be it Britain in its succession of wars with France and then with Germany, or the United States in the Cold War, the military strategy of an off-shore sea power is perennially liable to capture by the perspective of front-line allies. The value of superior sea power in war inevitably is at a discount in the minds of embattled continental allies, who do not understand how the control of sea lines of communication will help save their exposed national territories from landward invasion. This is a case where several perspectives are defensible. Britain's continental allies in the coalition wars waged against Revolutionary and Napoleonic France could no more be assisted directly and decisively by a Royal Navy thoroughly victorious at sea, than could France in 1914 or 1940.[3] However, it is no valid criticism of sea power as an instrument of war and diplomacy to chide it for failure to achieve the impossible. Great land powers cannot be defeated at sea. One looks in vain for historical examples of a great land power brought to ruin as a result solely of defeat in battle at sea, of the expulsion of land power's maritime commerce from the sea, of effective maritime blockade of continental naval assets, or of amphibious raiding. Robert Komer was substantially correct when he argued that "a peripheral maritime strategy gives up the chief prize of any U.S.-Soviet global contest—the resources of Eurasia."[4] In fact he was so obviously correct that traditional British, and later U.S., maritime strategy was designed and executed as an enabling complement to a continental balance-of-power policy, not as a blue-water unilateralist alternative.

The overselling of sea power is as detrimental to public education as is its undervaluation. In an authoritative description of the U.S. Maritime Strat-

2 On October 3, 1905, Colonel Charles E. Callwell (then of the Military Operations Directorate of the War Office) had written the following: "An efficient army of 120,000 British Troops, might just have the effect of preventing any important German successes on the Franco-German frontier, and of leading up to the situation that Germany crushed at sea, also felt herself impotent on land. That would almost certainly bring about a speedy, and from the British and French points of view, satisfactory peace." Quoted in Samuel R. Williamson Jr., *The Politics of Grand Strategy: Britain and France Prepare for War, 1904–1914* (Cambridge: Harvard University Press, 1969), 50. Also see John Gooch, *The Plans of War: The General Staff and British Military Strategy, c. 1900–1916* (London: Routledge & Kegan Paul, 1974), and David French, *The British Way in Warfare, 1688–2000* (London: Unwin Hyman, 1990), 166.

3. In this book I risk overemphasizing the strategic role of sea power, in contrast to its theater-operational and tactical roles. I accept that risk in the interests of clarity and focus. However, sea power frequently has been exercised for a direct military effect ashore. The argument that sea power is a strategic instrument is not an exclusive claim.

4. Robert W. Komer, *Maritime Strategy or Coalition Defense?* (Cambridge, Mass.: Abt Books, 1984), 67.

egy of the 1980s, then-chief of naval operations Admiral James D. Watkins asserted that "the Maritime Strategy is firmly set in the context of national strategy, emphasizing coalition warfare and the criticality of allies, and demanding cooperation with our sister services."[5] This statement can be supplemented by appreciation of the enduring geostrategic truth enunciated by Major General Sir Frederick Maurice in his 1929 study *British Strategy*.

> If, as the Field Service Regulations say, the prime object of the Army in war is, "in cooperation with the Navy and the Air Force to break down the resistance of the enemy's armed force in furtherance of the approved plan of campaign," *it follows that the Army can be most effectively employed and our military power as a whole be most effectively exercised when our Army is within comparatively easy reach of the coast.* Therefore in choosing the object of a war, when we have any liberty of choice, that particular feature of our power must be ever in our minds, and we should be very chary of going far inland unless circumstances leave us no option in the matter.[6]

Competent scholarship in strategy, like competent statecraft and strategy-in-action, must always keep in mind the essential unity of warfare. As Richard Pares wrote of William Pitt's conduct of the Seven Years' War:

> Pitt had a still stronger justification for revising his opinion on the continental war; he was not merely converted from America to Europe, but combined them. Having conducted the war during four years [Pares is writing of the state of play in 1760], he had come to understand the connection between all its parts. He saw that a diversion in Germany kept busy French troops and money that would otherwise be employed in Flanders, Portugal, America, or an [sic] invasion. He understood the necessity of a financial strain which he believed we could bear and France could not. *He insisted on the totality of the war.*[7]

---

5. James D. Watkins et al., *The Maritime Strategy*, U.S. Naval Institute *Proceedings*, Supplement (Annapolis, Md.: U.S. Naval Institute, January 1986), 4.

6. Frederick Maurice, *British Strategy: A Study of the Application of the Principles of War* (London: Constable, 1929), 85–86. Emphasis added.

7. Richard Pares, "American versus Continental Warfare, 1739–63," in *The Historian's Business and Other Essays* (Oxford. Clarendon Press, 1961), 167–68. Emphasis added

Pitt's comprehensive vision was the generic forebear of the global architecture of strategy designed, agreed, and executed by the Anglo-American combined chiefs of staff in World War II. Furthermore, those visions appeared in the U.S. Navy's Maritime Strategy in the 1980s, which called for, in the words of former secretary of the navy John Lehman, U.S. sea power to be "at once *global, forward deployed,* and *superior* to our probable opponents."[8] In its conduct of global war against France from 1756 to 1763, and again from 1793 to 1815, Britain did not have or seek to apply a rigidly detailed recipe for the concoction of applied strategy out of precisely measured, complementary continentalist and maritime elements. Steadiness of vision in grand strategy and in national military strategy, resting on a clear appreciation of the structure of the war, must accommodate the necessities of unpredictable events.

For example, periodically there has been a need to adjust to the situation created by the inconvenient defeat or defection of continental allies, or the failure of national expeditionary forces.[9] If we bear in mind the hazards of war, then we see that a vital practical test of the quality of a strategy is the degree to which it can continue to provide useful higher direction in the face of errors, or perhaps of superior enemy performance, at the operational and tactical levels of conflict. If the material balance is favorable, as it generally was for Britain over the centuries with its shifting continental alliances, superiority in strategy can offset many deficiencies in operational art and in tactics.[10] Williamson Murray wrote to the point when he said that

> The tragedy for Germany was that such slipshod thinking [Erich von Manstein's trust in Hitler's statecraft, and his belief that "strategy," narrowly understood, could be dominated by the army high command], passing all too often for strategy, helped launch the Second and Third Reichs on two great world wars that Germany had little prospect of winning. Ironically, the tactical and operational skills of the German Officer Corps then ensured that both wars would

8. John Lehman, "The 600-Ship Navy," in Watkins et al., *Maritime Strategy,* 36. For an excellent commentary, see Robert W. Love Jr., *History of the U.S Navy, 1942–1991,* vol. 2 (Harrisburg, Pa.. Stackpole Books, 1992), chap. 36. Emphasis in original.

9. Obvious examples of expeditions that failed include the British invasion of Holland in 1799, the invasion of Spain in September 1808, the "Great Expedition" to Walcheren Island (the Scheldt estuary, Flushing, and Antwerp) in 1809, Gallipoli in 1915, and the expulsion of the British forces from Norway and France in 1940 and from the Greek mainland and from Crete in 1941.

10. Note the interesting judgment in Michael I. Handel, "Clausewitz in the Age of Technology," *The Journal of Strategic Studies* 9 (June/September 1986): 87 n. 5

last almost to the point of destroying not only. Germany but also western civilization.[11]

Time and again, the global orientation and logistic flexibility of the leading sea powers have proved superior in the test of war to the operational temptations of swift conquest to which continental powers have succumbed.

DECISIVE EFFECT?

The major wars of the Western world in modern times typically have been conflicts characterized by large geostrategic asymmetries between the leaders of rival coalitions.[12] Furthermore, even in the rare cases when war at sea has been of equal strategic salience to both sides, the more maritime-oriented state inevitably has had a great deal more to lose at sea than has the continental foe. A case in point would be the Anglo-French (and Spanish) War of 1778–83. The unusual superficial symmetry of this war, the substantially maritime character of the struggle, was the product of Britain's involvement in a continental war an ocean away from its home base of strength, whereas France had assembled a united continental European front behind its war of revenge (for the defeat of 1756–63).[13]

11. Williamson Murray, "Clausewitz: Some Thoughts on What the Germans Got Right," *The Journal of Strategic Studies* 1 (June/September 1986): 284.

12. The most prominent exception is the Franco-Prussian War of 1870–71. The brevity of this conflict rendered a maritime dimension strictly moot. See Charles E. Callwell, *The Effect of Maritime Command on Land Campaigns Since Waterloo* (Edinburgh. William Blackwood & Sons, 1897), 218–23. Had France been able to avoid the most damaging of the defeats of its regular field armies (at Sedan and Metz) and forced a stalemate in the land war, then the maritime dimension could have been significant. In particular, both combatants would have cast about for allies and the result *might* have been a general European war. There would have been a "natural" geostrategic coalition match between Prussia and Britain on the one hand and France and Austria (and Denmark) on the other: in short a replay of the line-up in the Seven Years' War. The best study of the war remains Michael Howard, *The Franco-Prussian War* (London: Methuen, 1981). Howard observes that from the Prussian point of view, "rapid victory was vital to prevent the neutral powers of Europe enforcing a humiliating arbitration (389). Interestingly, he noted that although British public opinion veered toward France late in the conflict, probably as a result of the suffering of the people of Paris during the siege (454)—and possibly as France came to be radically redefined as the "underdog"—the British were willing "to acquiesce in a German hegemony of Europe which bore no resemblance to the pattern which they were traditionally supposed to cherish, of a European Balance of Power [at least for so long as Otto von Bismarck was at the helm of German policy]." Bismarck's European security order worked to the British advantage; the order apparently later intended by Kaiser Wilhelm II would not have been so benign.

13 France was seeking revenge for its wholesale defeat, in all theaters, in the Seven Years' War.

When viewed in their totality, wars between maritime and continental states or coalitions cannot usefully be dissected to determine the relative importance of sea power or of land power to their outcomes. One might as well endeavor to weight the respective importance of a boxer's left and right hands. An annihilating, or technically "decisive," blow by the right may be effected upon a body already weakened fatally in its powers of resistance and recovery by the left. A military literature that solemnly discusses the less-than-riveting issue of whether sea power, land power, air power, or economic warfare was or was not truly decisive in a particular war simply trivializes its subject matter. Any number of factors can be argued to have been decisive, in the sense that victory would not have been gained in their absence. In World War II the German army had to be beaten in the field because the political structure of the conflict precluded a compromise peace. Unconditional surrender was mandated as the overriding war aim by the burden of recent history (that is, the apparent lessons of 1914–18), the nature of the Nazi regime, its record of misbehavior, its grip on the loyalty of the German people, and the politics of coalition maintenance in London, Washington, and Moscow.[14] But unaided strategically by the Anglo-American siege of Hitler's *Festung Europa*, Soviet land power almost certainly could not have beaten the Germans. In its turn, that Anglo-American siege necessarily was a maritime siege, though it was a siege, and then a forcible irruption on land, utterly dependent for its feasibility on command of the air. Which arm then truly was decisive or most decisive? The question is absurd.

Until the development of long-range air and missile forces, the power of decision in war by land or by sea assets was attenuated or thwarted by the geostrategic mix of maritime and continental elements in rival coalitions. After the defeat of Austria at Marengo (June 14) and Hohenlinden (December 3), in 1800, and again after the defeat of Russia at Friedland on June 14, 1807, France decisively, indeed repeatedly,[15] won the war on land (for a

14. See Maurice Matloff, *United States Army in World War II, The War Department, Strategic Planning for Coalition Warfare, 1943–1944* (Washington, D.C.: U.S. Government Printing Office, 1959), particularly 37–42; Kent Roberts Greenfield, *American Strategy in World War II: A Reconsideration* (Baltimore: Johns Hopkins University Press, 1963), 4–5, 16, 23; Raymond G. O'Connor, *Diplomacy for Victory: FDR and Unconditional Surrender* (New York: W. W. Norton, 1971); and A. E. Campbell, "Franklin Roosevelt and Unconditional Surrender," in *Diplomacy and Intelligence during the Second World War: Essays in Honour of F. H. Hinsley*, ed. Richard Langhorne (Cambridge: Cambridge University Press, 1985), 219–41.

15 That France's enemies kept rising from the ashes, needing to be beaten again, reduces the authority of the adjective "decisive" attached to any of the battles prior to Waterloo.

while). Hitler was in a similarly favorable condition by mid-June 1940. The British case is too familiar to warrant recital, save to note that in war after war Britain won whatever there was to win at sea or easily reached from the sea. Enemy fleets and neutral fleets leaning toward the enemy either were sunk or effectively contained by blockade, and enemy commerce was sunk, captured, and driven from the high seas.

To achieve success in war, that is to say, to attain a tolerable political outcome, which may or may not encompass the military or political overthrow of the enemy, the center of gravity of the foe has to be assailed convincingly. In Clausewitz's words, "War is thus an act of force to compel an enemy to do our will."[16] War is not about the defeat of an enemy's military power. Such an achievement is simply a means to the political ends of conflict. Neither sea power nor land power can sensibly be considered separately as an instrument of decision in war, even with reference to a maritime-organized continental challenge to land power or a continentally based maritime challenge to sea power. Virtually by definition it is true that a great continental power can be overthrown only on land and a great maritime power can be overthrown only at sea. But the land power that did write *finis* to the French and German empires, or the sea power that might have terminated the thalassocracy of Venice or Britain, was, or would have been, power exerted in one environment that derived its strength primarily from the other.

Venice declined in its relative standing in the sixteenth century not because sea power generally was in decline—the reverse was true—but rather because a small city state with an insecure landward frontier could not compete with the sea power of an ascendant Spain and with Ottoman Turkey. Furthermore, the age of transoceanic discovery shifted trade patterns away from the Mediterranean. Similarly, Britain's decline as a great power in the twentieth century has been a measure not of any general decline in the diplomatic or wartime military value of sea power, but rather of Britain's relative material standing vis-à-vis other security communities.

Many of the generalizations about the importance of sea power favored by strategic thinkers and even by historians transpire on examination to be dangerously misleading half-truths, or true, but only from one strategic

---

16. Carl von Clausewitz, *On War*, ed. and trans. Michael Howard and Peter Paret (Princeton, N.J.: Princeton University Press, 1976; first pub. 1832), 75. Also of value is J. C. Wylie, *Military Strategy: A General Theory of Power Control* (Annapolis, Md.: Naval Institute Press, 1989; first pub. 1967). Wylie writes that *"the aim of war is some measure of control over the enemy"* (66). Emphasis in original.

perspective. Above all else, it is essential to specify whether a particular claim about the significance of sea power, for example its effect on the duration of a war, pertains to maritime effort by or against a continental state or coalition.

Georges Clemenceau once noted that "Napoleon was beaten at Waterloo, not Trafalgar." His accurate observation can be usefully juxtaposed to the following no less accurate observation by two of his countrymen, Paul Auphan and Jacques Mordal: "After Trafalgar the Napoleonic hegemony eventually crumbled—not because of the failure of Marshal Emmanuel de Grouchy to arrive on the field of Waterloo, as claimed by some, but because seapower little by little strangled 'Fortress Europe,' as Hitler's similar creation was to be called some hundred years later."[17]

Parallel judgment on the course and outcome of the First World War has been provided by C.R.M.F. Cruttwell, the most balanced of the historians of that conflict and certainly no uncritical spokesman for sea power. Cruttwell argues that "although the war was won as the direct consequence of an unexampled series of land battles, it is profoundly true that this result was attained only through the conduct of the war at sea."[18] Referring to the great German offensive of March 1918, he judged that "in the last resort it was the British fleet which drove Ludendorff to assemble his masses of offence in Artois and Picardy."[19] It is appropriate that Auphan and Mordal talk of the Napoleonic hegemony "eventually" crumbling, whereas Cruttwell qualifies his analysis with the phrase "in the last resort." It should be recalled that Callwell averred that "the effect of sea-power upon land campaigns is in the main strategical."[20] Callwell's plain meaning and the truth in his assertion notwithstanding, the influence of success by a continental power on land or on the sea and of similar success by a maritime power, requires careful treatment.

The influence of land power on sea campaigns is at least in part strategic. The course and outcome of combat on land determines both the geostrategic terms of reference of conflict at sea and the balance of resources that a continental power is at liberty to devote to maritime campaigns (whether available resources can be translated into naval strength is, of course,

17. Paul Auphan and Jacques Mordal, *The French Navy in World War II* (Annapolis, Md.: U.S. Naval Institute, 1959), 5.

18. C.R.M.F. Cruttwell, *The Role of British Strategy in the Great War* (Cambridge: Cambridge University Press, 1936), 94.

19. Ibid., 75.

20. Callwell, *Effect of Maritime Command on Land Campaigns Since Waterloo*, 29.

another question). A sea power lives by its maritime communications, but obviously not literally at sea. Defeat at sea, or even a condition of severely contested command, will have a much shorter audit trail to national defeat for a sea power than is the case for a land power beaten afloat. But the effect may still be strategic rather than operational or tactical. Actual military defeat, that is to say the loss of command through naval disaster, will lead a sea power to anticipate conquest by invasion or perhaps a maritime blockade that would cause an intolerable depression of economic activity.

It was Napoleon's mercantilist belief that by excluding British goods his Continental System would destroy the financial basis of the British war economy. Napoleon aspired to destroy that favorable balance of trade which mercantilist philosophy identified as the basis of economic health. In the words of Robert B. Holtman: "The mercantilist side of his thinking led Napoleon so far astray that he sacrificed the opportunity to starve England out in 1810, after two consecutively bad harvests. Napoleon sold wheat to England at this time because his attention was focused on draining precious metals from his adversary, so it would no longer be able to subsidize Continental coalitions."[21]

It was a recurring hope of continental naval powers that the vigorous conduct of *guerre de course*, as well as of selective import trade boycotts (which was the true character of the Continental System), would function strategically against the political center of gravity of a sea power's willingness to continue a conflict. Historically, sea powers, have tended to be commercial civilizations whose attitudes toward war have been much influenced by calculations of economic risk and of the likely balance of financial gain and loss. At least, this is what their land-oriented enemies have been wont to believe. Certainly one can find historical cases wherein commercial considerations dominated state policy, even in military circumstances where war was conducted generally successfully with reference to classical notions of maritime command. The less arguable cases, however, have tended to be ones wherein the contest was waged between two sea powers. For example, in the Venetian-Genoese wars of the thirteenth and fourteenth centuries, the Venetians discovered that naval victories could not reliably ensure the protection of vital seaborne trade.[22] Or, for the clearest case in modern

---

21. Robert B. Holtman, *The Napoleonic Revolution* (Philadelphia: J. B. Lippincott, 1967), 62.

22. See Frederic C. Lane, *Venice: A Maritime Republic* (Baltimore: Johns Hopkins University Press, 1973), 77, 84. William H. McNeill, *Venice: The Hinge of Europe, 1081–1797* (Chicago: University of Chicago Press, 1974), is also superb.

times, the Dutch Republic discovered in the 1660s that the conduct even of successful naval war with Britain could be a commercial disaster.

As a general rule, land powers have been unduly dismissive of the extent to which sea powers can offset their commercial losses by the short- and long-term gains secured in the particular conditions of war. Although war almost always disrupts traditional trading patterns, dominant sea power enjoys access to most of the world, even in wartime, and typically has adapted well enough to a new strategic context. Furthermore, land powers have exaggerated the commercial element in the policymaking processes of sea powers and have underestimated the financial strength and ingenuity of sea-based security communities. In addition, land powers have exaggerated their ability to disrupt and damage the commercial life of maritime enemies. Last but by no means least, land powers frequently have delayed determined resort to economic warfare in its many forms until too late in a conflict. The reason for this final error has lain in the hopes for, and expectations of, swift continental victory. Time after time, continental statesmen, true to their land-animal species, have failed to recognize in advance of events that success in land warfare need not equate to victory in war as a whole.

Preponderant continental power can function strategically for the intended ultimate humbling of offshore sea power. Because land power, in principle—out of specific context, that is—can achieve decision on and against the continentally accessible national territory of its enemies in a way that sea power cannot, it does not follow that it is somehow necessarily less strategic in character than is sea power. When confronted with the barrier of an uncommanded sea, land power ceases to be an instrument of prompt military decision. One could argue that modern history has shown the inability of preponderant continental powers to fashion potent enough instruments for the defeat of offshore sea powers. Alternatively, and more convincingly in my view, one could suggest that to date no land power has been sufficiently preponderant on land to have the surplus *and fungible* resources adequate for the conduct of successful war against great-power enemies offshore.

The issue is the role of sea power in the total context of war. It is no part of my purpose to seek out those rare instances when sea power played a decisive wartime role independent of national land power. Neither is it intended that this analysis should render necessarily tendentious judgments concerning either a leading or a subordinate role for sea power. By way of a relevant analogy, it is surely sufficient to know that Samuel Pepys, as secretary of the admiralty in Restoration England, "made the scabbard for the sword that Nelson, and the heirs of Nelson, used."[23] Also, "Pepys by his life-work had taught his country how to equip, regulate and maintain a fleet."[24] It is not sensible to inquire into the relative significance of Pepys's lasting achievements in naval administration, as contrasted with the achievements in strategy and tactics of the admirals and captains who actually wielded the naval sword. The complementary character of sea power and land power, and of naval administration and naval operations, should preclude any ignorant endorsement of a general preponderance in wartime significance of one or the other.

THE QUEST FOR WEALTH AND POWER

Few major conflicts in history have lacked an active maritime dimension. The basic reason has been the enduring advantage in efficiency and practicality of transport by water rather than by land. That practicality pertains to cost per ton-mile, security of cargo (notwithstanding piracy and weather), absence of political impediments, and to the physical uniformity of the seas. In Western perspective, strategic history has moved from the closed sea of the Mediterranean in classical and medieval times, to the Atlantic rimland of Europe as the scientific and technological advances of the Renaissance fueled the age of blue-water discovery and as new trade patterns traced outward from Europe. Strategic history then moved to a global stage with the rise of a continental-scale but maritime connected power in the United States, and in the post–Cold War 1990s to a renewed focus on shallow-water operations around the littoral of Eurasia (witness the need to operate in the Persian Gulf, in the Adriatic, and off the Horn of Africa).[25]

It is no accident that states oriented by geographical opportunity toward the sea have tended to be democratic in metropolitan political form and commercial in their approach to wealth. It is not true, however, to claim that sea powers have tended to be less bellicose than land powers. Rivalry

---

23. Arthur Bryant, *Samuel Pepys: The Man in the Making* (London: Panther, 1984; first pub. 1933), xiii.

24. Arthur Bryant, *Samuel Pepys: The Saviour of the Navy* (London: Panther, 1985; first pub 1938), 225

25. See the latest white paper by the Navy Department and the Marine Corps, *From the Sea· Preparing the Naval Service for the 21st Century* (Washington, D.C.: Department of the Navy, September 1992).

between maritime Corinth and maritime Athens provided a spark that helped ignite the Peloponnesian War; trade rivalry between Carthage and Rome's newly acquired Greek client cities in the south of Italy helped critically to fuel the First Punic War; and England self-avowedly and unashamedly chose to wage three aggressive trade wars against the Dutch Republic (1652–54, 1665–67, and 1672–78). This is not to draw any moral distinction between the English and the Dutch. By the middle of the seventeenth century the Dutch had secured the lion's share of the overseas carrying trade of northern and central Europe, having displaced Genoa and Venice when Europe's principal trade routes ceased to track through the Mediterranean.[26] English investors and sailors had every economic incentive to take the offensive against Dutch trade. Oliver Cromwell's Navigation Act of 1651 heralded England's arrival both as an aspiring great naval power and as a major competitor in the first league of mercantilist powers.[27]

England in the seventeenth century, like Germany in the late nineteenth and early twentieth (or republican Rome in the third century B.C.), was relatively late on the scene for economic, and political and military, self-aggrandizement. Halford Mackinder could write of the open world of the Columbian Era,[28] but in fact by the mid-seventeenth century English financiers, merchants, and sailors found the Portuguese, the Spaniards, and the Dutch already in place and in eminently challengeable maritime control of the overseas trade of Europe. By way of analogy, in the third century B.C. Roman profit from maritime trade could grow only at the expense of long-time commercially preeminent Carthage.[29] General Monk's reported explanation of the English motive for war with the Dutch in 1665 had the ring of truth about it: "What matters this or that reason? What we want is more of the trade which the Dutch now have."[30]

For the better part of two centuries the waging of successful maritime war

26. The classic treatment is C. R. Boxer, *The Dutch Seaborne Empire, 1600–1800* (London: Penguin, 1973; first pub 1965).

27. See Christopher Hill, *God's Englishman: Oliver Cromwell and the English Revolution* (London: Weidenfeld & Nicolson, 1970), 130–32, 155–58, and Bernard Capp, *Cromwell's Navy: The Fleet and the English Revolution, 1648–1660* (Oxford: Clarendon Press, 1989).

28. Halford J. Mackinder, *Democratic Ideals and Reality* (New York: W. W. Norton, 1962; first pub. 1942).

29. Valuable discussions include Chester G. Starr, *The Beginnings of Imperial Rome: Rome in the Mid-Republic* (Ann Arbor: University of Michigan Press, 1980), chap. 5, and William V. Harris, *War and Imperialism in Republican Rome, 327–70 B.C.* (Oxford: Clarendon Press, 1985; first pub. 1979), chap. 2.

30 Quoted in Alfred Thayer Mahan, *The Influence of Sea Power upon History, 1660–1783* (London: Methuen, 1965; first pub. 1890), 107.

was both necessary for Britain's national security and, on balance, highly profitable.[31] Such war functioned synergistically with the creation and augmentation of British trade monopolies. Profits from the latter helped finance the former, as well as subsidized continental allies who could keep the field and thereby distract France from the struggle at sea and in the colonies. Mercantilist and early-industrial Britain, like imperial Athens, republican Rome, and Alexander's Macedonia, discovered that when sensibly directed, war could approximate a self-financing enterprise.

Much has been made of the strategic necessity for Alexander the great to break Persian naval power before he plunged deep inland toward the enemy's continental heartland.[32] Persian naval power, based on the Levantine and Egyptian coasts, could both sever Alexander's lines of communication from Anatolia to Macedonia and create a major diversion far in his rear in a Greece that was none too securely under Macedonian control. All of that was true. But, of more immediate importance was the embarrassing fact that Alexander's imperial ambitions were threatened by imminent bankruptcy. He had prompt need of the profits that accrued to Persia's Phoenician allies from their maritime commerce.

Free trade and freedom of the seas are policy precepts that work to the advantage of a commercially dominant maritime power. British writers on maritime subjects late in the nineteenth century were wont to forget that the *Pax Britannica*, whatever its general benefits, was an overstated concept of an international order structured in its commercial underpinnings very much to Britain's advantage.[33] Germany's bids for continental empire during the First and Second World Wars were particularly bloody undertakings because the land at issue was already heavily populated by well-organized communities armed by modern industry and defended by patriotic citizens. In the case of the Russo-German War of 1941–45 the casualty lists were unusually high (particularly among civilians and prisoners of war), even by

31. See Richard Pares, *War and Trade in the West Indies, 1739–1763* (London: Frank Cass, 1963); Daniel A. Baugh, *British Naval Administration in the Age of Walpole* (Princeton, N.J.: Princeton University Press, 1965), chap. 1; and John Brewer, *The Sinews of Power· War, Money, and the English State, 1688–1783* (New York: Alfred A. Knopf, 1989).

32. For example, Arthur Ferrill, *The Origins of War: From the Stone Age to Alexander the Great* (New York: Thames & Hudson, 1985), 189–94, 204–7. Also see William Ledyard Rodgers, *Greek and Roman Naval Warfare: A Study of Strategy, Tactics, and Ship Design from Salamis (480 B.C.) to Actium (31 B.C.)* (Annapolis, Md.: Naval Institute Press, 1983; first pub. 1937), 218–26; C. E. Adcock, *The Greek and Macedonian Art of War* (Berkeley and Los Angeles: University of California Press, 1957), 46; and Chester G. Starr, *The Influence of Sea Power on Ancient History* (New York: Oxford University Press, 1989), 48–49.

33. See C. J. Bartlett, *Great Britain and Sea Power, 1815–1853* (Oxford: Clarendon Press, 1963).

the abominable standards of twentieth-century warfare, because of the ideological and racial character of the conflict.[34]

The societies of the North Atlantic rimlands, and the United States in particular, are the defenders of political values of great intrinsic significance. There have always tended to be important differences between the political values and habits of great maritime and great continental powers. Nonetheless, any British and American commentators tempted to moralize about the abortive German march of territorial conquest or the late and unlamented Soviet territorial empire should recognize that Britain's commercial supremacy in the nineteenth century and the growth of the United States to a continental superstate were gifts of God only in a strategic sense. Insularity and breakwater location across the sea routes to northern and central Europe enabled Britain eventually to replace the Dutch as the common maritime carrier.[35] Further, insularity enabled Britain to develop tolerably peacefully internally to the point where an overwhelming, if brief, leadership in industrialization created an all but universal demand for British manufactured goods. These historical trends were guarded and propelled more than marginally by the repeated and ruthless conduct of wars for Britain's net economic advantage.

The expansion of the United States from thirteen former colonies hugging the Atlantic seaboard to a continental giant may be expressed in American school textbooks as a plain case of manifest destiny, of God's will being done, or—in the jargon of some social scientists—of nation building and national development (at least prior to the politically correct views of the 1990s). The truth is that the United States became a territorial giant through the ruthless application of power, not to mention the good fortune that enabled the country, on credit, to double its size in 1803 with the purchase of the vast Louisiana Territory from a France unable to defend it against Britain. The urge for power and profit (and glory) has been common to great

34. This point is well developed and justified in Omer Bartov, *The Eastern Front, 1941–45: German Troops and the Barbarisation of Warfare* (New York: St. Martin's Press, 1986). Bartov reports that "the highest estimate of German POWs in Russian hands is 3,155,000, of whom between 1,110,000 and 1,185,000 (35.2–37 percent) died in captivity. Of about 5,700,000 Russian POWs in German hands . . . some 3,300,000 (57.8 percent) died in captivity" (153). Omer Bartov, *Hitler's Army: Soldiers, Nazis, and War in the Third Reich* (New York: Oxford University Press, 1991), also is relevant.

35. See Mahan: *Influence of Sea Power upon History, 1600–1783*, 29–32, and for an extended discussion, his essay "Considerations Governing the Disposition of Navies," in *Retrospect and Prospect: Studies in International Relations, Naval and Political* (London: Sampson Low, Marston, 1902), 139–205.

sea powers and great land powers. Geostrategic circumstances, political culture, and even ethical standards have varied, but the basic structure of international security has been common to land powers and to sea powers, as it has been to the nuclear and pre-nuclear eras.

Sea power, although not always a preponderance of naval power, naturally has been characteristic of the endeavor of small insular states, which have found great profit in maritime commerce. But sea power does not have to be based on small insular or coastal-enclave homelands. The Western Alliance of the Cold War, for example, was maritime both in geostrategic character and in the geographical dimension most crucial to trading relations, which helped bind it together economically. The sea power of the West, however, has been, indeed is, an expression of the economic and military strength of two continental-sized sub-blocs in North America and Western Europe, with distant but economically important allies in East Asia and Oceania.

The threat to U.S. security posed by a state or coalition preeminent throughout Eurasia would not be a threat posed in some generic sense by land power to sea power. Instead, it would be a threat posed by a land power to compete in ways that would enable it to engage U.S. strength, in all dimensions, both closer and closer to home and by methods ever more threatening to the survival interests of the United States. This reasoning lay behind the clear presidential statement that "for most of this century, the United States has deemed it a vital interest to prevent any hostile power or group of powers from dominating the Eurasian land mass. This interest remains."[36]

The Western Alliance of the Cold War era was not economically superior to the Soviet Union because it was a maritime alliance and in an aggregate sense was a great sea power. Rather, the West was the preponderant sea power because its economic assets of all kinds were so high in quality and large in quantity, because of its global geography, and because transportation economics pertaining to the efficient movement of bulky cargoes over vast distances mandated dependence on sea lines of communication. Maritime commerce can expand national and international wealth, as Alfred Thayer Mahan explained,[37] but as with the naval strength that protects that commerce, sea power is more a dependent than an independent variable in its relation to national prosperity and security.

36. George Bush, *National Security Strategy of the United States* (Washington, D.C.: U.S. Government Printing Office, March 1990), 1.
37. Mahan, *Influence of Sea Power upon History, 1660–1783*, 25–28.

As a general rule a sea power cannot develop and apply land power unless first it is secure at sea. Similarly, a continental power cannot go to sea with sufficient strength to challenge a sea power in its own most critical element with a high prospect of achieving success unless first it has secured its position on land. History shows the full range of relationships of net advantage as between sea powers and land powers—not *Sea Power* and *Land Power*. It could be difficult for regionally minded, land-focused policymakers both to build a navy formidable as a fighting instrument and to understand how to use that navy in a potentially global domain for grand strategy. Nonetheless, maritime expertise is not exclusively the possession of the dominant sea power; and if a country is strong in its resources base and its geostrategic condition, it can afford to make mistakes and learn from them (as Rome did in the First Punic War and Germany in 1916–17).

When contrasting land power and sea power, one often tends to forget that a sea power is also a land power and an air (and perhaps space) power as well. Some of the technological trends of the nineteenth and twentieth centuries advertised as heralding the demise of much of the strategic advantage enjoyed by sea power have, in fact, had no such result. The framework for strategic comprehension has been fundamentally flawed. Of course distances have been shrunk by the changes in transportation technology of the past century and a half. In amphibious operations, for example, the murderous conditions in the shallows and ground between the line of departure for beach assault craft and the first cover above the high-tide line (recall Tarawa),[38] have been much alleviated by the development of helicopters for tactical assault (vertical envelopment of beach defenses) and of hovercraft for rapid approach on the surface. Also, developments since World War II in the range of aircraft and, above all else, the coming of orbiting space platforms for reconnaissance and surveillance of wide ocean areas, have eased the problem of locating ships over the horizon.

Grave operational problems remain, however. Intelligence cycle time, the survivability in wartime of orbiting surveillance platforms, the endurance of reconnaissance aircraft, deceptive measures, the sheer quantity of maritime traffic, and the weather are but a few of the practical difficulties. Indeed, the evolving terms of engagement between sea- and land-based

---

38. See Jeter A. Isely and Philip A. Crowl, *The U.S. Marines and Amphibious Warfare: Its Theory and Its Practice in the Pacific* (Princeton, N.J.: Princeton University Press, 1951), chap. 6, and Patrick L. McKiernan, "Tarawa: The Tide that Failed," in *Assault from the Sea: Essays on the History of Amphibious Warfare*, ed. Merrill L. Bartlett (Annapolis, Md.: Naval Institute Press, 1983), 210–18.

forces have not shifted in favor of the latter since 1945. Furthermore, the structure of relative strategic advantage and disadvantage between a maritime alliance and a continental coalition has not evolved to the net benefit of the latter. New technology generally is an advantage, though it can be a curse as well as a blessing. The excellence of German radio in World War I, for example, prompted overuse, which proved unfortunate given British skills in cryptography and, later, in direction finding. The situation was even worse in World War II, when "wolfpack" U-boat tactics were controlled by Enigma-encoded radio messages, which, for long periods, were read in near real-time by the Allies. Moving to the present, surveillance from space can indeed be global in scope, but typically it is far short of continuous. Many of the emissions that lend themselves to being monitored from space can be suppressed by ships as a temporary matter of operational security. New technology invariably attracts countermeasures, which can take technical, tactical, operational, or even strategic and political forms.

It is ironic that Herbert Rosinski, a brilliant naval theorist, could refer in the middle of the Second World War to what he termed "the general crisis of Sea Power,"[39] at the very time when sea power achieved a success in the Pacific without obvious parallels in recorded history. In Europe, Anglo-American sea power was critically important to the logistic sustenance of Soviet land power, and—enabled by, and in tandem with, Allied air power—was the sine qua non for the forcible entry of (Western) Allied land power into Hitler's continental fortress. The years since the Second World War have seen neither a "general crisis of Sea Power," nor even the emergence of prospective conditions of war that might translate plausibly into a crisis of *surface* sea power.[40] The terms of strategic and tactical engagement between sea- and land-based forces have evolved more as a function of the general strengths and weaknesses of rival states—the geography of conflict, the technological base, economies as a whole—than of factors pertaining directly to sea power or land power per se. By way of illustration, the very ability of the U.S. Navy to operate six large aircraft carriers in the restricted and shallow waters of the Persian Gulf and the Red Sea during the 1991 war with Iraq attests only to the nearly absolute superiority of Allied sea-air command in that region vis-à-vis a top-of-the-line Third World country.

39. Herbert Rosinski, *The Development of Naval Thought* (Newport, R.I.: Naval War College Press, 1977), 43. The essay from which this quotation is drawn was first published in 1944.

40. An erroneous view propagated in John Keegan, *The Price of Admiralty: The Evolution of Naval Warfare* (New York: Viking, 1988), 266–75.

Although the total story is vastly complex, dynamic, and situation-specific, many of the developments in weapons and weapons-related technology since 1945 have strengthened the wartime ability of the country superior at sea to retain or enhance its maritime command. This is the case even with those technologies which shrink distances and in principle make it difficult for surface ships to hide over the horizon or in bad weather. Excellence in technology is a necessary, but not sufficient, condition for excellence in naval power; the human element is even more important. The military tools available for a Eurasian continental power to deny the United States a strategically meaningful maritime command, have been more than countered by U.S. exploitation of similar or offsetting technologies.

STRATEGIC MEANING

Wealth and power are positively connected. It is in the very natures of sea power and land power to express and pursue influence in distinctive manners. As I seek to illustrate, the key to national or coalition performance is the relative value of proficient sea power or land power for each other, together with the ever more potent contribution, and complication, of air power (and space power). In this chapter I have advanced the case for a unified view of sea power and land power; that is to say, for a view that declines to identify an allegedly decisive factor. The appropriate *leitmotiv* is combined arms for success overall in strategy and statecraft. This is not to assert a bland denial of leading-edge value to a particular form of military, or other, power in a particular conflict. Nor is this to neglect the ever arguable pace of change in strategic history. The information-age "hyper war" waged by the U.S.-led coalition forces, and particularly air forces, in the brief Gulf War of 1991, begs for intellectual appreciation, just as it may mislead with the attractiveness of an unduly magnetic single example.[41]

In these pages there is neither pusillanimous moral relativism nor any instant historical revisionism concerning the rights and wrongs of the contending statecrafts that organized the Cold War struggle. Nonetheless,

---

41. "Hyper-war" refers to a style in the conduct of military operations which accelerates interrelated events and compresses time in ways designed to produce the paralysis of the enemy. This ambitious concept has been advanced to describe the coalition's air war in the Gulf in 1991. It is all but a maxim that strategic theory and military doctrine should not be constructed on the evidential base provided by just one recent conflict.

the case has been advanced moderately in this chapter that all great powers, be they continental or maritime in primary orientation, have risen to that elevated status in good measure by their ability to prevail over serious rivals, or other inconveniently impeding societies. Whether or not the terms of engagement and the measures of success in world politics are in the process of significant evolution at the present time is uncertain, but improbable. Historians will look in vain to the ranks of political science for authoritative theoretical explanation of how and why the international political system works. Fashions come and go in international relations theory, but knowledge remains elusive.

In modern times, in sharp contrast to ancient and medieval experience in the Mediterranean, the leading sea power generally would appear to have benefited from a structural geostrategic advantage over the leading land power. This advantage has found successful expression in military strength both at sea and on land. There are reasons for skepticism over the explanatory power of sweeping cross-historical propositions. For example, consider an alternative history of World War II. Had Nazi Germany overcome British resistance in the summer of 1940, many people would have endorsed the idea that a new era of land-power dominance had arrived. But a victory for German land and naval power (with a critical air-power adjunct to both) over Britain as a sea power, would have told us a lot more about Britain's material strength and skill in statecraft and strategy vis-à-vis its continental enemy than it would about a trend of advantage between sea power and land power.

Between 1920 and 1940 the United States became the world's leading sea power. In the event that Britain had fallen in 1940 or 1941, how well might the Axis countries have fared in a global war with the United States? The importance to the United States of Britain and her empire cannot be doubted, any more than can the significance of the Royal Navy in the world balance of power. Winston Churchill sought to blackmail Washington in the summer of 1940. He implied, none too delicately, that in the absence of adequate U.S. assistance to the British war effort, Britain might be defeated and her fleet inherited by Hitler.[42] However, one has to beware of simple historical judgments as illustrations of an alleged trend in the strategic relationship between sea power and land power.

---

42 See Martin Gilbert, *Winston S. Churchill*, vol. 6, *Finest Hour, 1939–1941* (Boston: Houghton Mifflin, 1983), 591, and David Reynolds, "Churchill and the British 'Decision' to Fight on in 1940: Right Policy, Wrong Reasons," in Langhorne, ed., *Diplomacy and Intelligence During the Second World War*, 164–65.

Could the Axis coalition have presented the United States with an unanswerable challenge at sea? It is more likely that such strength of the Royal Navy as survived a desperate campaign to close the Channel and the North Sea to German invaders would have fled to Halifax, Nova Scotia, to evade seizure. Also, a necessarily maritime conflict between North America and the Axis powers would have been a struggle between two fleets founded on continent-wide resources, with many advantages on the U.S. side. Those advantages included an unmatchable breadth and depth of war-convertible industry, unity of political and military command compared with a very fractured, only loosely allied, Axis coalition, and the fact of a Soviet Union not exactly *hors de combat* in 1940–41.

Any sea power–land power theory that treats the quality of British national security as the test of the relative strategic clout of sea power has to be, first, modified, then adjusted massively, in recognition of the U.S. factor. Leadership of maritime-dependent coalitions in the West has shifted from the small islands of Britain to the continental-size United States. In its U.S. form, sea power was an ocean away from Axis strength in Eurasia and was and remains the product of the world's largest economy. The advances in continental-scale organization and transportation, which restored some of the Napoleonic power of rapid decision to armies, and which as a consequence might have permitted a dominant land power to bid for mastery at sea, also worked to the disadvantage of the Axis. The same industrial age that brought forth a Third Reich aspiring for continental (plus) hegemony, also summoned a Soviet Union already far advanced in the depth of *its* industrialization and a United States that could build the sea and air power of a true superstate.

The defeat of British sea power was a task immeasurably easier for the Axis to accomplish than the defeat of U.S. sea power would have been. The expedients of a boldly conducted machine-age warfare that might have enabled continental Germany to bridge the Channel for long enough to defeat Britain at home could not have worked against the United States. In the 1940s the United States alone was plausibly capable of sustaining one side of the global balance of power. However, the United States could not have fielded an army adequate in size to defeat a German army otherwise undistracted and substantially unattrited by active combat in Eurasia. The course of Britain's sea-dependent war with Nazi Germany should not be confused with the record of sea power against land power at some higher level of abstraction.

No law of history or strategy yields to Sea Power in the abstract, or to sea powers in general, inherent advantage in the conduct of war. Strength at sea is necessarily the product of the territorially derived resources of states and coalitions, whatever their primary strategic orientation. But states obliged by geography to look to their maritime defenses as the first condition for national security (second, today, after strategic nuclear deterrence) are by definition states not afflicted by immediate security problems for their national territories. In strategic terms, a tolerably commanded sea is a far-extended frontier. Such a frontier translates into time for mobilization for war and into choice for statecraft not vouchsafed continental powers. The details of relative strength among prospective enemies must always be important. But in geostrategic context, France and Germany were as fundamentally disadvantaged in their struggles with Britain as the Soviet Union was in its competition with the United States.

Some persistent themes and arguments merit highlighting. It would be absurd to argue for the superiority of land power over sea power or vice versa, but there can be no doubt that in modern times there has been a historical pattern of geostrategic advantage favoring sea powers over land powers. Contrary to the fears of some geopolitical theorists at the turn of the century, Eurasian continental powers have repeatedly failed in strategic competition with effectively insular, *but continental-sized* sea power.

Ancient, medieval, and even early modern times appear to reveal a pattern in sea power–land power competition which favors the latter. Sparta defeated Athens, Rome beat Carthage, and coastal control was the key to superior sea power in the narrow waters of the Mediterranean. One can argue that Mahanian notions of battlefleet-derived command of the sea cannot be applied to ancient Rome or medieval Byzantium, Venice or Ottoman Turkey.[43] There is, however, some danger that means and ends may be confused. Plausible assertions about the importance of coastal and fortress-port control are arguments about the paths to acquisition, not the strategic utility, of sea power.

Next, the all important and pervasive point that sea power has strategic meaning only for war as a whole, and only ultimately for events on land, is proved again and again by an abundance in all periods of positive and negative historical experience. In the words of a great American strategic theorist, Captain Dudley W. Knox: "History abounds in examples of naval effort misdirected because the naval mission was too restricted in its military

---

43. John Francis Guilmartin Jr., *Gunpowder and Galleys: Changing Technology and Mediterranean Warfare at Sea in the Sixteenth Century* (Cambridge: Cambridge University Press, 1974), chap. 1.

outlook."[44] Knox proceeded to balance his criticism with the claim that "more frequent still are the historical cases of army commanders failing to appreciate the vital importance of the naval element."

The frequent historical reality of an unduly separate conduct of wars on land, at sea, and in the air notwithstanding, as a rule decisions for war and decision in war are the results of combined-arms effects. Sea power, land power, air power, nuclear-missile power, and now space power are all complementary, but only in limited measure fungible. As deterrence and warfighting have been complicated in this century by the addition of the air and of earth orbit as military environments, so too have combined-arms theories of war. Julian Corbett began his great history of the Seven Years' War with an introductory chapter titled "The Function of the Fleet in War."[45] That focus is close to the spirit and content of this exploration of the influence of sea power and the advantage conferred by superior navies. However, consideration of the function of the fleet in war in the future has to take explicit account of nuclear-missle, air-power, and space-power elements, elements that did not trouble Corbett.

44. Dudley W. Knox, *The Naval Genius of George Washington* (Boston: Houghton Mifflin, 1932), 5–6.

45. Sir Julian S. Corbett, *England in the Seven Years' War: A Study in Combined Strategy*, 2 vols. (London: Longmans, Green, 1918; first pub. 1907), vol. 1, chap. 1.

Part III
THE FUTURE

7

Maritime Power and Space Strategy

.

Today the pervasiveness and scale of the challenge posed by the potential of space to the practitioners of sea power remains underappreciated. Both as opportunity and as problem the emergence of space power alters dramatically the geostrategic frame of reference for conflict. No longer can a navy defend its "high ground" with air power alone. The vertical flank of maritime operations can now be occupied, even perhaps fortified, by friendly or hostile vehicles in the earth orbits predictable by Johannes Kepler's laws of planetary motion. It is no small matter for a defense community to attempt to understand the implications of a new geographical environment. Navies in the twentieth century have been obliged to come to grips with the meaning of the submarine, the heavier-than-air flying machine, the electro-magnetic spectrum, and—virtually as an all-environment "wild card"—nuclear weapons. As if those broad-scale innovations were not enough, the utility of spacecraft is now limited more by money and lack of military imagination than by technology.

Not only is it difficult to come to terms with the still very much emerging technology for the space medium, it is also a challenge of the first order to understand how the five dimensions of war (underwater, sea surface, land, air, space, and electromagnetic)—plus the nuclear complication—should fit each with the others for an efficient blend of effects. History moves on, whether or not contemporary trends are well understood. It so happens that the U.S. Navy is no longer in a position to debate the broad advantages and disadvantages of the use of space systems, because a series of unconnected decisions over several decades has produced a current reality of truly massive space-system dependency. The Navy today places primary reliance on space systems for such nontrivial functions as communications, navigation (and therefore targeting), intelligence gathering (surveillance and reconnaissance), and meteorology. There is no longer any question of whether or not the Navy should repose major trust in orbiting vehicles; that decision already has been made in the affirmative, albeit by default. Indeed, it is no exaggeration to affirm that space power, friendly and hostile, will define the future of conflict at sea. The space age has come to stay.

Difficult as it is to come to terms with a wholly new geographical environment for war, there are persuasive historical precedents that can provide some guidance. By far the most significant point to be made about space power vis-à-vis sea power (or air power or land power) is that a common framework of policy logic and strategic reasoning unites them. The geophysical distinctiveness of space has inexorable and unique implications for technology, tactics, logistics, and operations, but not for policy or strategy. If a country, or a defense community perhaps, has mastered the art of thinking strategically about the sea, air, or land environments, then it can perform similarly for space.

Even at the level of operations, the structure of space warfare has more in common with the sea and the air than is widely appreciated. Just as a country's space power finds operational expression in (at least) three segments—ground facilities, up-and-down links to vehicles in orbit, and the satellites themselves—so maritime and air power have facilities at home, ships and planes, and (typically) some facilities abroad. The point is that space warfare need not focus on the destruction or harassment of orbiting satellites; instead, or in addition, it may well feature attacks on equipment on earth and data flows to and from satellites. Air campaigns can be won or lost on the ground, some great navies have been defeated by continental exclusion (loss of bases or of the hinterlands to bases), and space warfare assuredly will be waged on all geographical dimensions.

The common strategic logic that binds space together with the other environments insists that the significance of the exploitation of space to us must be the measure of its significance to our foes. The same reasoning that required the use of the sea to be protected, or assaulted, by fighting ships one day must work to insist that the right to use the spaceways be protected also. Space can no more be a sanctuary than can the deep ocean or the air environment. The more important space systems become for military effect, the higher will be the incentives to neutralize those systems in time of war. Space control is the master concept relevant here.

Analogous with sea control and air control, space control refers to a military condition wherein friendly forces are at liberty to operate in space, but enemy forces are not. Space control does not equate to a condition of absolute command wherein the enemy cannot launch any satellite at all. But this concept does point to circumstances wherein enemy policymakers and military planners cannot rely on assistance from space systems.

Debate over military space issues is prone to two characteristic, if opposing, errors. On the one hand, there is a tendency to emphasize the *adjunct* functions of space systems at the expense of the excellence of space power as space power. On the other hand, there is the familiar, and opposite, error of "space-cadet" thinking—when space power is praised and advocated virtually as an end in itself. Just for once, truth really does lie in the middle, or between these two classes of error. The attainment by space systems of excellence as adjuncts to terrestrial forces will increasingly depend on their quality as space systems. By analogy, for a navy to help its country's army it must, as a precondition, be good enough as a navy to beat off the enemy's navy. As the freedom of orbit is more and more contested (as a direct result of the military value derived from spacecraft) so defense planners will need to address seriously the problems of war in, as well as to and from, space.

The predictability of nonmaneuvering space vehicles in orbit and the popularity of particular orbits for particular missions has encouraged the idea that a space blockade might be easily achieved. Again, parallels from the maritime and aerial worlds beckon the imaginative, as well as threaten the unwary. There are good reasons to believe that blockade running would be at least as feasible for spacecraft as it has proved for ships and aircraft. A country may enjoy a meaningful control of space, but still not deny all hostile or ambiguous access to orbit. Moreover, it will probably prove easier to deny reliable use of orbit than to exploit the spaceways. Both parties to a conflict could find themselves with fairly effective means to deny the military use of space. That is not a prediction, but it is a warning. In addition, a

distinctly superior space power such as the United States would be well
advised to anticipate suffering a painful harassment of its space capabilities
by second-class space powers (or their friends). By analogy, the history of the
maritime world has registered distinctive strategies for weak navies as contrasted with strong navies.

The value of support from space systems to a navy must vary with the
conflict at issue. Although Desert Storm in 1992 demonstrated to many
previously inattentive people that space systems had become all but essential,
the conditions of that particular war allowed unilateral U.S. exploitation of
space. In the future, particularly in any superpower or great power struggle,
and perhaps even in some of the larger regional contests, war to, in, and
from space must be assumed to be bilateral. What is more, in a war where
the two sides have a generally comparable prowess on land, at sea, and in
the air (and in mutual nuclear deterrence, where relevant), a clear advantage
in space could well make the critical difference between victory and defeat.

A NEW ERA

Whereas the center line of this book thus far has been the relationship
between sea power and land power, this chapter breaks ranks and reaches for
the heavens. Lest readers come to believe that the author is unduly terrestrial
in his preoccupations and perhaps overly fascinated by the problems of past
eras, this discussion treats the strategic nexuses between the maritime and
space oceans. This chapter does not differ in kind from the rest of the book
thus far; it too is about the strategic meaning of prowess in one geographic
environment both for another environment and for deterrence or war as
a whole.

In some senses the war against Iraq in 1991 was the United States's first
"space war," but to date that experience has yielded tactical rather than
political, strategic, or what might be called "organizational" lessons. At the
inauguration ceremony for Naval Space Command in October 1983, then
chief of naval operations Admiral James D. Watkins issued the ringing
declaration that "space control is sea control." Speaking nearly four years
later, his successor, Admiral Carlisle A. H. Trost, advised as follows: "Today
we know that in wartime, even in a conventional war of limited duration,
the two superpowers would fight a battle of attrition in space until one side

or other had wrested control. And the winner would then use the surviving space systems to decide the contests on land and sea."[1]

The Watkins quotation has a rhetorical quality about it attributable to the circumstances of its delivery. Also, it might be noticed, 1983 was the year President Ronald Reagan startled Washington and the world by launching what was to become the Strategic Defense Initiative (SDI). The second quotation, from a chief of naval operations who unlike Admiral Watkins[2] was not one of the founding fathers of the revived legitimacy of strategic defense in the 1980s, explicitly and necessarily (for spring 1987) had a Cold War frame of strategic reference. With an SDI (Strategic Defense Initiative) vision that has evolved programmatically into a distinctly modest system for Global Protection Against Limited Strikes (GPALS),[3] a Maritime Strategy shelved in favor of coastal-water maneuver from the sea against the shore, and when the successor states to the U.S.S.R. are in the midst of incomplete revolutions, how much of yesterday's thinking about military space issues remains relevant for the U.S. Navy in the 1990s? Furthermore, which among yesterday's speculations on space power in its various alleged implications for sea power make much sense now? (Indeed, how many made much sense then?)

The title of this chapter intentionally raises large questions. Unlike the Air Force, the Navy has no basic doctrinal difficulty accommodating space forces as a set of support elements in aid of traditional missions. But like the rest of the defense establishment and for some understandable reasons, the Navy has yet to step up to what could be implied in the second concept in the title, "space strategy." In what senses can or should U.S. defense planners think about space strategy, if space systems essentially function in support of terrestrial forces?[4] Is there not a substantial peril that heavily space-minded people in space-dedicated organizations will, or would, be less than appropriately responsive to the practical needs of the Fleet? Could

1. Admiral Carlisle A.H. Trost, "ASW: The Challenge in Space" (speech delivered at the ASW Committee Banquet, May 20, 1987).

2. Admiral Watkins's role in the genesis of the SDI is emphasized in Janne E. Nolan, *Guardians of the Arsenal: The Politics of Nuclear Strategy* (New York: Basic Books, 1989), 164–65, 168.

3. See Dick Cheney, *Report of the Secretary of Defense to the President and the Congress* (Washington, D.C.: U.S. Government Printing Office, January 1991), 59–60. The definitive analysis of GPALS is Keith B. Payne, *Missile Defense in the 21st Century: Protection Against Limited Threats, Including Lessons from the Gulf War* (Boulder, Colo.: Westview Press, 1991).

4. "Space is an environment from which to support traditional naval missions, not a warfare objective itself." Vice Admiral Jerry O. Tuttle, "Navy Space and Electronic Warfare Programs Continue to Leverage Existing Force Levels," *Space Tracks Bulletin*, July 1990, 6.

the future effectiveness of the U.S. Navy be endangered by "space cadets" who, albeit for many of the best of reasons, would sever the links between the Navy and its orbital support vehicles?

It is my central purpose in this chapter to help clarify the proper relationship between the maritime and space environments, with particular attention to the prospective war-fighting needs of the former. William E. Howard III advises that "the 'battle space' surrounding all naval platforms must be redefined and extended beyond present limits. That battle space must extend to space."[5] He is correct, but what does this imply?

The scale of the challenge posed by the space environment for the U.S. armed forces is complex indeed. That challenge has political, strategic, operational, tactical, technological, doctrinal, and organizational aspects. It is scarcely surprising that this should be so, since it is not an everyday occurrence for a military establishment and its political masters to be confronted with the need to make sense of and use intelligently a wholly new geophysical environment for conflict. It is with that fact and its meaning that this discussion must begin.

FIVE DIMENSIONS OF WARFARE

By direct extrapolation from experience in coastal waters and narrow seas, understanding of the character of the deep oceans as an environment for war and of the strategic utility of sea power took perhaps half a century—from the 1520s to the 1570s—to coalesce into suitable concepts and doctrine. Unfortunately, the relevant sciences and technologies lagged far behind strategic insight. Indeed, it was really only in the 1780s and after that naval policy could employ a naval instrument capable of yielding the strategic effectiveness that had long been anticipated, but which typically was far beyond tactical attainment. Until sailors could be protected from scurvy and ships' bottoms could be sheathed in copper against the depredations of teredo worms in the tropics, ships had a range—and navies a practical reach—vastly more limited than policy needed. The mature conceptual, technological, and administrative-logistic mastery of sea power as a strategic contributor to national security took the better part of three centuries, from 1500 to 1800.[6]

5. William E. Howard, "Satellites and Naval Warfare," U.S. Naval Institute *Proceedings* 114 (April 1988) 44.

6. Colin S. Gray, *The Leverage of Sea Power: The Strategic Advantage of Navies in War* (New York: Free Press, 1992), explains and develops this point

Prior to 1500, "sea power" typically was short-range by design and of necessity, and was very much a close adjunct to land power.[7] It is probably no coincidence that the great wars of antiquity were won by land powers rather than sea powers (such as Sparta, Macedonia, and Rome) in the constricted geography of the Mediterranean basin.[8] Some scholars of ancient, medieval, and early modern naval power have argued quite convincingly that Alfred Thayer Mahan's conclusions drawn from the British practice of sea power do not apply in the different geophysical and geopolitical circumstances of galley warfare in the Mediterranean; at least they do not apply without considerable amendment.[9]

When Mahan published The Influence of Sea Power upon History, 1660–1783 in 1890, the strategic world, in the most macroscopic of terms, was elementally just two-dimensional. Had the great powers of the late nineteenth century employed unified (army-navy) defense staffs charged with the conduct of military planning, which they did not, the structure of strategic, operational, and tactical problems would have been understood to pertain to the synergistic uses of armies and surface navies. In peacetime all-but-invariably, and in wartime as a general rule, armies and navies waged their geographically separate wars with each paying only the most grudging of attention to the claims of the other. In 1914, for example, neither Germany nor Britain had or developed anything remotely resembling a combined army-navy approach to the conduct of the war,[10] and this for a simple context of only two geographically distinctive environments.

The first two decades of the twentieth century witnessed military-technical developments that rendered naval warfare itself three-dimensional, as surface combat was augmented dramatically with the complete novelties of subsurface and aerial assets and menaces. As the century progressed, technical, tactical, and then operational reality approached the more modest of the claims of airpower theory. By 1941–42—the evidence of 1939–41 was ambivalent—there was no further opposition to the precept that success at sea and on land required at the least a condition of disputed air control, and

7. See John H. Pryor, Geography, Technology, and War: Studies in the Maritime History of the Mediterranean, 649–1571 (Cambridge: Cambridge University Press, 1988).

8. A useful brief study is Chester G. Starr, The Influence of Sea Power on Ancient History (New York: Oxford University Press, 1989).

9. Preeminently, John F. Guilmartin, Gunpowder and Galleys: Changing Technology and Mediterranean Warfare at Sea in the Sixteenth Century (Cambridge: Cambridge University Press, 1974).

10. See the collection of essays, Paul Kennedy, ed., The War Plans of the Great Powers, 1880–1914 (London: George Allen & Unwin, 1979).

far preferably a condition of such undisputed air superiority to warrant description as command of the air. Effective air superiority did not mean that the enemy could not fly at all, but it did mean that he could not intervene in ground or sea campaigns in ways likely to shape their course decisively. In order to win at sea or on land it was not necessary utterly to destroy the enemy's air forces, but at the very minimum it was necessary to deny him the right to fly uncontested as and when he chose.

A U.S. Navy forcibly modernized at Pearl Harbor by the political, strategic and tactical errors committed by the still strangely overpraised Admiral Yamamoto responded to the airpower challenge and opportunity by co-opting that power on a massive scale, indeed by merging with it. Operationally, the U.S. Navy redesigned itself around fast carriers for the purpose of seizing island air bases from which the USAAF could batter Japan at home.[11] This policy of threatening to seize or actually taking island air bases obliged the Imperial Fleet to give battle under less and less favorable circumstances. At the same time the U.S. Navy's submarine force conducted a campaign of maritime interdiction that had the potential of being independently decisive. The campaign was a happy wartime invention—harking back to the old U.S. maritime preference for the *guerre de course*[12]—which, to the amazement of many people, yielded what could have been a conclusive defeat of the Japanese Empire.

By the close of the war in the Pacific it was plain that the strategic world had become unprecedentedly complex. People attempting to approach future war *as a whole* with a view to understanding how, with what, and to what strategic ends U.S. naval power should function, had to cope analytically—not to say politically—with an ever-expanding "team." Sea power itself was now four-dimensional (surface, subsurface, air, and electromagnetic),[13] while it had to operate in harness with the quasi-independent air power of long-range (and non-Navy owned) air forces. Moreover, there was the wholly novel complication of atomic weapons.[14] Those weapons,

11. The story is superbly told in Clark G. Reynolds, *The Fast Carriers: The Forging of an Air Navy* (Huntington, N.Y.: Robert E. Krieger, 1978).

12. An often forgotten choice of necessity which is given due prominence, if undue approbation in Kenneth J. Hagan, *This People's Navy: The Making of American Sea Power* (New York: Free Press, 1991).

13. See *Space and Electronic Warfare: A Navy Policy Paper on a New Warfare Area*, Final Draft (Washington, D.C.: Director, Space and Electronic Warfare [OP-094], Office of the Chief of Naval Operations, April 1992).

14. The Navy's strategic problems in the early postwar years are treated most competently in Michael A. Palmer, *Origins of the Maritime Strategy: American Naval Strategy in the First Postwar*

for a while at least, "belonged" to long-range, *land*-based air power, in that contemporary bomb design was not compatible with any aircraft capable of launch from an aircraft carrier. Of course, if what used to be called the art of war could be reduced to or had degenerated to the swift delivery of atomic, then nuclear, weapons by long-range aircraft or intercontinental missiles (space vehicles for most of their flight regimes), understanding of how the team of land, sea, and air power played together for the common goal of victory in war would be strictly moot. For a lengthy period, and for many people, it did seem as if the nuclear fact had effected a dramatic simplification of the architecture and strategy of major war. Armies, navies, and air forces would all be trumped by the new engines of mass destruction. Or so it seemed.

As instruments of deterrence, nuclear weapons appear to perform admirably. As tools for war-fighting, however, nuclear weapons suffer from the strategically fatal limitation that they cannot reliably eliminate the like weapons of an enemy. In other words, although nuclear weapons certainly cast a giant shadow over erstwhile superpower strategic relations in the Cold War era, the mutuality of deterrence rendered what once was labeled "the absolute weapon" all but absolutely strategically unhelpful *in use*. Nonetheless, nuclear weapons added an awesome complication to processes of defense planning already strained to the limit of intelligent management by the competing claims of the four military-power dimensions that, in distinctly arguable proportions, had delivered victory in 1945.

Two major points, which can be presented as working propositions, emerge from the historical tale. First, there are clear and direct historical precedents for the challenges and opportunities posed by the space environment. States had to learn how to conduct themselves as ocean-going sea powers, as air powers, and—to risk stretching the argument unduly—as nuclear powers. The space environment is geographically distinctive, but will not prove to be strategically so. Strategy is a general discipline.[15] Although technology, tactics, and operational ideas must be tailored for the space environment, a common logic of strategy will apply there. This means that the history of sea power and air power offer true precedents. Second, success in the deterrence or actual conduct of war is a team effort. What has happened since 1900 in particular is that the team's roster of distinctive

---

Decade, Contributions to Naval History, no. 1 (Washington, D.C.: U.S. Government Printing Office [for the National Historical Center, Department of the Navy], 1988).

15. A proposition argued forcefully and persuasively in Edward N. Luttwak, *Strategy: The Logic of War and Peace* (Cambridge: Harvard University Press, 1987).

dimensions or separable major elements has grown. The strategy coach for U.S. statecraft in the 1990s has to plan for the coordinated and synergistically efficient use of land, sea, air, electromagnetic, and now space power—all the while making careful provision to negate any prospectively table-overturning nuclear threats.

A focus on strategy and strategic effectiveness will help preclude unbalanced approaches to the subject of space power. Some vision of the objectives of the country during peace, war, or times of crisis is necessary, lest one of two incomplete tracks capture defense planning. Track One is the insistence, correct as far as it goes, that space be exploited strictly as a support realm for now-traditional terrestrial military activity. This track would deny the space environment the status of an operationally distinctive theater of combat. Track Two is the vision of the United States as a space power, with the practical nexuses between prowess in orbit and success on Earth left noticeably underexamined.[16] The historical precedents for the errors discussed here are formidable indeed. For example, Britain's Royal Navy waged World War II with desperately inadequate carrier assets and with only a fraction of the long-range maritime patrol aircraft that it needed. Germany had a powerful close-air-support *Luftwaffe*, but not the long-range air power that war with insular Britain and continental-size Russia required.

Assertion of the interdependence of land, sea, air, electromagnetic, and now space power (with, when appropriate, a nuclear counterdeterrent story, also) has to be appreciated as a general truth that accommodates some qualifications. All environments (land, sea, air, the electromagnetic spectrum, and space) will be important, but not equally important in all cases. Many military challenges lend themselves to alternative political, strategic, and operational solutions, wherein the mix of environmentally distinctive elements varies noticeably. Extraordinary strength in one or more dimensions (or perhaps subdimensions) of war typically compensates for weaknesses elsewhere. No country is equally competent across the board of military power. Fortunately, the United States (*inter alia*) is not tested in practice against absolute standards of true excellence, but rather against flawed foes.

Claims for "decisive" importance can be true (see Chapters 4 and 6), but most typically reduce under close examination to the status of statements of the trivially obvious. This topic, alas, is not trivial, because assertions for

16. For example, Simon P. Worden and Bruce P Jackson, "Space, Power, and Strategy," *The National Interest*, no. 13 (Fall 1988): 43–52. These authors offered the thought that "the Soviets seem to recognize that the primary measure of national power in the decades ahead will be the ability to place large vehicles up and out of the Earth's gravity well."

the decisive strategic importance of control of "the high ground" of space abound already, early in the "space age." U.S. defense planners today who wonder whether the space arena could yield a decisive military advantage should take comfort from a little historical perspective. Not only does history, even recent history, reveal that weapon systems, let alone weapons or weapons technology, do not win wars, history shows also that war is always a team game. The prophets of weapon-specific military "decision" tend to indulge in what amounts to self-negating prophecy to the degree to which their vision has potential merit. The truth of the matter is that decisive significance is a rare quality.

In his magisterial history of the Royal Navy in World War II, Correlli Barnett writes: "This [the German surrender on May 5, 1945 on Lüneburg Heath] was Britain's special moment of victory over Nazi Germany—a victory delivered in the end by armies, but which themselves had been delivered to the field of battle largely by the Royal Navy; a victory ultimately born of the Royal Navy's successful struggle to keep the sea-lanes to the British Isles open."[17]

Barnett also claimed that "for the Western Allies, therefore, seapower remained as ever the midwife of victory."[18] Nonetheless, there is much to recommend John Keegan's opinion that "in the final enumeration of Hitler's mistakes in waging the Second World War, his decision to contest the issue with the power of the American economy may well come to stand first."[19] Whether it be World War II or the Gulf War of 1991, all claims for the decisive significance of this or that advantage need to be approached with a healthy skepticism. Military success in one environment alone, be it land, sea, air, or space is likely to promote success in the other environments and may even be a necessary precursor for it. But it is improbable that success in one environment truly will be decisively significant, literally ensuring that the war as a whole will be won. Reasoning on the strategic significance of military space systems is no more immune to the claims for the importance of multi-environmental teamwork among land, sea, air, electromagnetic, and space power (with nuclear counterdeterrent cover), than are any other geographically specific categories of weapons.

War has a character unique to each geographical environment. The logic

17. Correlli Barnett, *Engage the Enemy More Closely· The Royal Navy in the Second World War* (New York: W. W. Norton, 1991), 857.

18. Ibid., 838.

19. John Keegan, *The Second World War* (London: Hutchinson, 1989), 219.

of war, however, is common to all of them.[20] Recognition of this point enables one to plan politically and strategically for the future of military space, even though much of the operational, tactical, and doctrinal detail remains obscure. The "grammar"[21] of war in space must be driven by Kepler's three laws of astrodynamic motion, but the strategic logic of that war is indifferent to geography and physics.

THE MARITIME AND SPACE OCEANS

Contemporary debate over the challenges and opportunities arguably posed by the space environment has some elements familiar indeed from the history of ocean-going sea power and, more particularly, of air power. Space power has three parts: ground, (up- and down-) links, and orbital segments. The sea power of great maritime empires often lent itself to parallel subcategorization as a focus for tactical, operational, and strategic debate. Specifically, the Spanish, Portuguese, Dutch, British, and French seaborne empires had an infrastructure of bases and ports at home, sea lines of communication (supported *en route* by a greater or lesser network of port-bases), and port-bases and/or colonies at the ends of those lines of communications. Politics, geography, and technology-tactics-doctrine largely determined how the maritime system in question was protected and assaulted.[22]

The annual *flota* of the *Carrera de las Indias* of imperial Spain was at least as important to Spanish power in the sixteenth and seventeenth centuries as space systems will be to any state or alliance over the next several decades. French, Dutch, and English sailors and maritime theorists long disputed whether Spanish treasure, and hence Habsburg credit, should be interdicted close to its source on the Main or at least in the Caribbean, at the chokepoint of the Azores, or on the approach to the Iberian Peninsula itself. In practice, none of these essentially maritime preferences proved

20. See Carl von Clausewitz, *On War*, ed. and trans. Michael Howard and Peter Paret (Princeton, N.J.: Princeton University Press, 1976; first pub. 1832), 605

21. Ibid.

22. See J. H. Parry, *The Spanish Seaborne Empire* (London: Hutchinson, 1966); Charles R. Boxer, *The Portuguese Seaborne Empire, 1415–1825* (New York: Alfred A. Knopf, 1969); idem, *The Dutch Seaborne Empire, 1600–1800* (London: Penguin, 1973; first pub. 1965); and D. B. Quinn and A. N. Ryan, *England's Sea Empire, 1550–1642* (London: George Allen & Unwin, 1983).

logistically, financially, technologically, or militarily feasible. Instead, imperial Spain was weakened by her protracted commitment to continental European wars, the conduct of which required a creditworthiness unsustainable even by the wealth extracted from the Americas and the Philippines. In short, by luck and by judgment Spain's many enemies contrived effective *grand* strategic responses to the menace of Spain's super power.

Turning to the history of air power, one finds that the threat posed by a putative enemy's air strength allows in theory a variety of active and passive responses. Specifically, enemy air power could be attacked indirectly at the source of its support, that is, the civil society behind it; attacked indirectly via its military-industrial support systems, that is, the aircraft assembly facilities and aviation fuel production, storage, and distribution; assaulted directly on the ground at airfields; intercepted *en route* to its targets by pursuit aircraft; confronted with powerful active point defense (anti-aircraft artillery as well as short-range aircraft) of likely targets; deprived passively of lucrative targets via facility dispersion, concealment, and hardening; and, finally, denied a whole-war context that could be influenced very significantly by the influence of air power of different kinds. The value of this complex airpower analogy, in common with the sea-power case above, is that it is historically familiar in all the aspects cited. A major difficulty with "space power" is that beyond narrow, albeit important, terrestrial support functions, it suffers from the weaknesses of extreme *specific* unfamiliarity.

Anyone able to think strategically about sea power or air power in times of peace, crisis, and war is amply equipped to consider the structure of the challenges and opportunities posed by space power. Strategic questions about the utility of maritime and space power for each other, as well as for the course and outcome of war (or deterrence of war) as a whole, are nested in issues and analysis at different levels. One has to be careful of overly neat distinctions, which can do violence to real continuities, as well as of interdependencies that should not be obscured. Nonetheless, it is important to appreciate that, again like land, sea, and air power, space power poses challenges and opportunities at the levels of policy, grand strategy, military strategy, operational art, tactics, technology, organization, and doctrine. On the one hand, there is a sense in which these eight levels of analysis all just point to different aspects of the same phenomena, an insight attributable to T. E. Lawrence in his reflections on Clausewitz's writings.[23] On the other

23. T. E. Lawrence, *Seven Pillars of Wisdom: A Triumph* (New York: Anchor Books, 1991; first pub. 1935), 192. Lawrence believed that "the first confusion was the false antithesis between strategy, the aim in war, the synoptic regard seeing each part relative to the whole, and tactics, the means towards a strategic end, the particular steps of its staircase."

hand, the possibility of compensation among some of these levels suggests that a differentiated view has merit. The degree to which it is important to think of, and plan for, operations and military strategy distinctly for the space arena is an open question, though not for long, one suspects.

The same reasons for wondering whether the concept of operational art can be applied to an ocean-going navy arise with even greater poignancy in relation to necessarily globe-girdling space assets. There is peril in borrowing a concept, in this case operational art, from its homeland (land power and land warfare) and force-fitting it to other geographical realms. Organized as questions, the levels of analysis present themselves thus:

1. *Policy:* What are the country's foreign policy goals and roles that generate demand for a quantity and quality of strategic effectiveness likely to require important contributions from space systems?
2. *Grand Strategy:* What are the implications of different mixes of policy instruments for the scale and character of demand likely to be placed on space systems?
3. *Military Strategy:* What is asked of military space systems as contributing agents to the conduct of war as a whole? With reference to the space environment narrowly viewed, which strategic objectives are necessary and feasible, and what are the means required to achieve them?
4. *Operational Art:* How can space assets be employed to generate the desired quantity and quality of support for terrestrial theater operations? Concerning the space environment itself, properly viewed *in toto* as a geographical "theater," how should a campaign be waged so that it serves the purposes of strategy and policy?
5. *Tactics:* How should space systems behave in order to succeed in a combat environment?
6. *Technology:* What technological options should yield the possibility of a tactical dexterity suitably supportive of operational, strategic, and policy goals?
7. *Organization:* Who should develop, acquire, operate, and direct space systems?
8. *Doctrine:* How do we fight with space systems? Basic strategic doctrine applies to space as it does to the other geographical environments. However, there is need of environmentally specific doctrine for space forces, because the range of operational and tactical choices and objectives are dictated by the technologically

unique circumstances of conflict in the medium of space.[24] Below
the level of strategy, there are significant differences among war
on land, at sea, in the air, and—prospectively—in space. This is
especially true of the relationship between offense and defense,
for example. An offensive style of war typically (*ceteris paribus*) is
advantageous in war at sea, in war in the air, and (probably) in
war in low earth orbit. A defensive style typically is advantageous
in land warfare and (again probably) in high earth orbit.

Particular difficulties with space assets—as with land, maritime, or air
assets—may lend themselves to alleviation by a variety of measures at
different "levels." Tactical problems of space-platform survivability can be
addressed at the levels of policy, grand strategy, strategy, and operations, as
well as tactically. This issue is not structurally that dissimilar from the
deterrence and war-fighting challenges faced by countries with strengths and
weaknesses in their maritime power. An important advantage in a holistic
approach to space power, as to maritime power, is that only in that way can
a sense of proportion be maintained and alternative solutions to problems be
identified in a timely fashion. Navies operate tactically, but they function
operationally and certainly to strategic effect. The building blocks for a space
force will be individual orbiting platforms (or ground stations). A satellite,
however, cannot be considered in isolation as a military asset without
reference to the orbiting constellation as a whole. No space force should
require what would amount to immortality in combat of an individual
capital unit.

Consideration of the effectiveness and survivability of military capabilities
of all kinds mandates multitiered analysis. Partial solutions from the technological, tactical, operational and strategic levels will all contribute to *mission*,
but not necessarily individual platform, survivability of the capability at
issue. Practical choices frequently are constrained severely. For example,
some sensor platforms have to operate in low earth orbit if they are to
perform tolerably. There can be no satisfactory, narrowly tactical solution to
the problem of, say, the vulnerability of radar and some other sensor

24. See David E. Lupton, *On Space Warfare: A Space Power Doctrine* (Maxwell Air Force Base,
Ala.: Air University Press, June 1988); General John L. Piotrowski, "Space Warfare Principles"
(June 1988), Colin S. Gray, *Space Strategy and Space Doctrine* (Fairfax, Va National Security
Research, March 1990); and, with specific reference to the doctrinal dilemmas of the USAF, James
A. Wolf, "Toward Operational-Level Doctrine for Space A Progress Report," *Airpower Journal* 5
(Summer 1991): 28–40.

satellites in time of war. Rather, one has to think operationally about how the enemy can be given severe *campaign* challenges, rather than a handful or less of rather elementary tactical engagement problems.

The novelty of space as an environment for war places a burden on the strategic imagination, not to mention on professional defense planners, which has yet to be borne very convincingly. For reasons of the immaturity of military threats to, in, and from space, the existence of the ABM treaty (which does *not* forbid dedicated antisatellite [ASAT] or theater defense systems), and the demise of the Cold War, forward thinking about military space is rare indeed. No matter what the contemporary politics of military space specify as feasible or infeasible to pursue now, and no matter how each service and unified and specified commander defines the bounds of the near-term practicable, there can be no excuse for an absence of strategic clarity.

Looking to the future, the familiar strategic logic of air power must apply for space power, though with some modification owing to the geographical uniqueness of the environment. The fundamental truth about space is as unsurprising as its recognition continues to elude many people. Namely, there are no free rides to strategic effectiveness. The more important the military exploitation of space to the United States, the more important it must become to the foes of the United States. Nazi Germany did not need to control, let alone "command," the North Atlantic in order to win its great continental struggle in Eurasia. But Nazi Germany did have to deny its maritime enemies a sufficiency of such control. The importance to Germany of the war at sea flowed directly from the sea's importance to the Grand Alliance. This is an illustration of why allegations of the "luxury" nature of sea power to a great continental state tend to be strategically nonsensical.[25]

This is neither an argument nor a plea for a particular kind of ASAT capability. Simply as a matter of basic strategic logic, the measure of U.S. military dependence on space systems has to be the approximate measure of the interest of potential foes in denying the United States reliable access to space. Similarly, the quantity and quality of threat that will repose in the use of space systems by enemies of the United States must dictate the extent and intensity of U.S. interest in neutralizing those systems. This argument is advanced strictly at the level of strategic logic, without prejudice to any among the wide range of candidate solutions.

25. Winston Churchill was wrong when he advised on February 9, 1912, that "from some points of view the German Navy is to them more in the nature of a luxury." Churchill, *The World Crisis, 1911–1918*, rev. ed , 2 vols. (London: Odhams Press, 1938), 1.76.

There is scope for debate over what fighting assets for space the United States will need, by when, and directed in battle by whom. There is no scope, however, for debate over the implications of the claim advanced here that the strategic logic of war in space is identical to the strategic logic of war at sea and in the air. U.S. space power will require a combat dimension, or adjuncts, for the same reasons that the United States has a navy able to fight for control of the seas and an air force capable of contesting control of the skies. The implications are that someone in the U.S. armed forces will have to be responsible for developing, acquiring, and controlling in action—or suitably delegating control—capabilities of all kinds relevant to the winning of a *space campaign*. That campaign need not be waged strictly in orbit, any more than maritime campaigns have been waged wholly at sea. When the RAF and the USAAF bombed the U-boat pens on the Bay of Biscay and disrupted movement by canal within and from Germany of the prefabricated hull sections of U-boats, they were waging the Battle of the Atlantic.[26] Similarly, the seizure of continental ground by Alied armies had a devastating effect on the effectiveness of German homeland air defenses, which enabled the bomber offensive to be very much more lethal . . . and so on. The point is that military operations in one environment can provide direct or indirect assistance to operations in other environments. Naval bases can be seized from the landward side and space systems can be assaulted via their ground or naval support facilities.[27]

The strategic logic presented here needs to be augmented by some important caveats. These are qualifications, they do not contradict the general logic advanced earlier. First, the United States may well engage in many different kinds of conflicts with different foes. The strategic utility and the practical vulnerability of U.S. space systems will vary from case to case. Second, as an extension of the first caveat, the fully successful exploitation of space, whatever that may mean in a specific conflict, does not guarantee victory in war as a whole. By analogy, control of the sea and the sky does not always guarantee victory (recall Vietnam). In other words, although the

26. See John Terraine, A *Time for Courage: The Royal Air Force in the European War, 1939–1945* (New York. Macmillan, 1985), 455.

27. A participant's account of the commando raid on the Normandie Dock at St. Nazaire in March 1942 opens with the accurate claim that "the attack on St. Nazaire was not just a Commando raid. It was an operation of high strategy, and was an important part of the Battle of the Atlantic. For St. Nazaire boasted the largest dry-dock in the world, the destruction of which was vital if Germany's battleships, pocket battleships and heavy cruisers were to be denied the safe refuge it then provided from attack." Stuart Chant-Sempill, *St. Nazaire Commando* (Novato, Calif.: Presidio Press, 1987; first pub 1985), xi

successful exploitation of space systems, directly contested or not, should always be useful, it will not deliver victory. Victory in war is a team achievement. Superior space assets, like an unmatchable navy, should limit the damage that friendly forces suffer. But by themselves, space systems (and navies and air forces) will not win wars.

Third, the strategic logic of conflict in and for space has to be augmented with recognition of the all but inherent weaknesses, as well as strengths, of space power. Again, this point is made easily if one considers the analogies with land, sea, and air power. For reasons of geophysics, each environmentally specific form of military capability tends to be relatively good and relatively poor at different kinds of activities.[28] Sea power, for example, is beyond equal at the task of moving bulky or heavy goods over great distances. But sea power is poor at moving men and material in hours or a few days. Similarly, sea power is a great enabling agent for the conduct of distant land campaigns, but itself is poorly equipped to project power deep ashore in the face of a great continental foe. Space power is beyond possible rival for truly global information gathering and dissemination (to ignore vulnerability issues for the moment), but it is impracticably expensive as a way to move heavy or bulky payloads. Also, for reasons more political than military-technical, there are severe limitations on what can be achieved by the global (not to be exaggerated, bearing in mind the laws of motion) passage and presence of space platforms. The same point can apply to air power. One can observe from the air, even bomb, but that may not be what the strategic circumstances require. With regard to space systems, one can observe but one cannot even bomb, at least not yet (to discount ICBMs as space vehicles).

SPACE POWER FOR EFFECTIVENESS AT SEA

Military Space: A Defining Factor

Space-system adjuncts for the U.S. Navy warrant collective description as a defining characteristic of the operating environment of the decades ahead. Space systems have not opened up new vistas of strategic opportunity,

28. See the discussion in Roger W. Barnett, *Regional Conflict: A Commanding Role for the U S. Navy* (Fairfax, Va.: National Security Research, 1991), 55–66.

however. Long before anybody's definition of the space age approximated contemporary reality, great powers intervened at oceanic distances in regional quarrels. To date space-system adjuncts to terrestrial operations have generally reduced the risks of poor coordination of forces through faulty communications and navigational error and have certainly provided a cornucopia of data of many kinds. One can claim that space systems have already had a grand-strategic, as well as strategic, operational, and tactical impact on defense planning and military practice. For example, it can be argued that President Bush's successive, contingent (on continuing political noncompliance) decisions to pursue a military solution to the Iraqi occupation of Kuwait were influenced critically by predictions of low casualties and rapid success, predictions that rested heavily, indispensably even, on the assumption of space-system aid to overall military effectiveness.

It is important to avoid a technology fetishism when claiming that space-system assistance is a defining factor for the U.S. Navy's operating environment. This is an appropriate juncture to register some points of enduring relevance about the relationship between technology and military effectiveness.[29] People matter most. Poorly trained, poorly led, poorly managed, poorly motivated, or grossly outnumbered people will neutralize the potential value even of the most effective systems. Next, superior equipment does not guarantee victory. Although notably inferior equipment will cause people to be killed and operations to fail, war and deterrence are very much team efforts. Also, the proper concern is with man-machine systems functioning in rich combinations with other man-machine systems. In the long history of success and failure in deterrence and war, technological inadequacy is only one among many relevant factors, and is not obviously the most important. In the last quarter of the eighteenth century, for example, Spain built fighting ships superior to comparable British or even French models. Spain's problem was that she lacked the seamen to fight in her excellent ships.[30]

Space systems must yield available data promptly and reliably, and terrestrial consumers need to receive and process it, and disseminate its meaning rapidly in useful form. Much of the value of space systems to the U.S. Navy depends not only on the equipment that is acquired but also on

29. A subject explored at length in Colin S. Gray, *Weapons Don't Make War: Policy, Strategy, and the Meaning of Military Technology* (Lawrence. University of Kansas, 1993).

30. See N A.M. Rodger, "The Continental Commitment in the Eighteenth Century," in *War, Strategy, and International Politics: Essays in Honour of Sir Michael Howard,* ed. Lawrence Freedman, Paul Hayes, and Robert O'Neill (Oxford: Clarendon Press, 1992), 48.

how it is used to help those who need it when they need it. If for reasons of security, cumbersome administrative arrangements, and too few terminals, critical data does not reach a naval task force commander, then from his point of view that data might as well not exist.

Finally, deterrence and war remain team enterprises. Space power needs to be co-opted as a vital adjunct, and contributor, to naval power, as happened with air power in the 1920s and 1930s. An aggressive approach to the development and acquisition of new space systems, however, should not lean on the kind of "dominant weapon" fallacies that have studded this century's military history.

Some Practical Difficulties

The Navy has faced few of the doctrinal problems that the Air Force has yet to resolve convincingly in the accommodation of space power to its core concerns. Certainly the Navy has not been obliged to invent some equivalent to the geophysically novel and bizarre concept of *aerospace*. Nonetheless, there are potentially severe practical problems of doctrine and organization that one day may seriously affect naval access to space systems. These are still early days, but there are, nevertheless, some general grounds for concern.

First, the principle of centralized control but decentralized execution of military space activity carries the risk of insufficient responsiveness to local need. The idea of space systems as national military assets is a compelling one. Nonetheless, the scarce national space systems of a global superpower, though plainly requiring central vision for, and discipline in, allocation, need to be responsive to short-notice, even unexpected, demands from far-flung tactical elements (that is, military customers).

Second, war at sea has characteristics unique to that environment and requires military space support crafted, or craftable, to fit them.[31] It is the Navy's responsibility to ensure that the distinctive character of naval warfare is taken fully into account in the relevant force planning and operational activities conducted by Unified Space Command and Air Force Space Command. If the Navy should eschew by choice, or be denied by fiat, responsibility for developing and acquiring (and possibly operating) space systems potentially critical to its ability to generate and exert sea power, at

31. See the terse comparison between land battle and sea battle in Wayne P. Hughes Jr., *Fleet Tactics: Theory and Practice* (Annapolis, Md.: Naval Institute Press, 1986), 143–44.

least it should ensure that some organization is "thinking Navy" to a suitable war-fighting degree.

Third, the history of land, sea, and air cooperation, as well as common sense, suggests that there is a more than trivial probability of Navy concerns over space assistance not being met adequately. There are several solutions or partial solutions. Aggressive Navy participation in Unified Space Command, adequate Navy representation on space topics in the joint arena, and assiduous, cooperative liaison with Air Force Space Command are but the most obvious of necessary measures.

Space Power a Rival?

For as far into the future as it is worth peering, it is difficult to identify a zero-sum relation between maritime power and space power. These two geographically distinct and distinctively focused kinds of power complement one another more powerfully than do any other combination of types of military power. In those cases the complementarity is strong, but there is a history of, and some limited basis for, claims of fungibility. If the arrival and maturing of air forces and of nuclear weapons could pose only transitory crises for the U.S. Navy, it is exceedingly unlikely that space forces, with the inherent strengths and weaknesses of systems functioning in that environment, will pose other than distinctly manageable challenges. Although both naval and space (and air) capabilities inherently support land-oriented policy, the laws of astrodynamics strictly delimit what orbiting platforms can accomplish at tolerable cost and with necessary efficiency.

Space Power as Sea Power?

Today sea power is close to implying space power, though the reverse need not be true. Similarly, it has been a truism for more than half a century that sea power implies air power, though—again—the reverse need not hold. The practical connections between naval and space capabilities have come to be so well known that they require no special emphasis. The implications of those connections, however, need not be taken wholly as givens. The U.S. Navy, like the other services, though to a greater degree, because of the nature of the maritime environment, has chosen to become critically dependent on space systems for warning, navigation, communications, and meteorology. "Dependent," like the adjective "decisive," should be employed with care.

For the time being, at least, advantage or disadvantage in space can have combat meaning for maritime events only through the agency of other military elements. Force application *from orbit* has long been recognized in principle, but—with the all-but-trivial and now lapsed exception of a Soviet fractional orbital bombardment system (FOBS)—it does not figure currently in any state's order of battle. This means that whatever advantage can be secured from space systems has to be translated into action by land, sea, or air forces. Unlike space forces for many years to come, naval and air forces can be described as "full service" military organizations. The direct and indirect synergisms among land, sea, and air forces notwithstanding, air power *itself* actually can exercise some control at sea. The long-standing capital-ship status of the aircraft carrier is recognition of this fact.

By way of contrast, space power *is* sea power only if that space power can cue or otherwise inform military executive agencies on land, sea, and in the air. It is not sufficient merely to cite what a potential enemy's space assets themselves can do as adjuncts. It is no less important to ask, "adjuncts to what?" In 1991, Operation Desert Storm demonstrated the total effectiveness of the American way in large-scale, non-nuclear regional war. U.S. space assets indeed were force enhancers, as the familiar phrase affirms. But the scope for that enhancement was driven by the quantity and quality of the terrestrial assets and the coherence in their orchestration in action.

The Trend

Defense analysts are wont to allow their studies to be captured by details, when trends are really what matter most. It is a fact of huge and obviously lasting significance that for some literally key military support functions, space systems have assumed primary status, with terrestrial (strictly, more terrestrial) systems slipping into backup roles.[32] This did not happen suddenly and neither did it occur as a product of a coherent central decision by the U.S. Department of Defense, but happen it did. It is a general truth that today the U.S. armed forces, *and particularly the Navy*, place primary reliance on space systems for early warning of attack, communications, navigation, reconnaissance and surveillance, and meterology. Primary reliance or dependence certainly does not mean exclusive reliance. But such dependence does mean in practice that the ability to pursue older alternative

32. A point advanced strongly in John W. Power, "Space Control in the Post-Cold War Era," *Airpower Journal* 4 (Winter 1990): 24–26.

approaches to the tasks now performed primarily by space systems tends to atrophy and eventually will vanish. The continuing growth of primary dependence on space assets mandates a clarity and urgency of thought on the subject of space control. The next section of this chapter addresses this still rather opaque, yet central, topic.

Argument about the meaning and implications of space power, and of space power for the Navy, occurs against the backdrop of generally short-of-stellar understanding of the strategic utility of maritime power and of how maritime strategy may be said to "work." The thinness of the analysis of space power and space control is really fully in step with a tenuous grasp of how land, sea, air, and nuclear-oriented forces function synergistically for strategic effect, let alone with the added complication of a space dimension.[33] A notable part of the problem the U.S. defense community exhibits in endeavoring to come to grips with space as a conflict environment is symptomatic of a more general difficulty.

SPACE CONTROL

Space control is the master concept for the military space environment, as are its direct analogues for the sea and the air. Deprived of rhetorical flourishes, space control refers simply to a condition wherein friendly forces can use the space environment on a reliable basis, but enemy forces cannot.[34] Control, disputed or otherwise,[35] is the concept that most usefully directs attention to the emerging status of the space environment as a (global) combat "theater." Also, no matter how demanding the military requirements of some meaningful approximation to space control (all orbits?) may prove to be, recognition of the salience of the concept is a necessary step toward prudent (force) planning for space operations.

Space control can be considered on a continuum with friendly command

33. See Colin S. Gray, War, Peace, and Victory· Strategy and Statecraft for the Next Century (New York: Simon & Schuster, 1990), 325–33.

34. "The function of maritime power is to win and keep control of the seas for one's own use, and to deny such control to one's adversaries " Stephen W. Roskill, The Strategy of Sea Power· Its Development and Application (London: Collins, 1962), 15. Also see Julian S. Corbett, Some Principles of Maritime Strategy (Annapolis, Md.: Naval Institute Press, 1988; first pub. 1911), part 2, chap. 1.

35. See Alfred Thayer Mahan, Naval Strategy, Compared and Contrasted with the Principles and Practice of Military Operations on Land (Boston: Little, Brown, 1919; first pub. 1911), 256.

at one pole and enemy command at the other. "Command," with its Mahanian overtones, [36] may well be neither feasible nor necessary, certainly not for all orbits of potential interest. Indeed, the prospect for U.S. space control as between a low earth orbit at 250–300 miles altitude and geosynchronous orbit at 22,500 miles, could be as different as were the prospects in the Cold War for U.S. sea control in the Eastern part of the North Atlantic and the Barents Sea. As with sea control, the concept, policy goal, or doctrinal requirement of space control raises almost as many issues as it appears to resolve. As a general objective there is everything to recommend that the United States seek the ability to operate where, as, and how it pleases in space and to deny like liberty to other states. Nonetheless, a veritable legion of issues and questions beg for clarification. Some of these are addressed in the paragraphs that follow.

Deterrence

Among the various aspects of deterrence that play in analysis and debate over space power, the most important is the most pervasive. Specifically, the course and outcome of particular military campaigns are rarely predictable in advance with high confidence. Similarly, the strategic effect on a war as a whole of an anticipated major advantage in combat at sea, in the air, or in space cannot be weighted and valued precisely in advance. It is possible, however, to craft systemic military advantage in a particular geographical environment for its deterrent as well as prospective war-fighting benefit. The deterrent value of such a military advantage should be a "free" gift of the latter, but that is not reliably the case. The actual war-fighting prowess of space (or space-related) forces for control of space, as well as the meaning of such control for the war overall, cannot be known with high assurance in advance. But it is probably the case that the very novelty of space warfare in all its dimensions encourages a prudent anxiety that is liable to err on the generous side. The expectation on the part of would-be foes that the United States will be able to impose and sustain space control is likely to yield a potent deterrent effect deriving from imprecise perceptions of pertinent causes and effects. Careful military analysis of the synergistic combat

36. Alfred Thayer Mahan, *The Influence of Sea Power upon History, 1660–1783* (Boston· Little, Brown, 1918; first pub. 1890), particularly 138, and, for a sustained treatment with regard to the value of command for the whole course of a war, his *Influence of Sea Power upon the French Revolution and Empire, 1793–1812*, 2 vols (Boston: Little, Brown, 1898; first pub 1892), vol. 2, chap. 19.

advantages to be derived from success in space warfare may well matter a great deal less for deterrent effect than does a deterree's general sense of critical inferiority in the space environment.

Foreign Policy

It might be thought that U.S. interest in space control, its achievement or denial to others, should express the character, even shifting direction, of foreign policy. Some objections to ASAT programs cite the changing threat environment as proof of the lack of need for such a capability.[37] (This is not to suggest that space control pragmatically reduces intelligently to debate over an ASAT interceptor.) Nothing could be further from the truth. Rather, the importance of space control flows directly from the importance of space, and that latter importance derives both from the geopolitical context of U.S. national security and from what might be labeled "progress." By analogy, it is as mistaken today to question the growing importance of space power as in times past it was mistaken to question the growing importance of ocean-going sea power and, much later, of air power. There is ample scope for argument over just how important space power is and will become, and over how it will play in the full team of instruments supporting strategy and policy. But the trend in importance of space power and hence, in principle, the importance of space control may be likened almost to a force of nature.

Different Approaches

There are as many ways to attempt to secure a tolerable level of space control as there are of sea control or air control. Obviously, the severity of requirements for the broad mission of space control can be reduced if and when more robust alternatives to space systems for key functions can be employed. The space arena offers some actual or potential analogues to such features of war at sea as the evasive routing of convoys, zig-zag sailing patterns, and armed escort, as well as self-defense capability by non-combat (-dedicated) platforms, electronic emissions control, and so forth. In common with war at sea, however, war in space could not be waged solely according to an environmentally distinctive logic. After all, war both at sea and prospectively in space are waged only because they have profound

---

37 "In current world conditions, the ASAT program appears to be an anachronism." Steven Aftergood of the Federation of American Scientists, quoted in Vincent Kiernan, "Pentagon Prepares for ASAT Flight Testing," *Space News*, August 5–18, 1991, 23.

meaning for ultimately land-oriented conflict as a whole. Seaborne convoys have to function according to an economic, political, geographical, military, and meteorological logic that is largely accessible to the enemy. One is reminded of the familiar point that secret agents have some measure of choice between being secure and being effective. The two aspects of space control, reliable use of the spaceways and denial of the same to the enemy, need not be of equal significance. By analogy again, it was far more important (and cost-effective) for Nazi Germany to deny the Allies uncontested control of the North Atlantic than it was to proceed beyond the negative goal of denial into trying itself to use the North Atlantic.

Space denial is not space control any more than sea denial is sea control, but either may suffice for the particular phase or character of conflict at issue. Examples of the potential for error in the discussion of space control are impressive indeed. The leading, sharply contrasting, errors to date comprise, first, an inappropriate focus on ASAT interceptor weaponry capable of reaching to, or perhaps across, orbit(s); second, a widespread overconfidence that potential space problems can be handled at or close to their source by assault on the ground segments of space-system architectures; and third, a powerful belief that space warfare reduces essentially to electronic combat. This third error provides a convenient and highly plausible excuse to downgrade planning for anything as crude and politically sensitive as physical assault on enemy facilities on the ground or platforms in orbit (or *en route* to orbit).

Needless to say perhaps, space warfare is very much a problem of electronic warfare, just as, more narrowly, satellite survivability primarily though not exclusively is a challenge for defensive electronic warfare. Nonetheless, at this relatively early stage of preparation for space warfare, it would be an error to close one's mind to dimensions to the space control problem beyond the obvious mandate of electronic combat. There is a need for open minds on the subject of how the two aspects of space control (denial and use) should best be treated. Almost certainly it will be discovered that a richly mixed approach is superior to the kind of single-focus solution that can amount all too easily to a requirement for heroic performance. The more single-minded the focus, necessarily the more competent one has to perform in that focus. Also, a narrow approach to space control and to space system survivability all but invites an intelligent enemy to design around that approach.

Blockade

A space blockade could be pursued by three complementary methods, each of which has close maritime parallels. First, enemy space systems could be menaced or attacked "in port." Second, those systems could be menaced or assaulted on their trajectory from earth into orbit. Third, they could be subjected to antipodal "chokepoint" control.[38] With some important exceptions—for example, space-reconstitution assets held more or less stealthily on mobile platforms of several kinds—the enemy's as-yet-un-launched space power, like his naval strength *not at sea*, poses an attractive set of targets. However, some of the same reasons why naval blockades can prove disappointing also apply potentially to a strategy of space blockade. At a critical period the adversary's space ports may be politically off limits for direct assault. Overall, some mix of inadequate intelligence, poor communications, bad weather, friendly assets off station, and plain bad luck could render the blockade an uncertain enterprise.

In addition, equipment key to information gathering and dissemination for enforcement of a blockade may be destroyed or harassed by the enemy. In a blockade—maritime, air, or space—the blockaded foe has the initiative. Proper use by the foe of surprise in space warfare could have fatal consequences for U.S. prospects for securing control in that environment. Moreover, it is not certain that the United States will acquire the weapons able to effect the launch-phase interception of space systems that a blockade strategy might require. It should be recognized that counter-blockade strategies and tactics are many and prospectively could be highly effective. For example, on-orbit spare satellites and mobile storage on earth of replacement platforms would frustrate the simpler of the approaches to space blockade.

Costs and Benefits

The costs and benefits of space control are not entirely to be likened to judgment on a force of nature. The extent of an enemy's space dependence and the overall balance of prowess in war-fighting capability must drive estimates of the stakes in space in any particular conflict. Desert Storm was a campaign wherein so many political, strategic, operational, tactical, and

---

38 See Aadu Karemaa, "What Would Mahan Say About Space Power?" *U.S. Naval Institute Proceedings* 114 (April 1988): 48–49, and D Nahrstedt, "The Case for a Submarine-Based Anti-Satellite System," *The Submarine Review*, January 1991, 50–55.

technological advantages were stacked on the side of the grand coalition that
the potential significance of space systems easily might be falsely assessed on
the basis of that experience. When an adversary is all but hopelessly
overmatched in all dimensions, it should be relatively easy to tie a knot in a
plan that comes unraveled, as General Eisenhower once said, and substitute
capabilities to compensate for major errors, weaknesses, or unpleasant surprises.

Radically different from the Desert Storm scenario would be a condition
wherein the balance of military prowess was even. For example, the Allies
probably were close to parity, or slightly below, with their German foes at
the water's edge of continental Europe in late summer 1943. That realization
was the basis of the British insistence for the launching of Overlord no
earlier than the spring of 1944. The military prospects for Overlord would
have lain firmly in the gamble category prior to the defeat of the Luftwaffe
in the winter of 1943–44. In a close contest a single major advantage—say
in the efficiency of tactical air-ground cooperation or the availability of
artificial harbors—literally might be decisive. For a historical case, by any
definition the British expedition to retake the Falkland Islands in 1982 was a
gamble. The political and military conditions for the success of Operation
Corporate were finely balanced on the brink of impracticability. Virtually
any important military setback, including the loss of one of the small carriers
or of the *Canberra*, could have doomed the entire enterprise. When
considering the strategic utility of the tactical benefits securable from space
control, defense planners should consider the hypothetical 1943 and actual
1982 cases, as well as Desert Storm 1991.

For a contest to be fairly even it does not have to be waged between states
or coalitions of nominally equal strength. Geography, that is to say, logistics,
and politics can more than compensate for apparent gross disparity in
military strength. For example, North Vietnam was a worthy foe of the
United States, given the unique geography and politics of that war. Similarly, the American colonists were no match for Great Britain, *on paper*.
But in the swamps of Georgia and the Carolinas and the forests of New
York, not to mention with an allied fleet massively complicating British
strategy, Americans obviously were very competitive indeed.[39]

The qualities of flexibility and discrimination which space systems can
improve in the performance of U.S. terrestrial forces are likely to be critically

39. See John Ferling, ed., *The World Turned Upside Down: The American Victory in the War of
Independence* (Westport, Conn.: Greenwood Press, 1988).

important for the political-military success of American arms in regional or local conflicts. Space systems can help dramatically to prevent some of the political fumbles that the traditional American way of high-firepower war was prone to commit. Precise navigation, generally reliable communications, and much improved target intelligence should translate into minimum scale, but still effective, options for the use of force.

In many of the conflicts that may absorb U.S. military attention over the next several decades, it is more likely than not that the regional foes of the United States will not have a noteworthy space dimension to their armed forces. Any space campaign in such a context effectively should be "no contest." As the post–Cold War world shakes down into new, or new-seeming, patterns of antagonism, the United States can be certain that any first-class adversary will work hard to neutralize as much of U.S. space-provided military advantage as strategic judgment advises to be necessary. The more critical the potential contribution of space systems, the more highly motivated will U.S. adversaries be to negate that contribution directly or indirectly.

Permanent and Ubiquitous?

Can space control be won at the outset of a war for all orbits of great military interest? If such control is attainable, can it be rendered permanent for the course of the war? As a practical matter, how much control is really necessary? And just what is it that is being controlled? Mahan and Corbett contributed mightily to confused thinking when they bequeathed a focus on sea *lines* of communication to subsequent generations of maritime thinkers, planners, and operators. Paradoxically, perhaps, the concept of lines of communication typically makes more sense for the spaceways, given the predictability of orbital mechanics, than it does for the seaways. With the exception of certain critical geographical chokepoints, it is the character of the sea to permit a wide variety of ship routing. In many cases, therefore, sea control cannot usefully be considered in terms of sea lines of communication, but rather in terms of *ships*.[40] In some respects the space environment is more like the land, with its main highways and railroads and the feasibility of fortifying key "lines," than it is akin to the sea or the air with the easy and unpredictable agility of vehicles in those environments.

40. This useful point is advanced in Eric Grove, *The Future of Sea Power* (Annapolis, Md.: Naval Institute Press, 1990), 22

Notwithstanding the differences between the maritime and space oceans, and the somewhat different range of practicable military objectives peculiar to each, still there is much of general value in the following words by Stephen Roskill:

> The aim of maritime strategy is therefore not so much to establish complete control of all sea communications, which would be an ideal hardly attainable until final victory was almost won, as to develop the ability to establish zones of maritime control wherever and whenever they may be necessary for the prosecution of the war. . . . And a zone of maritime control means no more than an ability to pass ships safely across an area of water which may be quite small in extent or may cover many thousands of square miles of ocean.[41]

Much of that statement could be applied sensibly to space. Orbital mechanics, however, albeit alleviated by a host of survivability measures (stealthy design, remote orbit, numerical proliferation, and so forth), in principle allows for a completeness and even a ubiquity of control rarely attainable by superior navies at sea. Remoteness of orbit alone, semisynchronous, geosynchronous, or higher, affords a transitory protection, which would be critical only if time were a critical factor. Even in its far-distant orbital segment, early-warning and communication satellites at geosynchronous altitude in principle will be vulnerable to space mines pre-deployed at like altitude, to ASAT interceptors allowed the time to ascend, and to directed energy weapons. There are no inherently secure orbits. Anywhere a friendly space vehicle can reach, so also can a hostile vehicle penetrate, and this is to sidestep the issues posed by challenges in the field of electronic warfare.

The possibility of a sky-sweeping campaign that, over days and weeks, yields a ubiquitous and permanent condition of space control, does not survive close operational scrutiny. Mobile deployment of spare satellites for reconstitution and the forceful degradation or careful evasion of launch-detection and space surveillance equipment should render space campaigning a distinctly two-sided enterprise. As Roskill noted of war at sea, "it is far more common for control to be in dispute than undisputed."[42] It is hardly necessary to add that the "grammar" of war in space is not confidently

---

41. S W. Roskill, *The War at Sea, 1939–1945*, vol. 1, *The Defensive* (London: HMSO, 1954), 3.
42. Ibid.

predictable. In the context of an absence of historical experience with space warfare, choices by states will matter vastly. The United States might be so inflexible in its provision for basic space transportation that in effect it could be blockaded from additional access to space. Intelligent planning for space as an environment for war, however, should render space blockade wholly impracticable.

THE SEA AND SPACE: A STRATEGIC RELATIONSHIP

The importance of space control for maritime operations cannot easily be overstated. The ability to exploit space and deny any adversary reliable use of it will be essential if the United States is to employ sea power as an instrument of statecraft in the future security environment. Not least among the many advantages of the coalition's cause in Desert Storm was the convenient fact that the enemy had no ability to contest the exploitation of the space dimension of the war. Much was learned, or relearned, from the war; for example, operational planners need a better grasp of what space systems can do to help them. Also, the utility of a space system has to be appraised fully from end to end. Technology is useful only if it can serve those in operational and tactical need *when they need it*. The war showed plainly that the path to the greater tactical utility of space systems lies in the training and equipment of all elements for direct connections between user and orbiting platform. Furthermore, Desert Storm provided evidence yet again that there is a flexibility in military affairs that flows from sheer quantity. Orbital mechanics can pose problems for commanders who need focused and timely terrestrial coverage.

Overall, the success of space systems as adjuncts to terrestrial military operations points to the trend of an increasing space-system dependency for navies that necessarily introduces novel vulnerabilities. It may be recalled that in both world wars the headlong progress achieved in radio communication proved to be a two-edged sword, particularly for Germany. Nazi Germany's appalling lack of operational signals security probably ranks only after Hitler's lack of skill in statecraft and the scale of the U.S. economy on the rank-ordered shortlist of why Germany lost.[43] A primary lesson of Desert

---

43. For the maritime dimension, see John Winton, *ULTRA at Sea* (London. Leo Cooper, 1988), and David Kahn, *Seizing the Enigma: The Race to Break the German U-Boat Codes, 1939–1943* (Boston: Houghton Mifflin, 1991).

Storm has to be that the undisguised and undisguisable utility of space systems will motivate potential foes to seek both to emulate and to offset the demonstrated U.S. prowess in space. The solution to this predictable problem has to lie in operational planning for the space arena as a combat environment.

The discussion in this chapter may be summarized in seven points. First, there is a need for the U.S. defense community to step up to the challenge of thinking about and planning for the use of space as an environment for war. There is scope for argument over the urgency of this need, given the current absence of a superpower adversary, but there is no reason to argue that space is, or will be, strategically different from the land, sea, and air. For reasons of physical geography and its technological implications, the tactical and operational character of space warfare must be unique. But unlike operations, tactics, and technology, which are environment-specific, strategic logic is generic. The U.S. armed forces should make proper allowance for the earliness of the hour regarding warfare to, in, and from space, but cannot begin too soon to train themselves to think soundly about this environment. Particularly challenging, as well as potentially rewarding, is the identification of parallels from the land, sea, and air arenas that can suggest ways to come to grips with the real as well as the only apparent novelties of space. At the level of strategy, people and organizations skilled in thinking about the utility of sea power or air power are better equipped than they may realize to cope with the challenge of space.

Second, "full-service," first-class spacefaring states can be inconvenienced, harassed, and perhaps even thwarted by second- or third-class space powers. Too little is known at present about the probable detail of space warfare for the United States to be complacent regarding the emergence of minor spacefaring countries. A maritime analogy may prove compelling. The infant United States of the War of 1812 could not build, or afford to build, line-of-battle ships. Indeed the U.S. Navy of 1812 was trivial in scale in comparison with the Royal Navy. It so happened, however, that pursuing intelligently and generally very competently the maritime strategy of guerrilla warfare at sea against British merchant traffic (the *guerre de course*), American privateers inflicted enormous pain.[44] Looking to the future, a U.S. defense establishment that expects potentially dangerous maritime harass-

44. The Royal Navy's blockade of the U.S. coastline was wonderfully efficient, as it should have been after twenty years' experience That blockade of U.S. commerce, however, did not prevent the problem with American privateers, who by 1814 were quite out of Royal Navy control. See G. J. Marcus, *The Age of Nelson: The Royal Navy, 1793–1815* (New York: Viking Press, 1971), chap. 16.

ment in, say, the Persian Gulf (from mines, missile-armed small craft, land-based short-range missiles, and also aircraft) should expect to confront equivalent problems vis-à-vis its space assets. This is not to suggest that a second- or third-tier space power would seek to contest for space control, any more than the United States sought maritime command in 1812. But it does suggest that there will be fewer and fewer potential conflict scenarios over the next several decades concerning which U.S. defense planners can afford to assume that the space arena will be an inviolable sanctuary reserved for unilateral U.S. military exploitation. *Guerre de course* against all segments of the space systems of a first-class space power is just one of the many topics that still awaits treatment by its Alfred Thayer Mahan.

Third, the Navy requires that the Department of Defense develop and enforce robust space control. If space control is in dispute or is lost to an enemy, the Navy, increasingly as the years proceed, will have great difficulty fulfilling its missions. That space control will be as important as air control, one must doubt, at least for several decades to come, given the prospective absence of spaceborne terrestrial bombardment vehicles. Nonetheless, of all the armed forces, the Navy is the most at risk to threats assisted by orbital platforms, just as it is the heaviest tactical user of information from space.

There is much scope for debate over just what space control could mean and just how it would be contested in practice. The heart of the matter, however, is as simply stated as is its sister concept of sea control. If sea control can be expressed colloquially as a condition wherein we can use the sea and the enemy cannot, so space control refers to a condition wherein we can use the spaceways and the enemy cannot. This elementary, even elemental, definition accommodates the minor qualifications both that our space/sea forces will suffer some harassment and losses in space/at sea, and that the enemy will be able to secure erratic and minor-scale access to some orbits/put to sea in a small way. The bottom line will be that friendly space forces will be mission survivable, albeit subject to some combat loss, whereas the enemy's space forces will not be so fortunate. The United States will be able to conduct operational planning in the knowledge that orbital assistance to terrestrial forces will be available, whereas the enemy will not be able to make such an assumption. That is what space control means and is all about—no more, but certainly no less.

Fourth, the conduct of war is a team effort; better understanding of the synergisms among land, sea, air, and space warfare is urgently required. A properly unified approach to deterrence and war exploits the fact that success or failure in each of the distinctive geographical environments for conflict can have great impact on the prospect for success or failure in the others and, ultimately, for victory, defeat, or stalemate overall. It is important and interesting to analyze what maritime and space power can contribute to each other's prowess. It is scarcely less important to broaden the scope of enquiry to embrace the sets of relations among activities in all environments. For example, the outcome of a space campaign could almost be predetermined by air power, sea power, or land power. Specifically, air strikes could cripple the ground segments of overcentralized space systems (and aircraft could launch ASAT interceptors into low earth orbit); naval vessels could impose a space blockade with antipodal ASAT weapons and could launch vehicles to reconstitute some satellite constellations; and land power could raid, or designate targets for aerial raids on, the ground facilities for space systems.

The relationship between maritime power and space strategy needs to be considered holistically. It is, of course, difficult to treat adequately the complex relations identified here, particularly since terrestrial combat experience with space adjuncts is so limited. Two points bear repeating. There may well be conflicts in the future wherein the adversaries are closely matched. In such cases an advantage in space could be the difference between victory and defeat. Also, virtually no matter how competent the United States may be in its exploitation of reliable access to orbit, the payoff from that competence can only be measured by the overall strategic leverage exerted on the enemy. Terrestrial forces have to make use of such advantages as success in space may yield. Like superiority at sea or in the air, superiority in space will enable victory, but alone will not win wars.

Fifth, for the indefinite future space power can only be an adjunct to terrestrial forces, but space warfare must be waged successfully on its own terms if it is to function reliably in that role. Because space is so novel an environment and space forces are so obviously an adjunct to terrestrial forces, the relationship between space control and (terrestrial) force enhancement from space tends to be neglected. Would enemy space power have to be defeated before U.S. space power could fulfill much of its promise? To date this question has been strictly hypothetical. In Desert Storm, however, all interested parties witnessed a live demonstration of the operational utility of space systems in war. Against a first-class adversary the United States will not have a space-system adjunct story unless it has a robust plan to seize and hold space control.

In World War II the Air Staff in London by and large subscribed to the strategically heretical view that long-range air bombardment could deliver victory without first defeating the German Air Force.[45] This "revolutionary" view opposed the "classical" principle that a country's fighting forces had to be defeated as the path to his general defeat. It may be recalled that Mahanian sea-power theory had emphasized the necessity for success in fleet battle as the condition for command of the sea. The same kind of strategic debate over the relationships among combat, control, and use which has been conducted concerning the sea and the air now looms for space. Much of the detail of a space campaign for the dispute of control remains obscure, but the applicable strategic principle is crystal clear. To secure and exploit reliable access to orbit in time of war, the United States will have to be prepared to defeat enemy forces of several kinds. The United States must assume that in some conflicts it will have to fight for the privilege of employing space assets as an adjunct to terrestrial forces. Moreover, a campaign to establish and enforce U.S. uses of space will need to be planned and waged on operational and tactical terms driven by the unique characteristics of the space environment and of space systems. The political and strategic logic of the space campaign will be provided by the total context of the war. The terrestrial clients of space systems have to be militarily empathetic to the distinctive nature of war for, in, and from space. In parallel, those charged with the planning of space campaigns should not be allowed to neglect the implications of the fact that space systems are only an adjunct to terrestrial forces.

Sixth, more thought is required on the issues of control and execution of military space missions in time of war. There is an understandable tendency for space systems to be regarded as inherently strategic in character. Those systems comprise relatively few, scarce, and valuable assets, and they serve military purposes literally on a worldwide basis. Assets this scarce and important, it is argued, must be controlled and tasked only on a highly centralized basis by an organization able to comprehend the entire scope of a conflict. The geophysically unique character of the space environment, the technically and tactically distinctive features of space systems, and the probable necessity to fight for space control would seem to leave little room for argument on this principle. When military value is distributed over only a few orbital platforms, it is entirely reasonable to insist on centralized control.

Beyond and behind the military logic that flows from the current character of U.S. space systems—low numbers of long-endurance, often multipurpose

---

45. See Charles Webster and Noble Frankland, *The Strategic Air Offensive Against Germany, 1939–1945*, vol. 1, *Preparation* (London: HMSO, 1961), 372.

vehicles with very slow reconstitution possibilities—lurk doctrinal and organizational preferences also. Moreover, doctrine can help drive force structure. Systems acquisition and operation is influenced by, for example, a
preference for central control and tasking for decentralized execution, as
contrasted with decentralized tasking for centralized execution. Those are
deliberately extreme cases. Plainly the appropriate story could be a distinctly
mixed one, system by system, or situation by situation.

The real issue is whether a centralized command and force structure for
space systems will be adequately responsive to the combat needs of tactical
land, sea, and air forces. A closely related issue is whether space forces can
perform well enough in the terms distinctive to space warfare to be sufficiently survivable to function as an adjunct to terrestrial warfare. The subject
is generally entirely familiar from the history of air power. Both a central
organization, that is, a unified space command, and major commands of
terrestrial fighting forces, such as CINCPAC and CINCLANT, have legitimate claims to authority over the operation of space forces. The challenge
is to develop space systems as an adjunct while ensuring that in "classical"
mold those systems can survive in space combat. Errors in that department
would be reminiscent of the oft-repeated French grand designs for the use of
their navy in support of their army without first resolving the fundamental
problem of sea control.

Seventh, sea-basing for some space launch vehicles (SLVs) and missile
defense elements could yield strategic benefits. That general flexibility of sea
power which derives from the mobility of ships able to utilize 70 percent of
the Earth's surface could be of major direct assistance in resolving the
inherently global problems of space combat. In addition to acquiring ASAT
weaponry complementary to air and missile defenses, the Fleet could
provide a highly survivable basing mode for vehicles stored for space-system
reconstitution. It could both defend itself at sea against most space threats as
well as contribute vitally to the general campaign for space control conducted
in a central way by the unified space commander. In addition, there may be
contexts wherein theater missile defense would have to be provided from the
sea if it is to be provided at all. Assuming an all-case, red carpet entry into a
region is as foolish as assuming a missile-free threat environment.

8

The Strategic Demand for Naval Power

The strategic value of naval power cannot be derived from the isolated study of ships, navies, or sea power. Naval power, on whatever scale of provision, is valuable only if a country needs it. It is the function of strategic reasoning logically to connect naval means and political ends. The history of a country's navy may be thought of as the dynamic product of a triangular struggle among domestic, foreign policy, and naval—which is to say professional military—pressures. Politicians with a domestic focus, people attentive to foreign policy questions, and defense professionals all have distinctive agendas with different implications for naval power.

Every period can be considered in light of the apparent trends of the day and the most persistent debates. Looking to the future, the strategic demand for U.S. naval power can be appreciated best in light of that future's likely defining characteristics. Prominent among the popular fallacies of this decade are the related notions that economic strength is becoming more important than military strength and that war between great powers is obsolete. In fact, economic power always has been, indeed has to be, the parent of military power, and the historical evidence for the proposition that major war is out of date is as yet inconclusive and unconvincing.

Policymakers and defense planners can be well advised by signs of the times, if they choose to recognize them. Claims for U.S. decline are quite persuasive, particularly in the linked economic and educational spheres, but declinist arguments need to be assayed in specific contexts. Relative economic decline or not, it is the case that the U.S. role as *the* essential leader for the undertaking of international peace and security duties is as plain today as ever it was. Those security duties have changed with the end of the Cold War, but the fact of effective U.S. military dominance (implying political leadership) is not really arguable. What has happened and what has failed to happen in Iraq, Somalia, and Bosnia all attest to the United States as the one essential, if not always effective, player for security in region after region after region. Unfortunately for those Americans who believed that victory over the evil empire in the Cold War would allow the United States a long "time out" from foreign security challenges and adventures, the post–Cold War world is characterized by disorder of increasing scope and on an increasing scale. Much of that disorder is the expression of what, generically, can be labeled cultural antipathy. The many tribes of humankind are in the process of showing just how innovative they can be in the prosecution of ancient hatreds. Peace is not breaking out in these 1990s.

National and transnational entities in conflict enjoy an ever widening range of opportunities to equip themselves with exceptionally lethal instruments. The world in which U.S. policymakers must operate, and for which U.S. defense planners must prepare, is one wherein weapons of great precision as well as of mass destruction are becoming more readily available to the less civilized of polities. The implications are troubling indeed for a naval power that may be the cutting edge of, but certainly will be an essential enabler for, U.S. intervention in regional conflicts. Some offset to the perils from local adversaries armed with late-model weapons can be secured by the aggressive U.S. exploitation of space. Enthusiasm for the potency that space systems can add to terrestrial forces does, however, need to be qualified somewhat by recognition that the space medium is not reserved exclusively for military exploitation by the United States. It is a safe prediction that space power will be a defining characteristic of the future for navies. In addition, indeed as a consequence, it is safe to predict that space will join the other geographical environments as a medium for conflict.

The strict limitations of air and space vehicles as carriers of bulky or heavy cargo translates as a permanent significance for U.S. maritime power as a servant of foreign policy and national strategy. Moreover, the temporary absence of any rival superstate renders that U.S. maritime power an asset of enhanced relative significance. During the Cold War decades it was always possible, and for a while it was plausible, to argue that nuclear use on a large scale would consign maritime endeavors to strategic irrelevance. In the 1990s the U.S. Navy is under no threat of being sidelined by nuclear menace, whereas the demise of yesterday's strategically worthy rival means that U.S. employment of its navy in regional conflicts is much less constrained than heretofore by fears of unwanted escalation. The detail of naval power, deployment, and action varies dramatically from era to era; but the structure of the strategic demand for effectiveness at and from the sea does not alter from decade to decade, or even from century to century.

The regionalization, even localization, of international security politics caused by the collapse of the Soviet superpower notwithstanding, assessment of the strategic value of the U.S. Navy has to encompass all segments of the spectrum of threat, regardless of apparent temporal proximity. It is necessary, therefore, to consider the strategic value of naval power with reference to three broad categories of demand: (1) the deterrence or conduct of *global war*, (2) the deterrence or conduct of *local and regional conflicts*, and (3) the support of *foreign policy*. The first category is plainly in eclipse—at present. Indeed, the United States has declared the primacy of a "regional defense strategy," but a navy built exclusively to handle regional and local rogues would fall far short of the needs of global struggle. This is not to suggest that a regionally focused navy could assume it would operate only in a permissive environment. As was noted above, the proliferation of high-technology weapons, not to mention the growing menace of weapons of mass destruction in local and regional hands, indicates the importance of U.S. military excellence across the board. One of the less controversial lessons of Desert Storm was to the effect that the more crushing the quantitative-qualitative superiority the lower the friendly casualties are likely to be. In an era when the United States will rarely have unarguably vital interests at stake in a regional quarrel, the conditions for U.S. military intervention will be certain to include the prospect that combat will be brief and casualties slight.

The uniformity of the sea and the flexibility of naval power mean that a future navy can be planned that will be less vulnerable than the future army to erroneous guesses about conflicts to come. The land is much more variable than the sea. In this decade the U.S. Navy will be reduced and reconfigured to be most effective in power projection against the shore, not for the conduct of blue-water campaigns to secure control of the oceans. The First Law of Prudence in Defense Planning, however, requires the making of provisions against the worst effects of unpleasant surprises. A U.S. Navy politically correct for the 1990s would be reshaped for modest regional conflicts and for constabulary duties in support of foreign policy. Unfortunately, such a navy would be both barely adequate to cope with strictly regional difficulties (how many simultaneous regional difficulties?) and dramatically unfit to deliver the strategic effectiveness the United States would need in the case of a new balance-of-power struggle in Eurasia. It would be much better for the all but insular continental United States to have a navy somewhat overprepared for regional commitments, rather than critically underprepared for a global scale of conflict.

The U.S. Navy today is emphasizing its new, actually renewed, orientation toward coastal, shallow-water operations. It does not follow, however, that such a coastal focus implies a navy of limited range. The coastal waters of most operational interest to the navy of the superstate guardian of international order are the coastal waters of Europe, Asia, and Africa.

The 1990s are proving no exception to the rule that scholarship follows official fashion, either to augment and develop or to oppose. Whatever the attitude adopted by such scholarship, the common denominator is a relative shortsightedness. The agenda for study is set by the trend in high policy. Without wishing "to boldly go" in a very large way whither others are not proceeding, I would like, nonetheless, to raise a question about the maritime future beyond tomorrow. Specifically, how might the current naval hegemony of the United States be challenged effectively and perhaps eroded or offset? This question needs to be posed, researched, and answered grand-strategically, not narrowly in naval terms. If for reason of military-technical vulnerability or because of political, legal, or sheer numerical constraints, the U.S. Navy were to cease to be a trusty instrument of order with a global range and reach, as a consequence the United States would lose a large fraction of her influence in world affairs. Bearing in mind the point registered much earlier in this book that U.S. and world trade is overwhelmingly *maritime* trade, a United States no longer effective globally in securing the freedom of the seas would be a United States electing to take major risks with economic well-being.

If the United States lacks transoceanic logistical excellence, it is a country confined to North America or to brief raiding strategies at great distances. States and coalitions anxious to neutralize, or at least reduce, the unique U.S. ability to reach around the world by sea and by air, can safely be assumed to be "red teaming" their U.S. naval and airpower problems. Future adversaries of the United States, no matter how imaginative their grand-strategic investigations, may find no plausible, reliable ways to deny U.S. air and naval power the quality of strategic effectiveness registered against Iraq in 1991. Nonetheless, U.S. defense planners should worry lest the strength of would-be adversary strategic motivation is the parent of effective invention. Bluntly stated, U.S. defense planners should not allow themselves the perilous indulgence of the assumption that the contemporary preeminence of U.S. naval and air power is permanent and irreversible.

It is no denigration of air power to claim that whatever might emerge as a world order later in this decade must, after the fashion of the Grand Alliance of World War II and of NATO in the Cold War, have a nervous system that is principally maritime. Given that large quantities of heavy and bulky goods can leave the United States only by sea, it is only through maritime power that U.S. policy can apply sustainable weight in any local, regional, or global conflict beyond North America. This judgment flows inexorably from the enduring facts of physical, political, and strategic geography.

AN APPROACH TO NAVAL POWER

The Cold War is over, but so also is what aptly has been called "the long peace."[1] From 1945 to the present has not exactly been an era of comprehensive peace, but it certainly has been the longest period in modern history wherein there was no war among the great powers of the age.[2] Why that was so is a matter of more than academic interest, as the structure of world security politics alters almost visibly.

Truly nothing fails like success.[3] For all its imperfections, real or just alleged, U.S. grand strategy and military strategy registered a historic

1. John Lewis Gaddis, "The Long Peace: Elements of Stability in the Postwar International System," *International Security* 19 (Spring 1986): 99–142.

2. Periods absent war among great powers: since 1945, 49 years; 1871–1914, 43 years; 1815–54, 39 years. These elementary statistics suggest that it would be an error to be overly self-congratulatory. The duration of "the long peace" is less extraordinary than some people have suggested. For historical perspective, see Jack S. Levy, *War in the Modern Great Power System, 1495–1975* (Lexington: University Press of Kentucky, 1983), and David Kaiser, *Politics and War: European Conflict from Philip II to Hitler* (Cambridge: Harvard University Press, 1990).

3. Or ". . . defeat is by far the better teacher." Edward N. Luttwak, *Strategy: The Logic of War and Peace* (Cambridge: Harvard University Press, 1987), 20.

triumph vis-à-vis the postwar Soviet threat both to the balance of power and to the humane values of Western civilization. The Atlantic Alliance named for an ocean geostrategically, as John Lehman notes appropriately,[4] has outlasted what warranted description as an evil empire. What now? What next? How many of the political attitudes and beliefs, strategic assumptions, and military and naval assets with which the United States entered the 1990s need to be discarded or adapted radically for the new post–Cold War world? Political and strategic vision and prediction is available in overabundant supply. The problem is to separate the sense from the nonsense and the prudent from the imprudent.

In his majestic study of Britain's Royal Navy in the long period of relative peace from the wars against imperial France until the Crimean War, C. J. Bartlett advises that "the formulation of naval policy is perhaps best viewed as a fluctuating, intermittent triangular struggle, with three main considerations, sometimes in conjunction, sometimes in opposition, determining the decisions. These three considerations may be described as domestic, foreign and naval."[5]

Bartlett's simple "triangular struggle" comprehends most of what is necessary for an understanding of the purpose of this chapter: to examine the strategic future of the Navy for the United States. The terms of debate over the future roles, size, and character of the U.S. Navy will shift among domestic, foreign, and naval—more generally military—arguments.

First, the *domestic* factor or consideration would allocate to the U.S. Navy scarce national assets on a scale utterly astrategic in derivation. Executive, legislative, and popular attitudes toward the Navy, its roles, size, and composition, are shaped in peacetime in part, and sometimes in good part, by stimuli that owe nothing to strategic phenomena. General political mood, the perceived health of the economy, and the relative political popularity of naval power contrasted with other objects for support by the public purse, all play in domestic consideration of the Navy.

Second, the *foreign* factor or consideration refers to the strategic or even political demand for naval support generated by foreign policy. Tanker escort services, the projection of major military-expeditionary power, and drug interdiction, to select three naval duties flowing from national foreign policy choices, all trigger demands for naval power. Of course, foreign policy demand for support can be precautionary as well as actually realized. The

4. John Lehman, "Half-Speed Ahead: Budget Strategy for a Strong Navy," *Policy Review* no. 53 (Summer 1990): 17.
5. C. J. Bartlett, *Great Britain and Sea Power, 1815–1853* (Oxford: Clarendon Press, 1963), 1.

terms of public and professional debate in the 1990s cannot be confined narrowly to the tangible contemporary needs of U.S. foreign policy; in addition, the United States has to provide prudently against possible future foreign policy needs.

Third, the broad *naval/military* consideration specifies that the U.S. Navy has to be retained with a combat prowess second to none, no matter how debates on foreign policy or domestic issues ebb and flow. To quote Bartlett again (on the 1815–53 period): "Naval supremacy could not be sacrificed, nor would the country have allowed such a thing, but many savings short of that point might be exacted."[6]

At least in principle, the politics of the naval budget in the United States in the 1920s and 1930s, as today in the 1990s, were in accord with Bartlett's characterization of the British context of the late 1810s. This third—really naval, certainly defense-professional—consideration points to the enduring need for the Navy to modernize; to take account of the naval and other maritime-relevant (largely air and space) capabilities of foreign countries. The U.S. Navy as an institution is the principal guardian of U.S. maritime capabilities. The making of high policy on the domestic scene or for the direction of foreign endeavor is not the responsibility of the Navy. But as an instrument of foreign policy, it is the duty of the Navy to be as ready as it can be, given resource constraints, for whatever the body politic chooses to order it to do. This commonsense point indicates a debating region of major difficulty for the Navy, since the subject here is the wisdom of preparedness, of being able to cope with more, or fewer, contingencies in a period of great uncertainty.

Following Sir Julian Corbett rather than Alfred Thayer Mahan, this chapter explores the future of the Navy from a unified perspective on likely U.S. defense needs. This discussion is less interested in naval strategy[7] than in the maritime dimension to U.S. grand and national military strategies. On the first page of his history of *England in the Seven Years' War*, Corbett referred to an aspect of his subject that did not alter with the evolution of military technology.

> Reaching higher and wider than what is usually understood by naval strategy [the category of action which Mahan claimed to be

---

6. Ibid.

7. There can be strategy for naval power, but it is not clear that there can be naval strategy (or nuclear strategy or air strategy). Strategy is strategy. This problem helped limit the value of Alfred Thayer Mahan, *Naval Strategy Compared and Contrasted with the Principles and Practice of Military Operations on Land* (Boston: Little, Brown, 1919; first pub. 1911).

unchanging], it is a branch of the art [of war] as vital for statesmen as it is for sailors, for diplomatists as it is for soldiers and by history alone can it be mastered. We may term it *the function of the fleet in war.* Marshalled in its place in the art of war, it will be seen to form, together with the functions of the army and diplomacy, a part of what is called the higher or major strategy [grand strategy, approximately], and to bear much the same relation to naval strategy as minor strategy does to tactics.[8]

Just as the sea, the air, and the space environments have no strategic meaning in isolation from the course of terrestrial events, so naval, air, and space strategies can be developed and assessed only with respect to a unified vision of national security in peace or war.[9] Unlike a work of art, a navy does not contain within itself the values that justify its existence. The merit, or lack thereof, in a navy is always relative both to the scale and character of burdens for foreign policy support placed upon it and to the quantity and quality of force provided by hostile polities that it may need to overcome.

Ultimately, the U.S. Navy, like the other services, generates potential *strategic effectiveness* over the ability or willingness of U.S. adversaries to take actions contrary to U.S. national interests. The terms of debate may seem to be over numbers of carriers or marine expeditionary brigades, or over dollars, but the true currency of debate should be the quantity and quality of potential strategic effectiveness the U.S. government will require from its navy. Yet the proper kind and scale of provision of strategic effectiveness cannot be debated intelligently out of context.

THE FUTURE STRATEGIC CONTEXT

A thirty-year span of concern is preferred here, both to reflect the operational longevity of major combat platforms and to capture the downstream legacy of decisions made in the 1990s. Imagination may be trumps, but trend-countertrend or characteristics-of-the-future analysis is a slippery project. Similarly, the "alternative futures" approach can swiftly degenerate into an

8. Sir Julian S. Corbett, *England in the Seven Years' War: A Study in Combined Strategy,* 2 vols. (London: Longmans, Green, 1918; first pub. 1907), 1:1–2 Emphasis added.

9. This is the principal theme in Colin S. Gray, *War, Peace, and Victory: Strategy and Statecraft for the Next Century* (New York: Simon & Schuster, 1990)

exercise in mere intellectual dexterity. For the purposes of this chapter, it is useful to discuss the future in terms of alleged characteristics judged to be false or very unlikely, as well as those characteristics judged probable or near certain.

Characteristics Rejected

- Rise of geoeconomics relative to geopolitics
- Decline in utility of force and military power

In a characteristically bold, though uncharacteristically unpersuasive, analysis, Edward N. Luttwak joined the ranks of those who discern and predict the progressive substitution of geoeconomic for geopolitical frames of reference for statecraft.[10] Unlike conditions in the heyday of mercantilist policy and military practice in the late seventeenth and throughout the eighteenth centuries, however, war is no longer profitable and cannot be approached as a business enterprise (as did the English promoters of war with Spain in 1739, for example).[11]

Even if people were strictly economic—that is, wealth-seeking—animals, the claims of geoeconomics relative to the concerns of geopolitics still would be limited. Proficiency in statecraft toward the latter should benefit those whose minds and calculators are focused on the former. Moreover, even when the case for the relative rise of geoeconomic concerns is stated with sophistication, still it generates the suspicion that carts and horses have been confused. Has the "Common Marketization"[12] of politics in Western Europe reflected or created the absence of recent geopolitical conflict among local states? People familiar with Norman Angell's *Great Illusion* should be excused some skepticism.[13]

The argument for the declining utility of force in international relations is as perennial as it is confused. Putting normative concerns aside, is it true to claim that the currency of force (by analogy, as credit or as cash) either is being devalued or has been devalued markedly? Unlike the situation two

10. Edward N. Luttwak, "From Geopolitics to Geoeconomics," *The National Interest*, no. 20 (Summer 1990): 17–23

11. See Daniel A Baugh, *British Naval Administration in the Age of Walpole* (Princeton, N.J.: Princeton University Press, 1965), 15.

12. Francis Fukuyama, "The End of History?" *The National Interest*, no. 16 (Summer 1989): 18.

13. Normal Angell, *Great Illusion: A Study of the Relation of Military Power in Nations to Their Economic and Social Advantage* (London: William Heinemann, 1911).

centuries ago, force is not very useful in current or future trade wars.[14] But no subject for statecraft and private commercial concern could be more geoeconomical than is access to, and the price of, oil, and no geoeconomical subject is more obviously dominated by the threat and use of force.

There is no doubt that the nuclear revolution has reduced, even removed, the policy utility of the massive actual use of force among great powers (by definition, today these have to be nuclear-armed), whereas at the same time the policy utility of the threat of such force has been stabilizing indeed in its apparent political consequences. Thus far, at least, which is to say with reference to the First and Second Worlds, nuclear weapons have favored the side of the status quo, the defensive camp in policy. But as nuclear weapons are more democratized in their ownership, it will become increasingly apparent that much of what U.S. defense analysts thought they understood about the utility of those weapons for policy and about nuclear doctrine was an understanding geopolitically and culturally confined to Soviet/Russian-American or East-West relations in an era now defunct.[15]

Arguments for the "obsolescence of major war" advertised and predicted by John Mueller[16] speak accurately enough to the debellicization of the societies of Western and Central Europe (always excluding the Balkans), to the all-too-obvious perils of actual conflict among nuclear-armed states (or their friends and allies), and to the long-recognized limitations to the utility of force for the resolution of economic problems. Nonetheless, trends can, indeed are wont to, be reversed. Current phases in East-West, let alone West-West, relations are special cases wherein, for different reasons, force indeed lacks utility, but from which simple and grand conclusions should not be drawn.

The period since 1945 has been one of violent peace and awesome proximate possibilities of catastrophe. With their eyes firmly, understandably, if in a blinkered way, fixed on the now secured prize of deterrence in U.S.-Soviet strategic relations, some defense analysts and scholars of foreign policy have reached conclusions about the prospects for a lasting peace that neither recent history nor reasonable prognoses for the future can sustain.

14	For example, see Richard Pares, *War and Trade in the West Indies, 1739–1763* (London: Frank Cass, 1963; first pub. 1936).

15. A point well made in Eliot A. Cohen, "The Future of Force," *The National Interest*, no. 21 (Fall 1990)· 15.

16. John Mueller, *Retreat from Doomsday: The Obsolescence of Major War* (New York: Basic Books, 1989).

Characteristics Accepted

- U.S. political and economic influence in decline
- U.S. military dominance, but not hegemony
- Increase in regional disorder
- Rise of cultural conflicts
- Proliferation of high-technology weapons and wider distribution of weapons of mass destruction (NBC weaponry)
- Growing importance of space
- The maturation of the environment as a national/international security concern
- The increase in the maritime dimension to U.S. national security as the post–Cold War world takes firmer shape.

In the last decade of the twentieth century the only true superpower is the United States. Nonetheless, for economic and political reasons the status of superpower means less than it did until recently. The apparent demise of the Soviet/Russian military threat to peripheral Europe and Asia is having the predictable effect of diminishing overseas demand and need for U.S.-provided extended deterrence vis-à-vis threats from the Heartland.[17] (The Gulf crisis was a different kind of case altogether.) As U.S. forces return from Europe, Washington will find it more and more difficult to be a true player, as opposed to an interested onlooker, in the politics of European security and hence in the politics of the balance of power in Eurasia. Players have to be present *on the ground*, otherwise they are tourists. Of course, the United States must always be a factor in the calculations of Europe's statesmen, but there is no substitute for local presence on a more than token scale. That, at least, has been the story of the past four centuries. The absence of a plausible Russian threat paradoxically limits the political influence of a U.S. superpower, which now appears to be more and more of an optional extra in the grand security designs of latter-day, would-be Metternichs.

Economically, the evidence for relative U.S. decline is unmistakable though in danger of overappreciation. In a nonmercantilist world the rise of new commercial blocs and new centers of manufacture and finance does

17. See Colin S. Gray, *The Geopolitics of Super Power* (Lexington: University of Kentucky Press, 1988)

not have to mean the relative impoverishment of Americans. The old formula of "political economy" points toward the nature of the U.S. problem and the problem of the world economy with its still very large U.S. component. Namely, Americans have made political choices, or are perceived to have done so, that have resulted in a protracted crisis of governance over their economy. Perception of this fact is well-nigh universal, at home in the United States as well as abroad. Having said that, it would be a most serious error to leap to the conclusion that the United States is in decline, à la Paul Kennedy.[18] That is not so and is not likely to be so. Imperial Spain in the seventeenth century, Great Britain in the 1960s and 1970s, Russia and Ukraine today: those were or are economies in decline. Nonetheless, there is no doubt that economic-financial leverage as a tool of U.S. statecraft is in peril as a result of the persisting lack of central grip in Washington on wise guidance for the U.S. economy. But U.S. problems in the field of political economy are more political and cultural than they are economic. The jury will be out for quite a while on the question of whether the domestically focused Clinton presidency can turn this situation around.

The classic definition of a great power is that it is a power that can stand up to any other great power in protection of its most vital interests. Russia retains much of the military arsenal that accorded the Soviet Union parity of political and strategic esteem with the United States, and undoubtedly is capable of deterring any U.S.-led encroachments on what its leaders judge to be vital interests. Nuclear weapons, being essentially defensive in their value for statecraft, are supremely persuasive instruments for the preservation of core values. If the strength of the Russian state were to be assayed solely with reference to the character and number of its strategic nuclear forces, then on this one dimension of a one-dimensional superpower Russia has lost little standing relative to the United States. The relative power of a state is not so measured, however. In Bartlett's triadic terms of analysis, it is evident that Russian foreign policy and some aspects of Russian military policy are securely hostage to the course of domestic events. Barring the appearance of some currently unimaginable foreign threat to Russian society, the Russian state lacks the requisite capacity for collective military action abroad. That condition will alter in due course, but in the meantime there is no East-West military balance to inhibit U.S. actions abroad. The course

---

18. Paul Kennedy, *The Rise and Fall of the Great Powers: Economic Change and Military Conflict from 1500 to 2000* (New York: Random House, 1987). A superb critical response is Samuel P. Huntington, "The U S.—Decline or Renewal?" *Foreign Affairs* 67 (Winter 1988/89): 76–96.

of U.S.-led action toward Iraq in 1990–91 would have been strategically impracticable under Cold War conditions. U.S. ratification of the START I treaty in October 1992 notwithstanding, it is not obvious that there is even a strategic relationship, let alone a strategic balance, between Russia and the United States today.

There is no hard and fast distinction between dominance and hegemony.[19] Nonetheless, the former is a reasonable description of the practical U.S. military condition in the mid-1990s vis-à-vis a wide range of global "ordering" duties. The United States has recovered a great deal of freedom of foreign policy and strategy action, at least with reference to a novel absence of external strategic restraints.

The political writ of the superpowers over regional friends and allies was always more or less tenuous, save with reference to Soviet control of its Warsaw Pact dependencies. Superpower–Third World alliances or other security arrangements were typically temporary marriages, or flirtations of mutual convenience. When regional quarrels were treated in Moscow and Washington as if they were subsets of the Great Game between East and West, however, there were often restraining hands provided by superpower statesmen and their proconsuls nervous lest some "Balkan trigger" for World War III might be lurking in a dark corner of the Middle East, Africa, or Asia. The central management of the "blocs" in, and bearing on, Europe, particularly in the East, served usefully to minimize the potential for crisis and war of strictly local or regional combustible material.

The occurrence of local and regional conflicts and the temptation or opportunity to intervene militarily will challenge U.S. statecraft and strategy increasingly over the next several decades. Even with its defense assets slimmed down dramatically from those extant at the close of the Bush administration in January 1993, the United States of the year 2000 and beyond will remain a military superpower with reference to all of the world's probable regional conflicts.[20] Removal of the partial harness of more or less distant Cold War connections, together with old and new political, cultural, and economic disputes, will help generate a distressing crop of regional crises and wars. The prediction of such disorder is easy. Though extreme cases, one can point to the recent unpleasantness in the Gulf and the current nastiness in the former Yugoslavia as the plainest of plain examples of just

19. But see John J. Mearsheimer, "Back to the Future: Instability in Europe After the Cold War," *International Security* 15 (Summer 1990): 13 n. 15.

20. For the grand design and details of the Clinton administration's "bottom-up" defense review, see Les Aspin, *Bottom-Up Review* (Washington, D.C.: Department of Defense, September 1993).

how conflictual local and regional politics can be. To cite the certainty of regional conflicts is a cliché. The difficulty is to decide what role or roles U.S. power of all kinds should play in some of those conflicts, *and for what purposes?*

The more subtle among strategic thinkers and practitioners through the centuries have been alert to the perils of ethnocentricity and to the salience of cultural empathy for strategic success. [21] In its celebrated chapter on the "Characteristics and Tactics of Various People," the classic text on strategy attributed to Byzantine Emperor Maurice (582–602), notes that "all nations do not fight in a single formation or in the same manner, and one cannot deal with them all in the same way." [22] It is ironic that a United States that belatedly but quite solidly had come to be culturally alert to a distinctively Soviet/Russian competitor by the 1980s, [23] now is faced with the daunting challenge to understand the cultures relevant to regional conflicts. There was wisdom for the ages in Bernard Brodie's well-known claim that "good strategy presumes good anthropology and sociology." [24]

In the twentieth century, as in the nineteenth, nationalism is proving to be the most potent political force. The distinguishable and more or less alien cultures of nations, or candidate nations, serve as fuel for conflict and impede conflict resolution. North-South issues in international relations are heavily about economics, but they are also "about" such cultural matters as ethnic or racial pride and identity, religious values, national or subnational political aspirations, and historical memories. As a continental-size but effectively insular superpower, which itself is a cultural melting pot (or at least, used to be), and historically has been accustomed to success, the United States is about as far removed from the Byzantine school of cultural empathy for foes in statecraft and strategy as it would be posssible to imagine. [25] For different reasons, Russians are similarly afflicted. If the United States anticipates a "defense" policy focused heavily on policing

---

21. See Ken Booth, *Strategy and Ethnocentricity* (London: Croom Helm, 1979), for a persuasive warning.

22. *Maurice's Strategikon: Handbook of Byzantine Military Strategy*, trans. George Dennis (Philadelphia: University of Pennsylvania Press, 1984), 113.

23. See Yitzhak Klein, "The Sources of Soviet Strategic Culture," *The Journal of Soviet Military Studies* 2 (December 1989): 453–90, and David R. Jones, "Soviet Strategic Culture," in *Strategic Power: USA/USSR*, ed. Carl G. Jacobsen (New York: St. Martin's Press, 1990), 35–49.

24. Bernard Brodie, *War and Politics* (New York: Macmillan, 1973), 332.

25. The contrast is even greater than that stated in the text. See Walter Emil Kaegi Jr., *Some Thoughts on Byzantine Military Strategy* (Brookline, Mass.: Hellenic College Press, 1983), particularly 10

duties in regional quarrels, let alone on "humanitarian interventions" (à la Somalia) it should ask seriously whether it has, or can acquire, the transcultural sophistication to be effective at tolerable cost. The failure of endeavors to "read" Saddam Hussein amply illustrate the point.[26] American modes of thinking, *mentalités*, need more adjustment for regional application than the structure or equipment of the armed forces do.

Until it ran afoul of Mauser rifles and Krupp artillery in the hands of the Boers, the British army's campaigns and expeditions in Africa in the nineteenth century were greatly eased by a gross level of military-technological superiority.[27] The same phenomenon enabled Portugal to dominate the Indian Ocean, Arabian Sea, and Persian Gulf in the sixteenth century in the face of well-established Arab sea power.[28] Unlike the British in Africa, or the Portuguese in the Indian Ocean, the U.S. Navy at the close of the twentieth century cannot assume that it will be able to operate in many truly low threat environments.

There are some heavily qualified parallels that can be drawn between the functions of Britain's Royal Navy for international order in the nineteenth century, and the functions for international order of the U.S. Navy in the post–Cold War world. However, the kind of U.S. Navy militarily appropriate for the global ordering duties that increasingly will be mandated by policy cannot be of the classic gunboat kind, though it will need to be able to operate extensively in shallow coastal waters.[29] This is not to imply that

26. Booth has noted that "strategists as a body are remarkably incurious about the character of their enemies and allies " *Strategy and Ethnocentrism*, 17. He approaches a good part of the truth when he advises that "strategy, society and culture cannot be divorced unless strategy is to be understood as a mere technique" (144). Military professionals are expert in the use, or in technically supporting the use, of force; they are not expert in the conduct of particular wars. For a concrete case, and all cases are concrete, rather than read Thomas Schelling on "compellence" (*Arms and Influence* [New Haven, Conn.: Yale University Press, 1961], 69–91) or Herman Kahn on escalation (*On Escalation: Metaphors and Scenarios* [New York: Praeger, 1965]), U.S. policymakers in 1990–91 would have been well advised to study carefully Samir al-Khalil, *Republic of Fear: The Inside Story of Saddam's Iraq* (New York: Pantheon Books, 1989).

27. See Brian Bond, ed., *Victorian Military Campaigns* (London: Hutchinson, 1967), and Daniel R. Headrick, *The Tools of Empire: Technology and European Imperialism in the Nineteenth Century* (New York: Oxford University Press, 1981).

28. See Charles R. Boxer, *The Portuguese Seaborne Empire, 1415–1825* (New York: Alfred A. Knopf, 1969), chap. 2.

29. See Antony Preston and John Major, *Send a Gunboat! A Study of the Gunboat and Its Role in British Policy, 1854–1904* (London: Longmans, Green, 1967), and James Cable, *Gunboat Diplomacy, 1919–1979: Political Application of Limited Naval Force*, 2d ed. (London. Macmillan, 1978) For the authoritative statement of the U.S. Navy's new coastal focus, see Sean O'Keefe, Frank B. Kelso II, and C. E. Mundy Jr., *From the Sea: Preparing the Naval Service for the 21st Century* (Washington, D.C.: Department of the Navy, September 1992).

there are regional conflict scenarios as stressful as would have been a campaign for control of the Norwegian Sea against a multidimensional Soviet threat. But the quality and quantity of naval power, with adjunct assistance from other dimensions of the military establishment, required by Britain in its campaign to retake the Falklands in 1982, and subsequent U.S. naval experience in the Mediterranean and the Persian Gulf, all serve to illustrate the global trend toward military establishments based on ever higher technology.

It is wholly improbable that useful regimes of restraint can be imposed on the international and transnational trade in high-technology, late model weaponry of all kinds. Such arms control vehicles as the Missile Technology Control Regime (MTCR) of 1987,[30] for example, falter under the malign effects of the sheer number of alternative weapon suppliers; the strength of states' (and even substate groups') motivations to be well armed; the profit impulse; and complex foreign policy goals on the part of many potential weapon supplier states. If the victors of World War I, some of whose political leaders were genuinely convinced that the "merchants of death" were at least partially responsible for the outbreak of the war,[31] were unable to achieve noteworthy controls over the international arms traffic in the 1920s, there is no good reason to believe that any set of governments could fare better today or in the future.

In addition to threats from advanced conventional munitions, U.S. forces operating in regional disputes will be at increasing risk to weapons of mass destruction (nuclear, chemical, and possibly biological). Many of the prognoses for nuclear proliferation drafted in the late 1950s and the 1960s have proved wildly pessimistic. Whether or not this was a case of a self-negating prophecy, one cannot be sure. Nonetheless, the perils of nuclear proliferation, certainly of chemical-weapon proliferation, seem to be a probable medium-term future. The apparent, though arguable, limited success to date of the Nonproliferation Treaty of 1968[32] should not be taken as a source of confidence for the future. Indeed, the extrapolation of regional

30. See Janne E. Nolan, *Trappings of Power· Ballistic Missiles in the Third World* (Washington, D.C.: Brookings Institution, 1991), and Kathleen C. Bailey, *Doomsday Weapons in the Hands of Many: The Arms Control Challenge of the '90s* (Urbana: University of Illinois Press, 1991), chaps. 8–10.

31. A representative period piece is Philip Noel-Baker, *The Private Manufacture of Armaments* (New York: Oxford University Press, 1937).

32. For sophisticated accounting, see Lewis A. Dunn: "Four Decades of Nuclear Nonproliferation: Some Lessons from Wins, Losses, and Draws," *The Washington Quarterly* 13 (Summer 1990): 5–18, and *Containing Nuclear Proliferation*, Adelphi Papers, no. 263 (London: IISS, Winter 1991).

military developments from the experience of the Cold War era needs to be treated with great caution. If world politics is moving at an accelerating pace toward, at best, a multipolar condition, the strength of local political motivation for the achievement of nuclear status is likely to rise dramatically; self-help for defensively motivated nuclear deterrence will be the order of the day. As the intervention, or forward, instrument of most frequent first choice, the Navy cannot afford to allow its political masters to make benign assumptions about the quality of military opposition it will have to face on behalf of U.S. foreign policy.

A world power, indeed *the* world power, has no prudent choice other than to exploit new technologies for the gathering and the transmission of information on a global basis. Military space systems are the supporting assets for which the generals and admirals required to operate far from home have been waiting throughout recorded history. Recent years have seen the coming of all-weather, day and night information gathering (of several different kinds) from orbit, in addition to the service functions that have been performed with increasing competence and reliability for the better part of two, and even three, decades (e.g., communications, navigation, attack early warning). As developed in detail in Chapter 7, these facts point to a significance of space-system "adjuncts" for the U.S. Navy that warrants description as a defining characteristic of the military environment in the decades ahead.[33] Of course, for every solution there is a problem, usually several.

As space systems move from the status of useful to essential adjuncts to terrestrial operations, much as aircraft did between 1920 and 1945, so they will be opposed actively by enemies no more willing to concede freedom of orbital use than they would freedom of the air or of the sea.[34] Of more immediate concern, the U.S. defense community needs to accelerate the pace of operational accommodation of support from space, come to grips with the probable character of conflict in the unique geophysical environment of space, decide critical issues of command and tasking for scarce space systems, and conduct timely integrated offense-defense planning so that the functions of military space benefit maximally from an evolving program of missile defense.[35]

33. See Chapter 7.
34. See Colin S. Gray, *Space as an Environment for Warfare* (Fairfax, Va.: National Security Research, April 1989).
35. Whether or not what used to be called the SDI ever leads to a deployed strategic defense system (SDS) with space components, there can be no doubt that it has had a beneficial impact on

By way of a partial analogy to the significance of space to a world power, one could cite the importance of the new technology of the telegraphic (particularly *submarine*) cable for the world-wide British Empire of a hundred years ago. In 1898, for example, Britain owned no less than 60 percent of the world's telegraphic cable and was ready, in time of war, promptly to cut the cables of rival powers. British determination in 1898 that it "ought to cut an enemy's cables wherever necessary for strategic purposes" has some nontrivial meaning for the antisatellite function today. [36]

There is some danger that citing the environment as a national and international security issue-area that could help characterize the next thirty years, might be seen as a bow to the merely fashionable concerns of the day. Yet the warning signs of possible cumulatively major climatic change are too serious to be ignored, and history should be allowed to alert us to the empire-shaking, or ending, consequences that can flow from such change. [37] The challenge here is to relate the early warning signs of possible global warming or cooling to the missions of the U.S. Navy.

If the Navy is likely to be the policy instrument of choice for the expression of U.S. interest in regional order, then the factors fueling disorder have to be subjects for attention in Washington. If the pessimists are proved more right than wrong in their prediction of adverse change in the global climate over the next century, then the political consequences are near certain to be massively unfriendly for the stability of any new world order and for the development of a global community of nations. Some countries could lose much of their most fertile territory, and already marginal food-producing regions could revert to desert. (Of course one should not discount the likelihood of an improvement of climate in some regions.) If one wished to write a script for worldwide social and political unrest in the next century, domestic and international, climate-driven insecurities would have to be a prime, if hugely uncertain, candidate.

---

thought and planning concerning space system survivability. The SDI program augmented preexist-ing interest in space surveillance and tracking systems; low-cost, high-volume space transportation systems; widely distributed value among orbital platforms for survivability; and all kinds of vulnerabil-ity reducing options, technical and tactical, active and passive.

36. Colonial Defence Committee, quoted in Paul M. Kennedy, "Imperial Cable Communica-tions and Strategy, 1870–1914," in *The War Plans of the Great Powers, 1880–1914*, ed. Paul M. Kennedy (London: George Allen & Unwin, 1979), 86. For Germany in 1914 cable use was "nice to have" but far short of essential for the conduct of grand strategy. After all, imperial Germany was expecting to wage and win a wholly continental war in the West in a period of forty-two days.

37. An outstanding study that (just) predates the current debate on global warming, is H. H Lamb, *Climate History and the Modern World* (New York: Methuen, 1982).

The U.S. Navy cannot and does not need to know today whether environmental catastrophe is science or science fiction. But people conducting defense planning in the 1990s should examine a broad canvas. After all, the investment decisions of this decade must support policy demands far into the next century. Anyone now inclining to a thoroughly commercial view of the future of international security politics needs to consider that a U.S. Navy inherited by policymakers in the early 2000s from the 1990s may be charged with deterrence and actual denial duties in the face of a truly global source of political disorder. The global power of the 1990s, the United States, already is on advance notice that an environmentally driven eruption could shake the content and ethos of world politics in the middle future. It has been the grim history of international relations to date to record the general preference of most countries to risk hanging separately rather than lose national control of policy choices through genuinely collective efforts at defense in the face of disaster. An accelerating environmental disaster would strain the potential for civility in international relations far beyond the point where any new world order would be likely to be able to cope. International cooperation for collective security is one thing when the peril is distant and the choices none too painful. But if the peril is here and now, and the plundering of other polities can provide near-term relief, let civility beware!

Finally, the maritime, including more narrowly naval, dimension to national security is likely to increase in significance as the post–Cold War world matures. Physical and political geography remain as key shapers of the structure of security policy. The passing of the Cold War left much of the framework of U.S. choice in grand strategy and military strategy intact. U.S. policy toward the U.S.S.R. after World War II was directed to thwart the menace posed by that state to the balance of power in Europe and Asia. The menace lay in a potential maldistribution of power, not in the U.S.S.R. per se. The Cold War, and the U.S. and Allied grand and military strategies applied to it, was about the balancing of power. The United States has a permanent need for power to be balanced in, not with, Europe and Asia.[38]

The scale of the maritime dimension to U.S. national security policy is indicated by the enduring facts of physical and political geography. Now that the danger of large-scale nuclear conflict has been banished for a while, the principal factor that long worked to limit the relevance of maritime factors for U.S. national security is similarly banished. Argument for the

38. For reasons developed in detail in Gray, *Geopolitics of Super Power*.

critical significance of U.S.—and Allied—maritime power in any general East-West war always had to be premised on the belief that there would be no major and prompt nuclear "exchange."[39] With large-scale nuclear exchanges, though certainly not all nuclear dangers, effectively removed from the defense planner's horizon as plausible possibilities, sea-based power is liberated to fulfill its historic missions.

One important reason why the maritime dimension to U.S. national security may wax rather than wane over the course of the next several decades is the possibility, or probability, of economic competition with Japan leading once again to political-military conflict. If the next great conflict in world politics is between coalitions led by Japan and the United States, a great deal of the military action would be at sea and about who is at liberty to use the sea. The logic in recent polemical tracts on the subject of the emerging renewal of the traditional Pacific rivalry between Japan and the United States is not thoroughly persuasive, but it warrants some respect.[40]

Time is, and has always been, a critical factor in the significance of sea power for the course and outcome of conflict. Whatever the form it assumed, sea power, as classically comprehended (that is, excluding sea-based nuclear bombardment of the land), functioned slowly in its strategic effect on the course of a conflict.[41] There is a "material" school of defense analysis that sees the strategic world remade anew with every noticeable change in military technology,[42] but the truth is rather different. Despite the installation of nuclear propulsion in many of the capital ships launched over

39. See Linton F. Brooks: "Naval Power and National Security: The Case for the Maritime Strategy," *International Security* 11 (Fall 1986): 58–88, and "Conflict Termination Through Maritime Leverage," in *Conflict Termination and Military Strategy: Coercion, Persuasion, and War,* ed. Stephen J. Cimbala and Keith A. Dunn (Boulder, Colo : Westview Press, 1987), 161–72.

40. The leading, well-argued polemic is George Friedman and Meredith Lebard, *The Coming War with Japan* (New York: St. Martin's Press, 1991). The title tells all. John H. Maurer, "The United States and Japan: Collision Course," *Strategic Review* 21 (Spring 1993): 41–51, provides a persuasive rebuttal, though there are grounds for apprehension lest the workings of "friction," Murphy's Law, and just poor statesmanship make a reality of the Friedman-Lebard thesis.

41. The bombardment of coastal fortresses and the harassment of coastal roads with naval artillery were commonplace features of naval action against the shore. It could be argued that the SSBN force is simply a modern example of weapons suitable for a class of naval activity which can be called shore bombardment. In strict logic such a claim has merit. Common sense, however, suggests that large-scale action against the shore by SLBMs would prove to be independently decisive to the course and outcome of a war. Quantitative changes, in range and destructive energy, beget qualitative changes.

42. This formulation is an adaptation of the argument presented in Clark G. Reynolds, *History and the Sea: Essays on Maritime Strategies* (Columbia: University of South Carolina Press, 1989), 12–13.

the past quarter-century by the United States and the Soviet Union, the fact remains that the contemporary speed and endurance of most of the sea-bound elements that comprise sea power are not significantly different from the figures for, say, 1945 or even 1918. Power projected from the sea, assuming it is ready to sail when so ordered, traverses oceanic distances in days or weeks. The geophysical characteristics of particular environments have recognizably persistent implications for technology, logistics, tactics, operations, and strategies.[43] Identity, and hence location, of the foe makes a difference for the application, indeed for the direct applicability, of maritime power. Also, changing technologies impose large adjustments on naval tactics and the design of naval operations. But the policy demand for the effectiveness generated for a maritime power by sea power has proved remarkably enduring over the course of centuries.

Historical analogies always require some measure of translation and a little imagination if they are to serve a useful purpose. Nonetheless, as Alfred T. Mahan put it: "Historical instances, by their concrete force, are worth reams of dissertation."[44] The closest analogy to the defense planning challenge for the U.S. Navy in the 1990s is the case cited at the beginning of this chapter; Britain's Royal Navy in the period after 1815. *Then* for the Royal Navy, as *in the 1990s* for the U.S. Navy:

- A great hot war (1793–1815), or cold war (1947–89), had been won.
- Yesterday's enemy, though no longer a super threat, remained heavily armed (it was the Spanish, not the French, navy that was destroyed at Trafalgar in 1805), was politically unstable, and might be needed in the future as an ally-of-convenience for the balance of power.
- Sea power was liberated, strategically, from the necessity to be ready to wage decisive fleet-scale action in home waters (or to confine the Soviet/Russian Navy to its fortified bastions), but considerations of European—major league—security politics

43. For an example of this phenomenon from a different technological era, see John H. Pryor, *Geography, Technology and War: Studies in the Maritime History of the Mediterranean, 649–1571* (Cambridge: Cambridge University Press, 1988). "I have become ever more convinced that certain aspects of the physical geography of the Mediterranean Sea, when considered in relation to the capabilities of maritime technologies of the time, exercised a profound effect on the course and competition between Islam and Christendom over a very long period of time [actually, nearly a millennium]" (xiv).

44 Mahan, *Naval Strategy*, 161.

meant that "big war" planning considerations were always present, if in a minor and generally rather relaxed key.

- It was possible, while assuming only minimal risks to core national values in home waters, to deploy and operate as a global arm of a foreign policy that pursued "order" and British/American commercial, humanitarian, and even ideological interests, worldwide.[45]

Anyone asking today "what use is the U.S. Navy in the post–Cold War era," should delve cautiously for inspiration into the roles of Britain's Royal Navy from 1815 to 1853.

THE VALUE OF THE NAVY

Understandably enough, the U.S. body politic has yet to come to grips with the implications of the dawning new age. Journalists, and others who are wont to focus on the new, tend to resist the idea that maritime strategy has a general content that comprises an enduring reality for U.S. security. Even with radical shifts in the international political system the country's need for a maritime dimension to its grand strategy, and the substance of what naval power typically can and cannot do, does not change.

It is necessary to ask whether the *structure* of the U.S. security condition is changing. To most people the answer to this question seems to be an all but glaringly obvious yes. Indeed, given that the Cold War is over, why would one need even to pose the question? The answer is that although the Cold War is no more, the concept of *the* Cold War was always a simple-minded notion that obscured as much as it clarified. Not unlike the misleading metaphor of "arms race," a convenient concept can distort reality. From the very time of its founding, the Soviet Union waged cold war, or war in peace, with the Western world. Moreover, a condition of war in peace, although unusual in international relations, is far from unique to the erstwhile U.S.-Soviet case (ask the Arabs and Israelis).

The enduring reality of a potential for hegemonic menace in Eurasia is more important as a guiding influence on defense planning than is the demise of the so-called Cold War. *In practice*, U.S. geostrategy from

45. For example, see C. J. Bartlett, ed., *Britain Pre-Eminent: Studies of British World Influence in the Nineteenth Century* (London: Macmillan, 1969), 172–93, and G. S. Graham, *Great Britain in the Indian Ocean, 1810–1850* (Oxford: Clarendon Press, 1967).

1947–48 until 1990 was organized primarily around the mission of containing Soviet power and influence within Eurasia. *In principle*, U.S. geostrategy was organized primarily around the mission of containing the current threat to the balance of power in Eurasia, which happened to be the U.S.S.R.

The problem for the careful student of strategy is not so much the identification of trends (the demotion, then removal of the Soviet/Russian threat, preeminently), but rather the interpretation of their meaning and determination of their probable consequences. Is the structure of the U.S. security condition changing radically? Technical, tactical, and operational errors generally can be absorbed and tolerated if the guiding policy and strategy have been well chosen. One recalls with profit the axiom that "errors in strategy can be corrected only in the next war."[46] History tells us that the United States will be surprised by some events and that many mistakes will be made in matters of detail. The U.S. defense community cannot avoid being surprised and cannot prevent error over details. But it should be possible for U.S. policymakers and defense planners to identify the structure of the future U.S. security condition correctly. To assist them in their search for a benchmark, one could say that a fundamental change in the structure of the U.S. security condition would be effected, or would be underway, first, if history has ended, Francis Fukuyama–style, if geoeconomics triumphs over geopolitics, and if "the obsolescence of major war" becomes a fact, as opposed to merely an interesting idea.[47] Second, the very structure of the U.S. security condition would alter if there is never again (say, for thirty years) a superstate or supercoalition menace to the balance of power, or to the tolerably free flow of world trade, in Europe and Asia.

It is not at all obvious that Russia, or some other entity (for example, a German-led *Mitteleuropa*), has vanished as a threat to the balance of power in Europe and Asia. The fact of change cannot be denied, that the change is necessarily and reliably benign certainly can be. What follows is discussion of the probable demands that U.S. policymakers will make on the U.S. Navy. In order to avoid the perils of a spurious precision, the categories are deliberately broad. There are many ways in which the purposes, functions,

46. For some related observations, see Michael I. Handel, "Clausewitz in the Age of Technology," *The Journal of Strategic Studies* 9 (June/September 1986): 87 n. 5.

47. Respectively: Fukuyama, "The End of History?"; Luttwak, "From Geopolitics to Geoeconomics"; and Mueller, *Obsolescence of Major War*.

and utility of a navy can be classified.[48] Too often, though, attempts to explain the uses of naval power reduce to mere typologies or even to a blossoming encyclopaedism, as impressive-looking lists of the obvious are presented.

A simple three-way approach is most appropriate to the possible and probable, active or residual, strategic demands by high policy on the Navy. Rank-ordered two ways, by inherent importance and by assessed likelihood, this elementary scheme captures what most needs to be captured about the subject of the prospective policy and strategic utility of the Navy, without venturing needlessly into distracting and arguable detail.

IMPORTANCE	PROBABILITY
1. Deter or defend in global war	1. Support foreign policy
2. Deter or defend in regional or local conflict	2. Deter or defend in regional or local conflict
3. Support foreign policy	3. Deter or defend in global war

"Support foreign policy" could refer also to the other two categories of Navy employment. The purpose here, however, is to distinguish generically among capabilities and activities designed: to help deter and defend in the context of a possible World War III—the principal focus of the Maritime Strategy of the 1980s (and, much earlier, of the thinking of Admiral Forrest Sherman in the late 1940s)[49]—to enable the United States to exert optimum influence to deter and, if need be, actually wage regional or local conflict, and to provide that forward local presence in support of foreign policy goals in cases other than those obviously covered under the categories of global and regional or local war. Needless to say, perhaps, there can be open boundaries among these three categories and the Navy's force structure can be built confidently with a view to the varied utility of particular assets among the categories of action, actual or potential.

In the 1990s, the dominant scenario for the Maritime Strategy has lost relevance. Global protracted non-nuclear war can be dismissed from the defense planner's consciousness because there is no live and malevolent enemy of superpower scale. Unfortunately, it is almost trivially easy to

48. A useful treatment is provided in Eric Grove, *The Future of Sea Power* (Annapolis, Md.. Naval Institute Press, 1990), chap. 11.

49. See Palmer, *Origins of the Maritime Strategy*, and Roger W. Barnett and Jeffrey G. Barlow, "The Maritime Strategy of the U.S. Navy: Reading Excerpts," in *Seapower and Strategy*, ed. Colin S. Gray and Roger W. Barnett (Annapolis, Md.: Naval Institute Press, 1989), 324–49.

mishandle the debate on this leading aspect of the subject of the utility of naval power to the United States. Prudent, history-sensitive argument readily lends itself to caricature as allegedly expressing a yearning for yesterday's threat, for the threat that functioned as the principal influence over the size of the U.S. fleet.

Global War

The course and outcome of any great balance-of-power, for which read "global," conflict in and for Eurasia would be shaped significantly by U.S. sea power, not just U.S. naval power. That statement assumes that nuclear weapons will not be used on anything other than a light and local scale. In its critical polemical dimension, yesterday's Soviet threat has evaporated along with the state that generated it. If the U.S. Navy, on anything remotely akin to its late 1980s scale and quality, is keyed for justification to a belief in the existence of a major foe or foes with malevolent near-term policy intentions, then the political and strategic case for a monumental scale of reduction in U.S. naval forces would be a powerful one. It so happens, however, that even if the politics of support for a large and diverse U.S. Navy are influenced nontrivially by trends in Russian-oriented news, there is a great deal to be said about the size and quality of that Navy that bears scarcely at all on those trends.

The Russian political future is exceedingly uncertain. In the context of economic collapse at home and political humiliation abroad, virtually anything is possible in Russia, provided it is broadly compatible with deep-seated Russian values. Moreover, some of the Russian military establishment, certainly its more technology-dependent, long leadtime forces, has been relatively unaffected by the current unrest. The structure of U.S. security concern with a giant, albeit politically fractured, reduced, and unstable military power in Eastern Europe and Asia is very much intact.

The perilous fragility of the post–Cold War world could be revealed by the events of a few hours. A successful conservative coup in Moscow would detonate a raft of American op-ed pieces "proving" that the new Russian Revolution always had to end in tragedy. Remember the new China and Tiananmen Square in June 1989? This analysis is only cautionary; it is not a prediction. There is a possibility that the empire could attempt a come-back, both domestically and in its international setting.

Short-legged armies and tactical air forces can be built or rebuilt consider-ably more rapidly than can navies. Regardless of the shifting tenor of political relations in Europe and Asia, the United States needs to be permanently watchful of the balance of power within those continents. Given the political and strategic impracticality of nuclear bombardment, [50] and notwithstanding the merits in air power of several kinds, *it is primarily through the maritime dimension to its grand and military strategies that the United States casts her weight for deterrence or defense in the security affairs of Eurasia.* The reason is so elementary that nonsailors are wont to forget it. The United States is an effectively insular superpower that can intervene militarily in Europe and Asia more than briefly only if it enjoys a working control of transoceanic lines of communication and only if it commands the services of a large pool of merchant shipping. There will be an enduring latent threat to the balance of power in Europe and Asia; that is the very nature of international politics. That threat may or may not be Soviet or Russian in identity, or principal identity, while in general land-power menaces to Eurasian continental security could mature and be executed relatively rapidly. The effective basis for decisive U.S. intervention to arrest the pace of such a dire course of events would have to be primarily maritime in nature. As always in sea power–land power confrontations, superior sea power functions primarily as a great enabling agent. In the future, deterrence of and defense against the use of weapons of mass destruction will need to hold as vital adjunct-enablers, lest the course of history be ambushed by some desperate continental statesman who suddenly discerns a bleak future and considers rolling the dice.

The U.S. policy need for the strategic services of the Navy in a World War III context does not hinge entirely on the reemergence of some *continental* would-be hegemon. John J. Mearsheimer overstated a fundamentally sound case to the effect that the prospects for conflict in the Europe of the 1990s and beyond are greater than obtained in the Cold War era. [51] Unlike the period 1947–90, the 1990s and beyond will not witness a European security order dominated by two superstate-coalition leaders who have no specific issues of contention between them. The possible fault lines

---

50. The United States has to provide nuclear deterrence because only nuclear weapons can deter nuclear weapons. However, nuclear-oriented, as opposed to nuclear-covered, deterrent and compellent strategy stories have little credibility today. The critical question of what use are strategic (nuclear) forces is a topic that typically attracts only superficial attention. The explanation is that it is politically inherently a "loser" as a subject to discuss, so politicians and officials shun it like the plague, whereas scholars find the subject too difficult as well as somewhat distasteful. See Robert Jervis, *The Meaning of the Nuclear Revolution: Statecraft and the Prospect of Armageddon* (Ithaca, N.Y.: Cornell University Press, 1989).

51. Mearsheimer, "Back to the Future."

in a future that could spawn "Balkan triggers" are many and beyond confident management even by experienced statesmen.

Despite the European focus of much of U.S. national security policy and strategy since 1941, it should not be forgotten that the United States entered World War II via hostilities in the Pacific and that virtually all of the actual combat waged by Americans during the Cold War occurred in Asia, and Pacific-rim Asia at that. As was noted earlier in this chapter, it would be as foolish to dismiss the prospect for renewal of the great U.S.-Japanese struggle as it would be to predict it with confidence. What matters at this late juncture in the discussion is to register the possibility of a maritime-air and generally high-technology East Asian challenge to a U.S. guarded international political, economic, and security order. That possible East Asian challenge, which could be Japanese, Chinese, or Sino-Japanese in form, need not preclude the simultaneous emergence of a would-be hegemonic continental menace in Europe.

Most of the U.S. forward military presence in and about Europe will be deactivated or redeployed back to North America over the next several years. Elsewhere in the world it is also plain to see that forward bases will be anything but politically locally secure as this decade matures (witness the demise of the long-standing U.S. bases in the Philippines). Given this trend, it is evident that transoceanic maritime power projection and logistic sustenance will be important in the postwar world as never before.[52] U.S. policy interests in seeing that power remains balanced within Eurasia is as high as ever. Nuclear strategy can provide no compensating strategic effectiveness for absent U.S. forces or an absent regional logistic infrastructure. If the possibility of major conflict in Europe and Asia is real if not imminent, if nuclear weapons cannot hold the fort, and if the side of order falls short in one or many dimensions of the capacity for collective action, then the deterrent and defensive value of sea power, and particularly of the U.S. Navy, has to be unusually significant.

It has been true for centuries that major warships have been the most complex machines produced by contemporary state and society. It follows that navies take many years to build or rebuild (see Chapter 5). The future being by definition beyond detailed foreknowledge, naval force planners and their political masters cannot possibly calculate precisely the risks to vital U.S. interests implicit in decisions to effect major reductions in the size and capabilities of the Fleet. Nonetheless, some discipline for policy and plan-

---

52. For complementary judgments, see Grove, *Future of Sea Power*, 202.

ning can be provided through recognition of the probable presence or absence of the political fuel with which a global conflict might ignite. This fuel has to be assayed geopolitically and geostrategically and not according to the tone of the latest speeches by politicians. History suggests that the structure of security and insecurity that feeds conflict has at its heart the distribution of power. [53]

Regional and Local Conflict

It is not controversial to assert the importance of regional and local conflict for U.S. national security policy, and of a large and diversely capable U.S. Navy for the support of national policy in such conflict. Because of the uniformity of the sea and the inherent flexibility of sea power, it is less important for naval than for army planners to be able to specify long in advance where they expect to be called on to exercise their trade. This is not to make light of sharply differing climatic and navigational settings, but it is to affirm that "all the seas of the world are one" in a sense that cannot be said of the land. [54]

Desert Storm meant nothing in particular for the future demands likely to be placed on the Navy. The conflict with Iraq was very stressing logistically, in that it was focused on the furthest region possible from the base of U.S. strength and could not benefit from the outset from much in-place local U.S. logistics infrastructure, not to mention the extreme discomfort to personnel and the strain on machinery created by weather and extreme terrain. However, U.S. forces were allowed a totally unopposed buildup in a friendly neighboring country; Iraq had no naval power (or allies with naval power); and the local terrain was relatively far more permissive of U.S. exploitation of its technological-tactical strengths than was the triple-cover jungle of, say, Southeast Asia.

53. A modern treatment is Kenneth N. Waltz's controversial text, *Theory of International Politics* (Reading, Mass.: Addison-Wesley, 1979), chap. 6. Robert Keohane, ed., *Neorealism and Its Critics* (New York: Columbia University Press, 1986), hits the whole area. The distribution of power is central to Colin S. Gray, "Strategic Sense, Strategic Nonsense," *The National Interest*, no. 29 (Fall 1992): 11–19. Owen Harries, "Fourteen Points for Realists," *The National Interest*, no. 30 (Winter 1992/93): 109–12, is a fount of common sense.

54. The quotation continues: "With a few insignificant exceptions—salt lakes rather than seas—they are all connected one with another. All seas, except in the case of circumpolar ice, are navigable. A reliable ship, competently manned, adequately stored, and equipped with means of finding the way, can in time reach any country in the world which has a sea coast, and can return whence it came." J. H Parry, *The Discovery of the Sea* (Berkeley and Los Angeles: University of California Press, 1981), xi.

There is no research-accessible objective truth about the United States and regional conflict. Eliot A. Cohen made a powerful and persuasive point when he asserted that "Saddam Hussein is a man who must be stopped, his sword broken, and his power wrested from him. Other nations must play their part, *but only the United States can lead the fight.*"[55] A conflict-prone world will witness many fights that "only the United States can lead" in the name of collective security, a new world order, and the like. But most of those fights should be left to the local principals. Moreover, it is as likely as not that the United States will decline to enter the lists in some cases of conflict where perhaps it should function as champion. It is virtually a matter of individual preference whether a possible U.S. intervention in the former Yugoslavia be labeled an example of "imperial temptation" or of responsible guardianship over human values and an emerging new structure of order.[56]

The Gulf War of 1991 performed the useful service of reminding critics of a large navy that the world contains increasingly powerful regional actors. It so happens that for pressing reasons of strategic geography Iraq has been very much a continental, indeed an all but land-locked, power. Unusually strong though Iraq was in land power, this potentially stressful case illustrated the point that Grenada and Panama were exceptions among possible military operations. When the United States chooses to intervene in a regional or local quarrel as leader of the posse for collective security, it should do so only with high assurance of achieving prompt success. When the superpower guardian of order chooses to intervene in a region it should do so only with a playing field sharply tilted in its favor.

Due recognition of the uniqueness of the current U.S. geopolitical role on behalf of international order, the diversity of potential policy demand for naval support in regional and local conflict, the day-in/day-out foreign-policy duties of the navy of the maritime superpower, and the residual anxieties about truly "big game" possibilities in Europe and Asia provide suitable perspectives on issues of naval force size and quality. An aspect of Desert Storm with enormous significance for U.S. military flexibility was the fact that it was the only crisis then extant. Should America's foes, deliberately or inadvertently, decline to present themselves *seriatim* for deterrence or coercion, the case for a larger navy would become all but self-

55. Eliot A. Cohen, "How to Fight Iraq," *Commentary*, November 1990, 27.
56. The title tells all in Robert W. Tucker and David C. Hendrickson, *The Imperial Temptation: The New World Order and America's Purpose* (New York: Council on Foreign Relations Press, 1992).

evident, even to those blind to the merit of mass, of numbers or brute arithmetic, in strategic affairs.

The argument presented here is primarily existential. One cannot presume to predict that the newly regional focus in the evolving U.S. defense policy of the mid-1990s must translate into further heavy military action around the globe. But there certainly will be many regional and local conflicts around the world in which the United States discerns national interests that are substantial, if rarely truly vital (that is, plainly worth fighting to protect or advance). If the United States wishes to imprint its policy preferences on the course and outcome of regional and local conflicts, by and large its instruments of persuasion will have to comprise, or be sustained by, maritime power.

Support Foreign Policy

This third broad category of naval function is far less controversial than even the second one. As a general rule there is scant room for dispute over the utility of sea-based power in regional and local conflicts; what controversy there may be pertains more to policy decisions to intervene in the first place than to the selection among grand-strategic instruments.

In a post–Cold War world the U.S. Navy—like Britain's Royal Navy after 1815—is likely to be reassigned, redeployed, and eventually even physically notably reconfigured for diplomatic and constabulary roles. In support of U.S. and the world community's interests in order at sea, the most powerful navy of the day will more and more come to assume the policeman's and diplomat's roles at the expense of the warrior's.[57] The logic of this argument is modestly persuasive, but it does beg for qualification. Prominent among the reasons why diplomatic and constabulary roles should not be permitted to assume anything resembling dominant status toward U.S. policy for its navy is the consideration that the global-war problem of deterrence and defense is not—at the moment—pressing, but it is by no means solved. Moreover, the demands of occasional regional conflict conducted half-a-world away from the U.S. Navy's home ports will far exceed the ability of a constabulary navy to cope. Also, the First Law of Prudence in Defense Planning forbids it. The Law states that defense planners, though surprised by future events, should have made provision to limit the damage that could

57. See Ken Booth, *Navies and Foreign Policy* (London: Croom Helm, 1977), and Geoffrey Till, *Modern Sea Power: An Introduction* (London: Brassey's Defence Publishers, 1987), chap. 10.

be wrought by the effects of surprise. How flexible is the chosen force posture in the face of major and unexpected unpleasant events? A constabulary navy could not adjust to cope with a significant regional crisis, let alone with a great-power quarrel pregnant with the potential for global conflict. A global navy, however, designed—following mobilization or reconstitution—to cope with world war and certainly with a regional crisis, certainly could cope well enough with the day in, day out needs of foreign policy support. It is true that U.S. naval operations over the decades ahead are more likely to focus on shallow coastal-water environments than on the deep ocean, but the legacy value of overdevotion to readiness for the former truly could be catastrophic. U.S. naval operations may well have a coastal focus for some years to come, but that prediction does not imply the need for a navy with only a short reach. The coastal waters in question most likely will be half a world away from the United States. Therefore, although shallow-water constabulary work should not be dismissed merely as lesser but included duties, neither should the merit, albeit limited merit, in that dubious principle be rejected out of hand.

The complementary concepts of general and immediate deterrence offer important insight into how naval power serves U.S. national interests.[58] On the one hand, often there can be no effective substitute for a local, forward naval presence, perhaps of a highly specialized kind. It is important that the United States Navy actually be seen, as well as just appreciated, to exist. These days, port visits are witnessed not only by the local population, but also often by all viewers of national television newscasts, as well as by viewers worldwide, courtesy of CNN. On the other hand, a local U.S. naval presence derives most of its value not from its inherent fighting worth but from what it represents. One has to think synergistically of forward deployment and forces in reserve.

Much of the civility in the world is a simple function of self-interest. A truly Hobbesian world would be a world of general impoverishment. To the limited but still important extent to which U.S. interests benefit from the implicit, if generally distant, sanction of force, one can think of the U.S. Navy as contributing massively to a general deterrence. That world-class

---

58. Patrick M. Morgan, *Deterrence: A Conceptual Analysis* (Beverly Hills, Calif.: SAGE Publications, 1977), chap. 2. "*Immediate deterrence* concerns the relationship between opposing states where at least one side is seriously considering an attack while the other is mounting a threat of retaliation in order to prevent it. *General deterrence* relates to opponents who maintain armed forces to regulate their relationship even though neither is anywhere near mounting an attack" (28). Emphasis in original.

navy may frequently provide immediate deterrence or defense, but the principal way it will serve U.S. foreign policy interests is simply by "being" (not to be confused with the old concept of a "fleet-in-being"). Would-be maritime and other malefactors of all political hues and sources of motivation do not necessarily need to see a U.S. naval vessel on the horizon to know that "out there" is a large stick committed to international order.

Five discrete, interlinked conclusions worthy of highlighting stand out from this discussion.

First, policy objectives shift dramatically, but what can and cannot be achieved by maritime strategy does not change. Americans contemplating the maritime dimension to their struggle for national independence or to the Civil War would be considering the very structure of conflict, while changes in the key elements of the relationships that constitute that structure vary little over the centuries. "The function of the fleet in war," to paraphrase Corbett,[59] varies greatly with the identities of the parties, with particular material and human strengths in different periods of history, and with the wisdom or otherwise in policy and strategy, but the structure of the subject does not.

Second, although the strategic value of sea power must always fluctuate with local historical circumstances, the sea power–land power nexus has endured in its basic character through the centuries. Ignorance of the strengths and the limitations of sea power continues to mar the discipline of strategic studies and to detract from the potential effectiveness of U.S. national security policy and strategy. Whatever the new order that emerges in this decade, with the United States of necessity functioning in some respects as sheriff, that order will be maritime in the nervous system of lines of communication (ship movements)[60] that enable it to work. The strategic relations between sea power and land power will always be individual to discrete cases, but historical education in statecraft and strategy provides the basis for sound choices on policy and strategy. Of course, that basis needs to

59. See note 8.

60. "Such terms as 'sea communication' or 'sea lines of communication' are dangerous in that they tend to mask the fundamental truth that maritime strategy is about *ships*, defined as the *means of movement* on or below the surface. One does not defend the sea as it is usually a matter of indifference whether explosions take place in empty water." Grove, *Future of Sea Power*, p. 22. Grove is criticizing the formulation of the theory of maritime strategy by Julian S Corbett. "Command of the sea, therefore, means nothing but the control of maritime communications, whether for commercial or military purposes. The object of naval warfare is the control of communications." *Some Principles of Maritime Strategy* (Annapolis, Md.: Naval Institute Press, 1988; first pub. 1911), 94.

be complemented properly with due consideration of airpower and space-power adjuncts, and with the story on nuclear cover, where appropriate.

Third, in the context of the analysis and judgments provided above about the improbability that History is ending à la Fukuyama, political and physical geography mandates the proper roles of maritime power in U.S. grand strategy. It does not much matter that the exact locus and occasion for U.S. military interventions in the future cannot be predicted with certitude, because it is known that such interventions will be distantly *overseas*. Material large in volume or that is heavy has to move by sea from North America to Europe, Asia, or Africa. If the seas must be important for U.S. national security, then *ipso facto* the seas must be no less important to other countries motivated to impede U.S. use of them.

Fourth, geography, history, and culture indicate clearly that a United States determinedly exploiting its comparative competitive advantages would choose to be a sea power, air power, "strategic"-forces and space power, rather than a land power. The current timeout from, or disorderly reshuffle in, the balance of power in the security politics of Europe and Asia, should allow the United States to reconsider the grand and military strategies with which the old Soviet empire was contained for four-plus decades. For different reasons, the U.S. Army in World War I, World War II, and then in NATO-European deployment for conduct of the Cold War lacked the sustainability necessary for first-class performance in protracted continental warfare.[61] In 1918 the lack was in equipment as well as tactical and operational skills; in 1944–45 the principal lack was in quantity of high-grade infantry; whereas in recent decades the lack again has been in numbers. Accepting some risk of giving offense, the United States has excelled as a sea power, air power, and strategic forces' (and space) power—it has never excelled as a great land power despite its continental-scale homeland.[62] Victory in the Cold War provides a historic opportunity that

61. See Timothy K Nenninger, "American Military Effectiveness in the First World War," in *Military Effectiveness*, ed. Allan R. Millett and Williamson Murray, vol. 1., *The First World War* (Boston: Allen & Unwin, 1988), 116–56; Allen R. Millett, "The United States Armed Forces in the Second World War," in *Military Effectiveness*, ed. Allan R. Millett and Williamson Murray, vol. 3, *The Second World War* (Boston: Allen & Unwin, 1988), 45–89; and Russell F. Weigley, *Eisenhower's Lieutenants: The Campaigns of France and Germany, 1944–1945* (Bloomington: Indiana University Press, 1981), chaps 1 and 2, and the epilogue.

62. But for a different perspective see Geoffrey Perret, *A Country Made by War: From the Revolution to Vietnam—the Story of America's Rise to Power* (New York: Vintage Books, 1990; first pub. 1989); and *There's a War to be Won. The United States Army in World War II* (New York: Random House, 1991).

should not be missed for the United States to restructure its military posture in favor of those strategic functions at which it tends to shine. Blessed geostrategically with what amounts to a central location between Europe and Asia, the less fixedly precommitted scarce U.S. military power is to a particular continental theater, the greater the scope both for discretion in policy and strategy and for true flexibility and agility in operational art.

Fifth and finally, any responsible student of history has to warn today's policymakers and defense planners that bad times assuredly follow good. Rephrased, history is not a linear process in favor of progress. The United States is so significant a political, economic, military, and even cultural player in international relations[63] that U.S. statesmen can aspire to play some modest active role in the shaping of the future international security condition. However, no statesman or succession of statesmen ever has succeeded in shaping a "new world order" that on reasonable definition was both benign in general effect and durable. Bismarck and Disraeli performed admirably in the 1870s, but their world order dissolved noticeably after two decades and catastrophically after four. As Edward Gibbon (among others) observed, the first nearly two centuries of imperial Rome probably constituted the finest achievement in what amounted to a purposefully shaped "world order" that history has witnessed, before or since; *an order imposed by military preponderance.*[64] It is improbable that the politicians of the 1990s will perform as competently in statecraft as did the increasingly autocratic rulers of Rome from the time of the formal accession of Augustus Caesar in 27 B.C. to the death of Marcus Aurelius in A.D. 180.

---

63. Joseph S. Nye Jr., *Bound to Lead: The Changing Nature of American Power* (New York: Basic Books, 1990), eloquently advances many fashionable fallacies.

64. Edward Gibbon actually was more precise than this. "If a man were called to fix the period in the history of the world during which the condition of the human race was most happy and prosperous, he would, without hesitation, name that which elapsed from the death of Domitian [September 18, A.D. 96] to the accession of Commodus [co-emperor with his father, Marcus Aurelius, from A.D. 177]. *The History of the Decline and Fall of the Roman Empire*, 7 vols., ed. J. B Bury (London: Methuen, 1909), 1:85–86.

Index

Lightning Source UK Ltd.
Milton Keynes UK
UKHW03f1642170418
321211UK00001B/25/P